PRAISE FOR
THE LEADERSHIP

"A refreshing book of real substance that explains negative personality traits that, left to the unconscious, can quickly derail today's leaders. Great research is discussed with real-life examples to create compelling insights. There are plenty of practical suggestions to deal with your own risks as well as a way to reframe irritating behaviours from others into something more useful. A must-read for professional coaches, talent management professionals and leaders who are serious about career development." **Chris Humphreys, CEO, Advanced People Strategies**

"While epic leadership failures capture headlines, the underlying reasons usually lurk in the shadows far from view. This timely book does a masterful job of throwing light on the dark side of leadership by synthesizing a growing body of research and distilling concrete, actionable lessons any leader can use to avoid coming off the track." **Rob Kaiser, Kaiser Leadership Solutions and Editor of** *Consulting Psychology Journal*

"There are always two reasons for doing anything: a good reason and the real reason. Anyone who desires to know more about these real reasons, about what creates leadership pathologies, and what makes for leadership's core qualities, would do well to study this book. Not only will they become more knowledgeable about the shadow side of leadership, but they will also acquire a profound insight into how to overcome the various pitfalls that accompany the leadership journey." **Professor Manfred Kets de Vries, INSEAD**

"In the *Leadership Shadow*, Erik de Haan and Anthony Kasozi provide a welcome antidote to the usual overblown presentations to be found in the enormous number of books and research papers on leadership. Most writing on the matter of leadership presents an idealized, sanitized view of leaders which does not mention the pathologies and neuroses of those who take up leadership roles; because of this they provide very unrealistic and unhelpful views on leadership. *The Leadership Shadow* provides a much more realistic and helpful account of the problems leaders face and how they need to take into account their own leadership shadow. Leaders can do enormous harm if they do not sustain an awareness of the dangerous psychological states it is so easy to be sucked into as a leader. It is to this task that *The Leadership Shadow* provides an important contribution." **Professor Ralph Stacey, University of Hertfordshire**

*Many of us will have to pass through the valley
of the shadow again and again before
we reach the mountain tops of our desires*
Jawaharlal Nehru

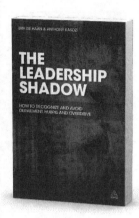

The Leadership Shadow

How to recognize and avoid derailment, hubris and overdrive

Erik de Haan and
Anthony Kasozi

KoganPage

LONDON PHILADELPHIA NEW DELHI

Publisher's note

Every possible effort has been made to ensure that the information contained in this book is accurate at the time of going to press, and the publishers and authors cannot accept responsibility for any errors or omissions, however caused. No responsibility for loss or damage occasioned to any person acting, or refraining from action, as a result of the material in this publication can be accepted by the editor, the publisher or either of the authors.

First published in Great Britain and the United States in 2014 by Kogan Page Limited
Reprinted 2014

2nd Floor, 45 Gee Street	1518 Walnut Street, Suite 1100	4737/23 Ansari Road
London EC1V 3RS	Philadelphia PA 19102	Daryaganj
United Kingdom	USA	New Delhi 110002
www.koganpage.com		India

© Erik de Haan and Anthony Kasozi, 2014

The right of Erik de Haan and Anthony Kasozi to be identified as the authors of this work has been asserted by them in accordance with the Copyright, Designs and Patents Act 1988.

ISBN   978 0 7494 7049 4
E-ISBN   978 0 7494 7050 0

British Library Cataloguing-in-Publication Data

A CIP record for this book is available from the British Library.

CIP data is available.

Library of Congress Control Number: 2014016508

Typeset by Graphicraft Limited, Hong Kong
Printed and bound by 4edge Limited, Essex, UK

CONTENTS

PREFACE: LEADERSHIP IN THE 21ST CENTURY

> *He who has great power should use it lightly.*
> **LUCIUS ANNAEUS SENECA (CA AD 60)**

In today's fast-paced, interconnected, and mercilessly competitive business world, senior executives have to push themselves and others hard. In order to succeed, leaders have to live the paradox of closely attending to others while following as deeply as they lead. They have to listen well to followers, understand their concerns, give them useful and bespoke support, and at the same time motivate them for results or take decisions on their behalf.

It is precisely those leaders who can adapt to these conditions and who can develop a tough and relentless focus on competitive advantage who are most at risk of appearing to become 'overcooked' as they adopt unhelpful and ultimately unproductive patterns of demand, stubbornness, or frenetic activity. Instead of being open to possibility and ambiguity, and willing to engage in continuous and creative conversations with themselves and others, these executives instead become obstinate, resentful, inarticulate, or intense. They become a caricature of themselves. They go into 'overdrive'.

In this way the qualities executives have relied on to get them to the top and to achieve outstanding results, can overshoot under stress and challenge, into unhelpful drives that lead to business and personal catastrophes. Hitherto high-performing executives suddenly find themselves facing the prospect of relationship breakdowns, strategic failures or the risks of derailment.

This book takes up the opportunity to respond to some pressing questions and needs that leaders in today's organizations really grapple with:

- how to provide sound, ethical leadership in an increasingly transparent and interconnected workplace;

- how to understand the rift that the leader's activities open up between their bright, action-oriented, inspirational or caring sides – and their much more personal yet universal darker side: in other words, how to overcome their own leadership shadows;
- how to distinguish between what really matters and what is only peripheral to their jobs;
- how to escape the unhelpful and corrupting patterns that so many of our leaders succumb to;
- how to foresee and forestall some of the personal risks in taking up a leadership role;
- how to discover and actually adopt ways to integrate their anxieties with their confidence, and their toughness with their care for others.

This book offers the opportunity for busy professional executives to find practical ways of restoring their faith in the quest for balance; it represents what many executives have indicated to us as missing today from their business knowledge and leadership bookshelves:

1 a text on leadership that is both robust from an empirical research point of view, and yet steeped in practical leadership experience;

2 a balancing act that is enduring and not a quick fix, because if it were, they would probably have already seen it, tried it and applied it;

3 a voice and a vision that is authentic and resonates with their real everyday challenges.

This book, *The Leadership Shadow*, draws on the lived experience of executives engulfed in this paradoxical challenge in today's business world. Its aim is to help hard-pressed executives to make sense of what actually happens when their drivers overshoot and they find themselves acting out the shadow side of leadership. The book attempts to show how executives can find stability in the face of uncertainty, resilience in the face of gruelling demand, and psychological well-being in the face of contextual and internal turbulence.

Never before has leadership come under more criticism and distrust than in this second decade of the 21st century. After the disillusioning behaviour and practices of democratically elected top political leaders throughout the nineties; after the major catastrophes in the financial services sector in the first decade of the 21st century; and alongside the string of management and leadership debacles in practically every walk of public and private corporate life, there has been an ever-growing consensus that it is time to reassess leadership. To reassess what it is and what it should aim for as appropriate outcomes for industry, organizations and for both individuals and society at large. With this need and demand in mind, this book will help you understand more deeply and live more truly the critical aspects that shape your leadership performance: your leadership 'input' (you as a person) and your leadership 'outcome' (your impact).

For more than 20 years, as we have worked and specialized in the field of leadership and organizational development, we have repeatedly been challenged to admit that we could not really define precisely what 'leadership' was. Despite the many thousands of books and articles about leadership (eg according to Morris, Brotheridge and Urbanski, 2005, there were almost four hundred thousand articles and books on leadership at that time and this number has only been growing) we could not find a definition that was rigorous and able to capture the essence of leadership, although we have to admit that we may not have scrutinized all of those books. We therefore maintained that probably the best book about leadership is Plato's *Meno* (*ca* 380 BC), in which Socrates interviews the famous leader and general Meno about the essence or excellence of leadership and how to learn this excellent leadership. After several attempts at definitions, both have to admit that not only do they not know what leadership is, but they could not authoritatively teach other scholars or practitioners about the art of leaders. This has been our condition as executive coaches and organization development consultants, until very recently. As executive coaches we worked alongside senior executives and managers to reflect on their leadership practice. But if we were really honest we did not know *a priori* what effective 'leadership practice' is. As Socrates and Meno found, we too find it much easier to define our own role and practice as executive coaches than the role of our clients as leaders.

Getting to grips with leadership

Our work in preparation for this book taught us why we faced this challenge. We believe we understand now why we were so confused. The definition that most people implicitly use to understand leadership, goes something like: 'The leader is the person who occupies the leadership role. Whoever it is, that is your leader. Now live with it...'.

Therefore – we all think we can be leaders; in fact, we *are* all leaders and managers – at home in our families, at our clubs, and at work; be it of projects, divisions or organizations. A conductor is a train manager. An administrator is an office manager. A technician is an IT manager, and parents are family leaders and managers – all by nature of their role.

However, this implicit definition is problematic. It unintentionally leads to the assumption of leadership of a team or organization as being inevitably a scarce resource, and hence something we all need to compete for. And if we win control over the resource, it tells us to seek improved emoluments (a better salary, even a bonus too). It also implies that there may be no particular skilled practice or talent involved, and no particular qualities to look out for when appointing a leader. We can all do it, which is the same as saying that nobody can do it, or that the strongest bloke or the greatest bully will end up doing it. This brings us back to the negative conclusion of Plato's *Meno*.

About a year ago we found a way out of this quagmire when we 'stumbled' onto a much more satisfactory definition of leadership (which you can find at the beginning of Chapter 2). We started thinking about leadership as the function that helps a team to perform better and increase its output or impact. We began to see leadership impact as a means by which the team or organization is able to outperform other similar teams or organizations. We discovered that it is the team that needs to be competitive, not the leader. The leader just helps it to compete better. We also realized how important the 'right' definition is in practice, because a change in the definition makes leaders place the emphasis differently and therefore act differently. For one thing the new-found definition made us realize that as team members we can (and therefore should) act and behave as leaders alongside and in tandem with the formally designated leader of the team. This choice of definition also has other profound implications, which this book explores further in the following chapters.

Finally we discovered that we were not alone in our confusion when trying to appreciate the leadership literature. We discovered that Rost's (1991) analysis of a vast array of leadership studies from the early 1900s onwards has lost nothing of its accuracy and relevance. Rost shows convincingly that the 20th century has seen very little usable theory on leadership; in fact, truly encompassing, interdisciplinary studies only started in the 1980s. Until the 80s leadership studies were mostly limited to 'school leadership', 'military leadership', 'business leadership', etc, without recognizing an overarching profession or discipline. Even as late the 1990s there were still three fundamental and intractable problems remaining, to prevent further development of leadership theory and models:

1 Most of the literature emphasizes peripheral issues such as traits, skills and outcomes, without coming to grips with what leadership *is* and what leadership *is for*. Also, the existing literature focused on the *content* of leadership rather than the much more important *process* of leadership or the understanding of leadership as a dynamic relationship between stakeholders.

2 Neither leadership scholars nor practitioners had been able to define leadership with precision, accuracy and conciseness. As a result there is an astounding variety of views and opinion without any criteria to compare them and separate the wheat from the chaff. Most writers and practitioners do not even see this as a problem. More than half of the books, studies and articles on leadership do not bother to define the topic of leadership.

3 Following on from the lack of clarity and definition, there was no integrated domain or profession of leadership.

Rost (1991) himself analyses 587 original publications from 1900 to 1989 in detail and summarizes all leadership definitions in the minority of 221 publications out of those 587 that contain a definition of their subject.

Because we agree with Rost (1991) that 'scholars who want to write books on leadership must think deeply about the nature of leadership, articulate their thoughts about what leadership is, and then be very consistent in their writing so that what they write flows from their definition' (1991, page 82), we have made every effort to focus on the true nature of leadership, considered as a relational process; and we have consistently worked from concise definitions which can be anchored in leadership praxis and in the wider literature. We have attempted to rise beyond and inquire beneath the 20th-century literature on leadership. Hence we do not summarize Taylorism, Great Man, group, traits, behaviourist, situational and excellence leadership models, all competing schools in the 20th century, but instead attempt to get closer to the intractable realities of leadership. Virtually every other leadership book will give you that historical summary over a limited timeline and we agree with Rost (1991) that the idea of progress in those leadership models is more myth than reality. Instead, in the Epilogue of this book, we will try to anchor our own leadership thinking in older schools of leadership as they emerged in the Greek Warring States period, the Chinese Warring States period, and the beginnings of the African Rainbow State.

However, even when approached with a helpful definition and with sound understanding, leadership comes with inevitable anxieties, doubts and projections. As leaders we feel the tension of taking responsibility. We feel the uncertainty and unpredictability of outcome. We feel self-doubt or overconfidence. We will succumb to the vicious cycle of 'impotence' versus 'omnipotence' that many leaders feel on a daily basis. In order to step into the role of leader and serve our teams, we need to 'step up to the plate', face up to and deal with these and other similar anxieties. Even then, as we try to face our demons and anxieties, we can be certain that our vulnerabilities and pathologies will re-emerge whenever we have the audacity to 'lead', ie to express ourselves on the performance and effectiveness of our own organization. The main purpose of writing this book was to share our insights into how you as an executive or senior leader can help yourself deal with these struggles and challenges, with anxieties and frustrations, as effectively and productively as you can, on an ongoing basis.

So in this book we will work with you on what we can do about your very own working relationships and leadership pathologies, by drawing attention to your core qualities as well as your ingrained patterns of behaving and habitual relating to others. We recognize your unique drivers and competences as the key assets that drive the creative dynamic of your leadership practice. We recognize that these personal talents can settle into patterns. We note that those patterns can be productive *and* problematic, and most often both at the same time. The very same patterns that lead to opportunity and success will of necessity lead to shame and failure as well. Our experience of the reality of working in complex organizations made up of diverse human beings in a dynamic external environment, suggests that your unique core qualities and personality patterns matter. The ever-present challenge executives face lies in their ability to *work with* those patterns and cycles simultaneously and in a dynamic way, whilst also living the challenges and changing the patterns, and thus embracing uncertainty and realizing possibility.

We work mainly as executive coaches and organization-development consultants. That means we have worked for many years with individual executives, teams and organizations. This book is our attempt to 'open up and scale up' the work that we are doing with them, making it accessible to a wider audience. Consequently, for us, writing the book has been an exercise in understanding our clients' roles and responsibilities more deeply. Where we struggled to define their profession we are now slowly getting to grips with what leadership is there for and what is required of leaders to do their job well.

The structure of The Leadership Shadow

The Leadership Shadow is in three parts.

Part One: The way leaders thrive explores when leaders are at their best. It also presents the core concepts and frameworks of this book, and what relevance they have for you as you are engaged in demanding roles in organizational life today. The chapters in this section place the issues of the book into the wider context of socio-economic and techno-political change experienced by most early 21st-century organizations and executives.

Part One examines how our wider context has dramatically changed. It describes the escalating demands for personal performance, engagement and responsibility that are in turn implicated in shaping further challenges. It shows how today working environments trigger, stimulate and drive contradictory patterns of executive behaviour. Finally it looks at the implications of addressing issues as part of an executive's learning and developmental journey. In doing this it presents how it is possible to approach leadership as either a one-off expedition to be endured, or as part of a longer-term and continuing journey to be lived with, actively and with intent. It shows that this is a journey that cannot be pre-planned at the start. It reveals that the journey can only be guided and left to unfold as new situations and challenges arise. This may feel at times precarious and contradictory, or tough and unrewarding; it can also be a growing experience of mastery and a real sense of personal and professional maturity.

Part Two: The way leaders come to grief focuses on the 'other' side of leadership, the shadow side of our talents and competences. It illustrates core qualities and driven behaviour in practice by introducing cameos of ambitious executives and the patterns that they portray when they come under great pressure. Part Two comprises three chapters focusing on well-defined personality patterns and how these patterns respond to pressure. Each of the personality patterns comes with illustrative profiles and descriptions of

FIGURE 0.1   Reading this book: the more you invest, the more you will take from it

associated behaviour that the authors have experienced in practice and portray in case studies, using commonly understood psychological descriptions (based on the psychiatric Diagnostic and Statistical Manual DSM and the Hogan Development Survey; Hogan & Hogan, 1997).

Part Two enables the reader to engage with the 'shadow side' of his or her own personality and to reflect on how core anxieties and challenges, personal drives, relational effectiveness and personal achievement may all be related. The final chapter in Part Two is a practical one that invites you to explore your own personality adaptations and patterns. This chapter also offers guidance through which you can initiate a personal journey and find unique core strengths and accompanying pitfalls, challenges and allergies.

It offers practical suggestions as to how best to work with executive realities and relationships as healthy and creative orbits, rather than as unhealthy and destructive spirals.

Part Three: Overcoming the excesses of leadership presents findings from leadership research more broadly and then shifts the focus from the individual to the individual's realities and challenges within teams and groups. In this part we consider overdrive and its impact in teams and groups, and examine the question of 'balancing' in executive drives, relationships and experiences.

Part Three considers how individuals in groups can engage with, and rely on, the resources and support of others to strike a healthy balance in their experience of success and failure. This part of the book addresses how to bring humility and hubris together in a balanced way. It suggests how to nurture self-development, resilience and healthy relationships in a way that is productive as well as sustainable. Part Three also connects the ideas we raise there with related research from the relevant organizational literature.

At the end of several of the chapters in the book we have reproduced one of Aesop's fables. Some 2,500 years ago this legal expert used his acute perceptions of leaders and their frailties to create these short fables in which he exposed leaders' habits and patterns. We quote the translation by Olivia and Robert Temple in the Penguin Classics edition and also take the numbering of the fables from that edition.

We recognize the challenges busy executives experience in finding time to read anything that is not directly relevant to the businesses they hold responsibility for or indeed anything that is more than one or two pages long. In appreciation of this, and to make this book accessible to you, we have structured it for easy reading. So each part starts with a short introduction to the section. Likewise, each chapter (1–14) has a short introduction at the beginning and a brief summary at the end. This should help you navigate swiftly through the book – focusing on what is most interesting and relevant for you. Reading only the summaries of all the chapters can give you a quick taste of the content of the book in less than 15 minutes. The introductions and summaries are also designed to draw you into aspects that may be less familiar to you and to help you to identify easily what are most relevant chapters to you or which aspects you might do well to pay more attention to.

As coaches, dedicated to encouraging you to extend your personal learning precisely where it is most needed, we would also encourage you to challenge yourself to find the time and space to take a more reflective and inquiring walk through the entire book. We think both approaches (speed reading and slow reflection) are valuable and useful, and we know that you will, initially at least, be the best judge of what will help you best.

It is probably helpful to say that the initial chapters of this book move slowly. This is because we want to start at the very beginning. The first chapter explores the unique context of leaders in the 21st century, focusing on the changes we are experiencing in our globalizing economy. The second chapter offers a rigorous definition of 'leadership' and looks at the consequences of that definition, in particular from a relational perspective. This means that the 'leadership shadow' can only make its entry in Chapter 3. We believe however that it is important to set the stage in some detail before we can begin to understand 21st-century leaders' pressures, overdrive patterns and effectiveness.

Acknowledgements

We are profoundly grateful to the many colleagues, leaders and coaches, who have helped us with the material, and would like to name a few of them in particular. Our consulting colleagues John Higgins and Gerard Wijers who have kindly offered us feedback on an early draft of the book, and Marlyn Young, Mike Grant and Ruth Evers-Cacciapaglia who have been very generous with relevant case material that they had written up for other purposes. Alex Davda has shared a short version of his Resilience Questionnaire (Appendix B). Alison Greene, Ashridge's legal manager, has helped to protect us from the risks of potential defamation in our case material. Christine Aebli has helped with logistical issues and the selection of the cover picture. Richard Bamsey has captured the core content of the book in evocative illustrations and Ashridge's graphics experts Danee Miller and Michelle Moore have produced the clover leaf diagram in Chapter 5 and the two diagrams in Chapter 12. Last but not least we wish to thank our editor, Liz Gooster.

PART ONE
The way leaders thrive

Introduction: the importance of framing the leadership dance

> *All the ills of mankind, all the tragic misfortunes that fill the history books, all the political blunders, all the failures of the great leaders have arisen merely from a lack of skill at dancing.*
>
> **MOLIÈRE, *LE BOURGEOIS GENTILHOMME* (1670)**

In the lighthearted quote above, Molière, being the great artist that he was, ventures a very risky communication about something that is much more profound, existential and unsettling than first appears at face value. He is alluding to the fondness for *dancing* of the absolute monarch Louis XIV (the self-styled 'Sun King'). Louis loved ballet and during the early half of his long reign he frequently danced in court ballets. He was a brilliant professional dancer and had a profound knowledge of music. He often had a new ballet written for him and presented in the palace in which he appeared in the central role. Louis had danced in three of Molière's own *comédies-ballets* and of all the aristocrats he danced the best. Moreover, since the beginning of his autocratic rule in 1661, he organized large festivities in which the aristocracy was forced to dance in the shadow of the monarch's talent. Louis set the rhythm and the courtiers had to follow him in a line. As Louis insisted on such royal ballets the aristocracy were obliged to participate in order to stay in the king's favour. At the same time, being allowed to participate was a royal honour. Not just the courtiers but the whole political establishment had to dance to the king's tune.

In the quote above Molière is trying ever so gently, behind the protection of frivolous comedy aided by King Louis' passion for the arts, to open up the field of leadership in his country and make a comment, however indirect and however ironic, about leadership practices at court. He wonders aloud – yet subtly disguised – whether it is good for the state of France that the main focus of court gatherings is dancing and that all courtiers need to dance to the tune of the king, feigning admiration whilst making sure they display less dancing talent than the Sun King himself.

The quote has remained famous as a poignant example of Molière's great courage in contributing to a discussion about leadership in a place where the norm was that nobody but the king leads, under the motto *L'état, c'est moi*. It did not always work out well for Molière and his fearless efforts to speak truth to power in the context of Versailles cost him dearly as it resulted in several banned plays, biting opposition and ill health.

Part One of this book will look at the context in which leadership thrives, which in our view is a context different from that experienced in the court of Louis XIV where leadership was the prerogative of one single man with absolute power. We will argue that it is precisely where many can be involved in leadership that better decisions are made, where the positive impact of decisions is greater, and the excesses and extravagance of leadership are avoided.

Whilst exploring the context for good leadership we will spend time on *definitions* of leadership. Through hard experience, we have learned that how one defines leadership, even if implicitly, matters immensely and determines to a large extent how one behaves as a leader and as a follower.

In the mind of the Sun King the implicit definition of leadership was: 'All power resides with me, the state and the organization are synonymous with me, and they dance to my decrees'. From this absolute power something may occasionally trickle down to lower levels, for example when the king is in a good mood or feels particularly safe. There is absolutely no obligation on his part to do anything specific, not even to occupy himself with any affairs of the state. His definition affords Louis XIV complete freedom and his followers none. In recent times we have seen plenty of other absolute dictators who cynically did not bother to occupy themselves with the responsibility of the office and the fact that their word was 'law', until something 'interesting' happened like a big sporting event or something 'challenging' like a revolt.

In such a context of 'absolute leadership', accepting the prevalent definition means resigning yourself to insignificance. And it also means resigning yourself to having no say whatsoever on what you do, with whom you collaborate, or how you are led. Adopting a different definition of leadership, where possible, provides you with a completely different outlook and offers a means to change and influence your own affairs. It is not just the case that your personal definition of leadership and its particular validity in your current context determine how you act and influence as a leader. Such an (implicit) definition also determines how you conduct yourself within leadership conversations. Such a productive view of leadership and your own role as a leader means that you can have a *vision* for the circumstances and a leadership contribution for most opportunities that arise. In other words, your (implicit) definition of leadership determines how you lead in practice, on a day-to-day basis.

After looking at characteristics of the modern business world in Chapter 1, we will provide our own definition of leadership in Chapter 2 and explore what consequences flow from this definition and what criteria for good leadership we can deduce from it. In Chapter 3 we will look at how participating in leadership brings out a dance of the 'Sun' and the 'Shadow', of the light and dark sides of our personality. Finally, in Chapter 4 we offer help with reflecting on your own leadership practice by inviting you to ask yourself questions that we believe are relevant for your personal journey as a leader.

The context that produces a leader

01

> *Of all creatures that breathe and move upon the Earth, nothing is bred that is weaker than man.*
>
> HOMER, *THE ODYSSEY* (CA 850 BC)

The 21st-century world of work: not a place for wimps

If you are working as a senior executive and are actively engaged in managing and leading an organization today, your experience of top leadership probably suggests that the 21st-century world is not a place for equivocating wimps.

As an executive you are expected to be decisive. The problems you face are presented to you as needing deliberate, quick and intelligent action. You have been trained and repeatedly encouraged to be 'tough' and to prevail in the face of challenge and adversity. Everywhere you go you face situations that require physical and psychological resilience in order to navigate the complex and contradictory challenges as well as the massive workloads.

But what has created the tremendous demands you face? Why are you (like many others) so severely stretched? What is it about the context within which you work that has created the experiences you and others face? Why do you have to adapt to this?

As we have worked with senior executives facing these questions we have looked back over the last 30 years and into the last quarter of the 20th century. We can see that today the world is very different from the place where we started our working lives when one of us was selected as a young corporate recruit to join the fast-track management trainee development scheme at Unilever and the other was a researcher studying for his PhD. We were told that we should apply ourselves to solving problems quickly, be skilful and succinct in our written and verbal communication, and work on our specialist expertise in a key area. We were trained and encouraged to lead and motivate others younger than ourselves to enable them also to achieve demanding goals.

Although much has changed in the world of work since then, we notice that many a top executive faces similar demands in the 21st century. They are still expected to be in charge, in control, and high-performers in very similar ways. It is the case, however, that executives today need to contend with quite different realities....

The world is a much more connected and interconnected place than it was 30 years ago. Organizations span more lives and enter those lives more deeply and through more channels. Faster, more versatile communications have led to greater linkage and intimacy between suppliers and consumers. Concern for relationships, ethics, environmental impact and fairness has grown as media (new and old) have driven forward access to information and transparency of leaders' decision making. Work is no longer confined to 'working hours' or contained in the narrow confines of factories, offices, buildings, farms and plantations. The 'brute world' of extraction and manufacturing is lithely connected with the 'sleek world' of finance, fashion and celebrity. Working virtually, and working daily in close contact with different people living in different time-zones, is a growing norm.

At a macro level the business world of today's senior executives is larger, more diverse and widely spread. It calls for much faster and greater changes of focus than when we started work some 30 years ago. Then, we still had time to think and to reflect on what we were doing. 'High performance' now more than ever requires that you have to be able to solve problems quickly, to be skilful and succinct in written and verbal communication, and to have a specialist expertise in at least some of the key functions of the organization that you are supervising. However, today high performance also means that you have to be able to do this 24/7, with people you have never met, taking greater responsibility for your actions, taking into account new and different risks and hazards and using a multiplicity of technologies to stay connected, in touch and available. In other words, it is not the case

FIGURE 1.1   Critically reviewing our thirst for speed, pace and excellence: is it giving us the best results?

that demands have changed. It is the scope and content of work that is completely different.

As an executive today you have a multiplicity of factors to consider when taking even the simplest of decisions. You have to consider more stakeholders (internally and externally), more socio-political perspectives, more regulatory requirements, a greater range of cultural sensitivities, fuller transparency to the media and civil society, higher levels of accountability (for the decision as well as the consequences of the decision), more specific and rigorous governance standards, and more exacting performance criteria.

Your world of work is a fast-moving global marketplace. It is a marketplace of commodities, interconnectedness including stakes in companies, ideas, and resources of all kinds, information, technology, ideals, as well as products and services. Communication and media have shrunk the world. Your executive decisions have to be made in an instant, and soon after they are made, they are transmitted around the globe, for others to respond to and comment on. As an executive you rarely have the time for lengthy contemplation before deciding, or the luxury of separate spheres of influence within which you can study the consequences of one decision before you have to make the next one.

At a personal level, the context of your business world is rapidly changing and putting new demands on you to adapt and change swiftly. Many demands challenge our human evolutionary capacities. We know today that most of our DNA goes back millions of years and is shared with all other animals. The adaptations we have achieved and that make us quintessentially human (allowing us to read and reflect and blush, for example) have been hundreds of thousands of years in the making. Moreover, as adults we learn and adapt much more slowly than when we were infants or teenagers (just try to learn a new language or to play another musical instrument when you are over 40). So undoubtedly we bring a lot less flexible, adaptive, learnable and malleable person to the table than our 21st-century working environment is calling for. It would be no exaggeration to say that the main obstacle to meeting the challenges demanded by our present-day context is ... *us*.

This is not just a 21st-century issue – truly we have never been on top of things in organizations, even in times of less complexity and speed of change. We are only 'satisficing' our actions because we are unable to optimize them, as March and Simon (1958) already noticed:

> This, then, is the general picture of the human organism that we will use to analyse organizational behaviour. It is a picture of a choosing, decision-making, problem-solving, organism that can do only one or a few things at a time, and that can only attend to a small part of the information recorded in its memory and presented by the environment.

Although we can be proud to have the most complex and connected adaptive processing organ in the universe (the human central nervous system), we cannot make changes with the speed and irreversibility demanded by present-day computing systems, market movements and global trends. We cannot easily and seamlessly respond to questions such as:

- Given that the epicentre of the world economy is shifting thousands of miles from the west (and northern hemisphere) to the east and south with every passing year, what will the consequences be for your business?

- Following the emerging trend, can you transplant your livelihood to 'where the money is'?

- Will you be able to learn Russian, Mandarin and Arabic within the next few years so that you can respond effectively to your new clients?
- Do you have the ability to repeatedly transform the way you work with every passing year?

No we cannot. We each have our own pace of change and adaptation, which is at a significantly slower pace than the current context appears to demand. Yet we need to adapt in order to survive, let alone to thrive in this postmodern world.

We would argue that, rather than entertaining the fantasy that our central nervous system can ever catch up with the pace and complexity of change in business, we should not waste effort on developing an even faster-adapting human being. We may quite rightly bemoan the fact that the speed of our thinking is not as fast as our contexts call for. On the other hand, perhaps we do not need ever more speed and computing power; perhaps we need something else. In our view it is more important to anchor ourselves in our vulnerable yet stable human nature than to try to learn and adapt more quickly all the time.

Rather than *quick change* we believe we need more radical and *deeper insight*. In other words, what we think we need in this day and age is an ever better understanding of what drives us, what informs our responses at the most visceral level, and where our limitations lie when adapting to change. If we were furnished with reliable psychological insight that is adapted to the demands placed on us, then we may at least be able to understand the shocks and frustrations that we experience, and gradually learn to work and live effectively through the changes and challenges that this fast-moving world presents, regardless of our innate incapacity to match the speed of contextual change and demand. We can learn about our own measure or range of action, the limitations of our very own 'human condition'.

In other words, insight and understanding may give us the edge we need as so-called 'high-performers' who are at risk of rapidly losing that very pre-rogative. Such insights may also give us a basis for guiding others in their own journeys through the pressures and changes of the 21st century.

At a deeper level, our society and (western) culture, whilst evolving rapidly into more and more complex and powerful technologies, have also suffered a profound and hurtful loss of status. The last few centuries have demonstrated the power and presence of human ingenuity based on reflection and insight. Human sciences have insightfully arrived at ever more truthful and humbling models of our own place in the world. Freud (1917) neatly summarized our 'progress' in the sciences in the form of three 'injuries' to our naïve self-love. Since Galileo we know that our little planet is indeed not the centre of the universe as most of us thought previously. Since Darwin we know that we are not the apex and measure of life on our planet, but in fact we are just another (rather late arriving) species intimately linked through evolution with other contemporary species. Since Freud himself we know that we are not even masters of our own minds, because a great many things go on in our minds of which we have no idea but which are nevertheless highly relevant for how we make decisions and perform our actions: unconscious, primary-process thinking.

The latest chapter in this account of humbling discoveries and narcissistic injuries to our self-love and the realization of our very modest place in the universe is our growing understanding of our relational being (Mitchell, 2000; Gergen, 2009). We do not 'exist' outside the relationship network that we are embedded in. This essential insight provided by 'relationality' is that we are not the singular autonomous units (person, thinker, decision maker, entrepreneur etc) that we thought we were, despite the prevalent illusion that we are. Too much of our psychological make-up is located *between* us and others and is thus represented by our relationships as well as by our 'selves'. We will come back to this relational turn in psychology in the next chapter.

Organizations have changed beyond recognition

Organizations have also changed. On the face of it, in form, they may appear very much the same types of organizational units as they were 30 years ago. There are small proprietary businesses, small and large partnerships, private and public limited organizations, large public institutions, international organizations, and multinational global corporations. So what has changed?

Even if they are not immediately apparent, there are fundamental long-term shifts that are noticeable in 21st-century multinational corporations. For one thing the average lifespan of large corporations has reduced by some 75 per cent over the past fifty years: the average lifespan for S&P 500 largest corporations in the V.S. was more than 60 years in 1957 and is only around 15 years now. That means that looking ahead from 2014 it is likely that three quarters of the leading corporations on the S&P 500 will not exist in 2028. Similarly, life-cycles of products and services have, according to economists, 'collapsed' over the same period to such a degree that throughout most industries more than 50 per cent of revenues are made on products that are less than three years old.

Not just the largest corporations have profoundly changed. At the other end of the spectrum, the small proprietary organization (such as Cath Kidston, see below), is now internet-enabled and accesses markets across countries and geographies. Multinationals, brands and branding organizations not only still have a presence around the world, they also have to be meaningful and accessible wherever they are. All kinds of alliances and joint ventures, formal and informal, have been created between different organizations in different countries. Private and public limited corporations as well as international organizations have to have multiple faces and interfaces in multiple locations. Large public institutions are now often challenged to develop and maintain subtle combinations of government-funded and public–private partnerships. New entities are emerging as international organizations that are based on a combination of non-governmental, charitable trusts and foundations, and philanthropy-based initiatives. Multinational global corporations are bigger, more diverse and have multiple locations in different jurisdictions and with a multiplicity of staff and customer realities.

The remarkable Cath Kidston

In the year to April 2012, Cath Kidston, the UK-domiciled retail purveyor of household 'vintage kitchenalia' is reported to have had a turnover of £89 million obtained through its network of UK and overseas stores and internet-based sales. Whilst the size of the turnover was, in the greater scheme of things, quite unremarkable, what was notable was the way it had been achieved. During a recession in its core markets the business had in the previous year managed to grow turnover by nearly 40 per cent. Overseas business was reported to have grown by nearly 70 per cent. The number of stores had also been increased by 33 to 85, with the overseas network of stores growing to over 35.[1] This growth has been sustained into 2013. In the year to April 2013 the business increased its turnover to £105 million, the number of stores to 118 and the overseas network of stores to over 60.[2]

This story of remarkable meteoric growth has an even more remarkable history. In the 20 short years since the first Cath Kidston store was opened in 1993 'as a junk shop full of curtainalia'[3] off the fashionable King's Road in London, the retailer had gone from scratch to develop into a small but perfectly formed worldwide retailing sensation. By the end of 2011 the retailer was reported to be employing over 650 staff and delivering a variety of products worldwide through multiple channels and across retailing cultural and geographical boundaries. In an interview with Kirsty Young on the BBC Radio 4 programme *Desert Island Discs*, the founder Cath Kidston said that she realized that 'it is not me playing shop any more, it is about looking after the wider picture and the wider people'.

This remarkable entrepreneur had started an organization which had created a niche ('cheerful and practical with a nostalgic nod to the late 50s') and was now taking it across merchandise boundaries and into different cultures whilst remaining essentially true to a distinctive and quite narrow definition of vintage design, creatively translated into everyday living and homeware. In an elegant description of what she felt the Cath Kidston brand offered, this modest self-deprecating and be-medalled[4] entrepreneur explained that Cath Kidston customers simply felt that 'the product cheers them up'.

Transforming Unilever

In the 30 years between the 1980s and the end of the first decade of the new millennium, the global multinational Unilever has been transformed from a diversified lumbering giant into a streamlined global heavyweight with sleek divisional lines and a new green, more socially connected image which in some ways harked back to its founder William Hesketh Lever's aspirational origins: 'to make cleanliness commonplace; to lessen work for women; to foster health and contribute to personal attractiveness, that life may be more enjoyable and rewarding for the people who use our products'.[5]

Unilever in 2011 is a very different business from the one that the Lever Brothers would have recognized – but arguably one that they would have been mightily proud of. The post-millennial Unilever is winning sustainability and green awards, partnering with the UN's World Food Programme, and trumpeting its Unilever Sustainable Living Plan. Its commercial credentials are also impressive. By 2011 the organization had a massive turnover of £46.5 billion and returned an operating profit of over £6.4 billion. The organization is present in 190 countries worldwide, employing 174,000 people and reaching 2 billion consumers every day.[6]

Most remarkably, however, has been the organization's continuous adaptation to meet the challenges of countless decades across three centuries. Created in the 1890s the business has not only survived for over 100 years: it has in the last 30 years undergone a remarkable metamorphosis from being an industrially diversified, fragmented giant conglomerate with a variety of locally focused and managed businesses into a streamlined business concentrated around three essential core divisions (food, hair care and personal care), managing aligned businesses around the world, and supplying carefully managed global consumer brands all under the single Unilever corporate identity.

Adaptable International Finance Corporation

A legal and financially independent part of the World Bank (created in 1944 after the Bretton Woods conference) the International Finance Corporation (IFC) came into being in 1956, starting with a small core full-time staff of 12 and charged with providing finance to private enterprise in developing countries. In doing so, the IFC was to ensure that it would 'take no government guarantees; always work alongside other private investors; never manage its investees'.

The IFC was initially conceived around the idea and commitment of senior banking executive Robert L Garner's insight into the importance of the role played by private enterprise in economic development. Expressing remarkable foresight that has stood the test of time he stated: 'It was my firm conviction that the most promising future for the less developed countries was the establishing of good private industry.'

By 2011 the IFC had become a key player in the international development finance and banking landscape. The organization had developed into three distinct aligned and connected streams of business, namely investment services, advisory services and asset management. It had over 3,400 staff worldwide, half of whom were distributed around various key centres in the so-called International Development Association (IDA) countries.

The organization's business performance has also been impressive. In the financial year to 2012, IFC invested a record $20.4 billion in 103 developing countries. IFC reports that in 2011 IFC investment clients helped support 2.5 million jobs in 2011, and made 23 million loans totalling more than $200 billion to micro, small and medium-sized enterprises.[7] In addition to being responsible for numerous investments and business initiatives, the organization has also been credited with materially influencing and shaping the international development policy agenda. The IFC did not only coin the term 'emerging economies', but also guided a lot of their development strengthening policies that enhanced regulation, such as the so-called 'Equator principles'.

Some underlying patterns beneath these vignettes

Underlying each of these corporate vignettes is of course a much more intricate story of leaders and executives facing the real challenges of making change work within a complex and challenging context. In each of the cases, executives will have had to put forward suggestions, make decisions or take actions with which others disagree. Inevitably they will have had to work hard, deal with conflict and recover from mistakes they or others have made.

Cath Kidston notes for example that for five years she was working so hard on the business she was too distracted to finish selecting and changing the curtains in her own bedroom. Consequently she lived with the irony of having black-out blinds in her own home while making it possible for other people to furnish and design their own.[8] In Unilever, the story is told of how Niall FitzGerald (Chairman of Unilever between 1996 and 2004) resorted to mild subterfuge to draw the attention of the marketing community to the new Marketing Academy that was part of the refocusing strategic effort and to which Unilever was committed in order 'to reinvigorate Unilever's traditionally strong approach to marketing training and development'.[9]

The IFC organization has had to continually review its own processes and structures as well as training and organizational development to ensure that it has the people with the skills, capabilities, motivations and relationships to support dramatic change and growth. Leadership at all levels has been required. And executives have had to make tough choices about careers, reporting lines, promotion of staff and relocation of offices and people to align with client needs and developments. Underlying the rather innocent declaration that over 51 per cent of IFC staff is field-based is an ongoing commitment and drive to be more relevant and proximate to IFC's clients and their needs and issues. This has no doubt been a challenging requirement that inevitably stretches leadership across different organizational levels and functional boundaries.

Here is a brief overview of how we believe organizations have changed only in the last few decades:

1 Different funding models underpinning organizations, generally leading to more stakeholders through, for example, crowdfunding and crowdsourcing, so that there are more potential gainers and losers looking into organizations where ownership and accountability are increasingly democratized.

2 Shifting ownership models and domicile realities, calling for different controls and legislation which challenge national taxation and corporate accountability.

3 Ever-decreasing lifespans of corporations, products and services, accelerated by the ongoing digital revolution, leading to an average lifespan of the most powerful corporations of only 15 years now.

4 Implementation of better supervision and independent governance of (aspects of) organizational life.

5 Greater transparency, with decision making and implementation being forced to be more open and under constant scrutiny.

6 Greater reach and interdependency across geographies and cultures (note for example China announcing in 2013 their future sourcing of raw materials from the Moon representing a new frontier of competition to add to the wrangling over the Arctic, the Antarctic and the ocean beds.)

7 Collapse of boundaries between organizational entities: more interrelationships, dependencies and cross-boundary and virtual-team leadership.

8 Masses of data that have to be processed and taken into account and also that cannot be easily erased or hidden. As a result, leaders can come across as being somewhat sluggish, leaving behind them a very visible and slithery electronic trail of all that they have looked at and worked on in the organizations that they have ever touched or been involved with.

9 Organizations being less likely to be mono-cultural, with more mixed talent from various places and backgrounds across the globe. Increasingly organizations being occasionally without a single dominant culture. Many organizations branching away from the European or western model as being the dominant influence.

10 Continual re-invention taking place, with a sense of constant change and flux, both in terms of products and services and of the support mechanisms that facilitate execution (such as communication and information technology or customer relationship management).

All in all, organizations have become more complex whilst becoming more transparent; they have become more interconnected whilst becoming more technology driven; and they have become more democratic whilst becoming more accountable. In other words, with greatly enhanced complexity, functionality and reach have come increased responsibility and accountability. Not the kind of context in which the Sun King, whom we mentioned in the Introduction to this part of the book, or any of the 'Great Man' leaders that we all know, would flourish. It is clearly time for a different kind of leader, a leader who can remain connected, relational and open to scrutiny from all directions (see also Brown, 2014, who performs the same analysis in the domain of political leadership).

FIGURE 1.2   The constant pressures on executives

The new demands on executives are leading to cycles of hubris and humility

All these significant contextual changes place tremendous demands on you as an executive. As a 21st-century executive you have to develop a way of working, living and being that will enable you to survive and thrive in these demanding environments.

You have to be incredibly hard-working. You have to be decisive. You have to be intellectually, physically and emotionally resilient. You have to be productive and be seen to be productive. You are on parade and on display at all times. You are open to criticism and expected to be responsive (constructively so) at all times. You have to work across bandwidths and across time-zones, and remain available and fresh, at the tinkle of an e-mail, the ping of an iPhone or the bleep of a tweet – and this includes evenings, weekends and holidays.

Beyond that, the personal demands on you abound. As a 21st-century executive you have to work well with ambiguity. You need to have a style that is adaptable across cultures and across conversations. You are expected to be highly self-aware. You are required to be flexible, comfortable with conflict, and adaptable to ever-increasing and complex demands. You have to have a strong strategic sense, be able to rise above it all; and then be able to switch mode and quickly and effectively engage, deeply and constructively, with the detail. You are called to have a strong sense of self and to offer up your values for inspection. You have to be a hard-working team player as well as a strongly independent individual. You often need to be a motivator and assessor at the same time. You have to be part of the organizational push, rush and tumble as well as a pacesetting runner, able to avoid the kerfuffle and venture out confidently ahead – to lead the way for others.

To do this you have to be comfortable to work with *knowledge* of all kinds. You have to be on top of the facts of your organizational unit, your larger organizational landscape, and the context of your organization. But you also need to understand the personalities that you work with and the psychological landscape around them. You need to know about allegiances, unwritten rules, present but changing 'no-go areas', and about who needs to know what. Beyond this, you need to have some rudimentary understanding of *why* you are there and what you are up to: what is your longer-term purpose;

which objectives are you aiming for, and which might you compromise on. Quite apart from your specialist training, therefore, in addition to being a 'knowledge worker' or an 'educated person' (Drucker, 1993), with a view of where society is heading and what challenges the global economy is posing, you also have to be an aware and insightful 'empathy worker' with some understanding of the psychological make-up of your nearest and dearest.

To be a high performer in today's world of work, it is necessary for you to be engaged and collaborative, as well as tough and uncompromising. You have to protect the individual as well as look after the whole. You must work at the core whilst being present at the periphery. You are responsible for the detail yet are expected to stay out of the detail to be able to imagine the future.

In a word, you have to be incredibly present to a great many people. You have to be erudite and action-oriented; reflective and initiating; flexible and warm in relationships and decisive in your stance. This means you have to embrace quite a few paradoxes and transcend as many contradictions. It appears superhuman, yet around the globe entire hierarchies of executives are engaged in precisely this tough yet flexible dance.

In our work as coaches and consultants, we are essentially working in 'real time' with similar questions of aspiration and frustration with clients who are seeking and achieving (or suffering and recovering from) what they may perceive as episodes of balance or imbalance. This book addresses the commonly known reality that in modern life, and its challenging circumstances, and in the midst of a hectic career, we can, as managers and professionals, go into *overdrive*. We can be pushed or push ourselves into a balancing effort that overshoots, and that we have difficulty recovering from. This experience may be seen as unhealthy because it has an immediate negative effect on the quality of our work and relationships. For instance, such an overdrive may be accompanied by perceptual and cognitive biases. It may lead to increased stress and burnout. In the extreme, it may result in a decrease in physiological and psychological resilience. Ultimately, overshooting may lead to a negative spiral that can cause physiological and psychological illness or collapse.

Central to these rather extreme experiences of overreaching is the idea of *hubris*. Hubris may be described as a sense of overbearing pride, defiance or presumption not justified by the circumstances or the perceptions of others.[10] Hubris, while being implicated in the spirals of unhealthy experience described above, is itself associated with a cycle of experience. In this hubristic cycle, excessive pride and pig-headedness is generally associated with public displays of overconfidence, which hide associated private and deeply held feelings of remorse and doubt. The oscillation between excessive pride and deep shame and self-doubt can become a repeating cycle that may well spiral out of control.

What makes this process most challenging, assuming even that we recognize it within ourselves and subsequently address its causes and symptoms, is its association with other relatively healthy processes of noticing our own strengths and actively developing them. They are two related and mingled processes: one a process of *growing our talents* or *growing our business*; the other an intertwined process of *growing our hubris*. The primary developmental task here is to grow our talent without succumbing to the rupture or the exhaustion, the pride or the stress, that are the essential concomitants of the very process, leading to excessive and unfounded self-assertion. For growth and balancing to take place effectively we must pay attention as objectively as possible to our progress and the influences of our changing roles and relationships. This requires the ability to face failure or the possibility of failure with self-awareness and fortitude whilst continuing to relate effectively with others. Learning to lead requires humility in the true and original sense of the word, which is being lowly and grounded, including being in touch with what the base of your organization thinks and open to your own experiences of incompetence (*impotence*) and over-competence (*omnipotence*). Humility in this sense has little to do with a lack of self-confidence or with self-abasement and may be a quality that can support confidence as well as authenticity in leadership (Collins, 2001).

We observe that the risk of overdrive or hubris is particularly great in modern organizations. In these complex, fragmented and global settings, talented individuals may be elevated to leadership positions which nourish, reward and exploit strengths and at the same time fuel particular hubristic processes that their personal make-up and biography exposes them to. Placed in those situations they might conclude, 'I must be a really exceptional talent because this big, powerful organization is recognizing my contribution and propelling me into ever more senior ranks'. This risk is ever the greater in publicly exposed yet paradoxically highly isolated executive leadership positions. Similarly, in large professional service organizations such as investment banks, law firms, accountancies and the medical professions, individuals are singled out for reward and recognition as well as for performance and achievement. Even as we write following the debt crisis of the early 21st century, we see evidence of grandstanding and hubristic behaviour as a normal part of our everyday experience.

In order to understand and help professionals work through the unhealthy effects of such intense experiences including hubris and humility, it is necessary to understand the undercurrents that inform them. Specifically, we need to understand how these processes relate to and depend on the expression and overdrive in our core qualities. We need to understand more deeply what core qualities and personality patterns are and how such qualities conspire to develop our abilities by building on what we do well and by connecting us more intimately with others. In other words we need a model that allows us to integrate core competences with the reality of relationships and interactions with others. Such an understanding combines the essence of who we are, with the dynamics of what we are, and with the potential that we are becoming. This would enable us to understand and explain the critical aspects that lead to episodes of imbalance and the associated opportunities to recover and deepen our own self-awareness, ability to adapt, resilience and capacity to sustain recovery.

We come back to the risks of hubristic cycles in leadership in Chapters 3 and 12.

Summary: the context that produces the leader

The 21st-century workplace is placing high demands on executives. Aided by globalization and communication technology, change is becoming so rapid and complex that it is now impossible to keep up with all relevant developments, and demands seem to be overstretching anyone's competences for information processing and adaptation.

In response, our organizations and businesses are also changing more rapidly than ever before. Some of the core changes include:

- greater scrutiny, shorter lifespans and growing needs for transparency;
- greater complexity and interdependence;
- more cultural diversity and more permeability at their boundaries;
- further democratization of ownership and accountability.

All of this change is humbling for leaders and requires them to 'step up' in a new way, not by developing more capacities, more strength and more toughness, but by developing the ability to work with change in a less driven way and acquiring more balance. It is becoming ever more important for leaders to sustain the changes, offer containment and foster insight. The following chapters will look into how this can be done.

For the individual leader it becomes very tempting to take up all these challenges unquestioningly or at face value, and as a consequence to become extremely driven and focused. This may start off what we call a *hubristic cycle* that reaches out for *omnipotence* but often oscillates back to *impotence*. More than ever leaders need a place to reflect on the demands and expectations that are put on them, a place where they can rebalance and reconnect with their personal vision and home base.

Notes

1 See article by George MacDonald in *Retail Week* at: http://www.retail-week.com/home/fashion/profits-rise-at-cath-kidston/5043246.article.

2 See article in the *Telegraph*: Graham Ruddick, 12 August 2013: 'Cath Kidston sales clear £100m for first time', http://www.telegraph.co.uk/finance/newsbysector/retailandconsumer/10238314/Cath-Kidston-sales-clear-100m-for-first-time.html.

3 Cath Kidston products have been variously described as 'Kitchenalia', 'Curtainalia' and 'vintage'. See Zoe Wood's article 'Queen of Florals' in *The Guardian*. http://www.guardian.co.uk/lifeandstyle/2009/aug/09/cath-kidston-recession-floral-empire and the BBC Desert Island Disc archive: http://www.bbc.co.uk/radio4/features/desert-island-discs/castaway/685808b9.

4 Founder and creative director, Cath Kidston, was honoured in December 2009 for services to business, and was awarded an MBE in 2010.

5 See Unilever history: http://www.unilever.co.uk/aboutus/ourhistory/

6 See Unilever Annual Reports and Accounts: http://www.unilever.com/images/FinancialreviewAR11tcm13282793.pdf and http://www.unilever.com/investorrelations/annual_reports/AnnualReportandAccounts2011/Financialreview 2011.aspx

7 See IFC Global Results Report 2011: http://www1.ifc.org/wps/wcm/connect/CORP_EXT_Content/IFC_External_Corporate_Site/Annual+Report/2011+Printed+Report/Global_Results.

8 Story recounted by Cath Kidston in interview on the BBC's *Desert Island Discs* programme, http://www.bbc.co.uk/radio4/features/desert-island-discs/castaway/685808b9.

9 Niall FitzGerald is reported to have written to the Unilever Marketing Community an e-mail entitled 'Salary Increase'. When it was opened the e-mail said 'Gotcha – I thought that would get your attention' (Bird and McEwan, 2011, p 259).

10 Some well-known whistle-blowers, whose actions we shall review in later chapters, have been extremely and courageously defiant and proud against immense countervailing forces, but in their case at least the outcome of their actions has borne out the ultimate justification of their proud struggles.

Patterns of leadership

02

It is time to rethink. Business schools should – with urgency – adopt approaches to leadership education that are more critical, relational, and reflective.

DENNIS TOURISH, *THE DARK SIDE OF TRANSFORMATIONAL LEADERSHIP* (2013)

Leadership is one of the most widely written-about activities in the business literature, whilst arguably remaining one of the most obscure. This is possibly because leadership is so core to our functioning as human beings that it has become very hard to understand and conceptualize. Strong leadership is mostly present from the first moments after we are born and remains crucial for any baby's survival. Leadership is also traceable to the prehistory of human endeavour, from as soon as humans started to live in organized settlements in the Upper Paleolithic or Later Stone Age, some 50,000 years ago.

Present-day leadership in organizations is an equally fundamental concern for all who take part in business life: 'Who holds leadership?', 'How do they carry leadership?', and 'How can I influence leadership?' being some of the core questions that we can encounter in organizations on a daily basis. As this is such a core theme for all of us, it has been hard to take a good step back in order to observe the phenomenon, make sense of what it is and find criteria for effective leadership. In this chapter we will nonetheless attempt to step back, define and provide criteria for measuring the quality of leadership as offered in modern work organizations.

What is leadership and what makes good leadership?

A definition of leadership

It took us 20 years of not knowing and doubting, before the blindingly obvious, a workable definition of 'leadership', finally dawned on us:

> Leadership is the function that is devoted to enhancing an organization's effectiveness.

Retrospectively we discovered that although this definition is not widely used in the minority of books, chapters and articles in the leadership literature that do offer definitions (Rost, 1991), it does have important precursors, starting with Campbell (1956) who suggests: 'Leadership may be defined as the contribution of a given individual to group effectiveness, mediated through the direct efforts of others rather than himself' (page 1).

From this very straightforward definition, a process description can be derived, as well as criteria for measuring leadership, and measures of success for leaders.

The immediate implication of this definition is that leadership does not reside with a leader, but that anyone inside or outside an organization can contribute to this function.

Also, it immediately follows that leadership is an immeasurably complex function: 'effectiveness' can be measured on a plethora of dimensions for most organizations; similarly 'organization' can be understood in a vast variety of ways, not least in terms of the varying perspectives on it from any of its members; and finally the same is true for what is meant by 'enhancing', which again may mean a whole complex of activities, some of which are contradictory.

Finally, it is important to realize that leadership stretches all the way from the ordinary, predictable and repetitive 'management' of an organization to what might be extremely radical interventions that call into question the very existence of an organization or even its marketplace. We all know examples of new organizations that have risen out of the ashes of old ones and organizations that have decided to be taken over by others. These can be monumental leadership decisions, and for that reason perhaps 'effectiveness' in the definition should be replaced by 'efficacy' or even 'raison d'être'.

Let us look at criteria for measuring the quantity and quality of leadership first, then at a deeper understanding of our definition of leadership, and finally at what all of this implies for measuring the success of a leader. In the business of leadership the definition adopted is not arbitrary. On the contrary, any leadership definition, implicitly or explicitly, will lead to correspondingly different behaviours through the implied criteria of the definition – as we shall show for another popular definition ('leadership consists of the contributions of the leader') in Chapter 11.

A criterion for measuring leadership

In the case of our fairly obvious definition above, the main criterion for measuring leadership that would match our definition of leadership is the organization's or team's *output*. If the team's output goes up beyond baseline or beyond expectations, then leadership for the team is performing well.

So in order to measure leadership for a particular team or organization, we would have to measure the team's or organization's output under this present leadership and compare with the team's output with all circumstances the same except for how the leadership function is implemented. So we could compare the same team under a different leader (although it is never certain that the team has not 'moved on' and that many other important characteristics of the team have not changed as well). Or we could compare the team with another, similar team in similar circumstances. In Chapter 11 we will show how this is being done, eg at a company level.

It could also be argued that interviewing the team's members, in confidence, within a safe, trusted relationship, would give a helpful estimate of the performance of the team's leadership. The team members would arguably be the first to notice any signs of good or bad leadership and change their output accordingly. This way of measuring is regularly attempted with 360-degree-type, multi-party feedback instruments or interviews. Team members are bound to realize when the leadership function is not working for the team, or when their effectiveness is significantly enhanced by their formal leader.

One simple heuristic that we have picked up along the way to check whether anyone is receiving 'good enough' hierarchical leadership, is the following question: 'If you are in a meeting or a presentation or engaged in any other work activity, and all of a sudden your boss joins you in the room, how does that feel?' If you feel strengthened or appreciated, then you are experiencing 'good' leadership. If you feel inhibited or exposed, then you are experiencing 'not so good' leadership.

What this means for the business of leadership and the leadership of businesses

Before we embark on identifying measures for success based on the criterion found (output), ie before exploring what leaders can do to perform the 'leadership' function really well, we would like to review some other important implications of our simple definition of leadership.

1 *Leadership is the same as followership; and leadership is also the same as management.* 'Followership' is simply one way of implementing leadership, one way of doing our best for the effectiveness of the team. Any leader can choose at any time to contribute either more directively or rather non-directively, ie as a dominant leader or as a laid-back follower. Both options can be leadership strategies and are therefore not fundamentally different. The same is true for formal and informal leadership roles, for managers and leaders, and for designated and emerging leaders. In the literature, a lot has been made of the distinctions between leaders and followers, between leaders and managers, between formal and informal leaders. However, in terms of our definition of leadership, in terms of their contribution to leadership, there is no difference. Of course, each of these may be very different in how they take up their leadership role – that they have one is self-evident. Even for the distinction between 'leadership' and 'management', which seems so important in much of the literature (see eg Rost, 1991), we would argue that there are only gradual differences. The manager is perhaps more interested in the fine operational detail and the leader perhaps in the longer-term strategic vision: however, both remain essentially devoted to enhancing the effectiveness of the organization.

In our view there has been a lot of unnecessary confusion in the leadership literature through differentiating leaders and managers, leaders and followers, and formal leaders and team members. Although unequally distributed in organizations through role and personality differentiation, leadership is a function that *everyone* partakes in, just like, say, holding the door when someone else needs to pass or delivering on work targets.

2 *Leadership is always intimately linked with power*. Every leadership 'act', every communication that is intended to enhance a team's output in some way, even every communication that just turns out to have an impact on the organization and its output, can be seen as one individual taking authority over themselves and other individuals. This is irrespective of the individual being the nominated 'leader' of the team. Leadership is therefore always a contribution to a discourse, or a conversation, which is infused with power, with power of all kinds – position power, personal power, charm, rhetoric, resistance... In very real terms leadership amounts to an ongoing power struggle over *meaning* for the team (Mumby, 2001).

The fact that leadership is infused with power has also been noted in the *servant leadership* literature (Greenleaf, 1970); however, what we mean here is of an entirely different order. It is not enough for a leader to place him- or herself in the service of the team; in fact, that is what any leadership gesture amounts to anyway in our definition. It is also necessary to open our eyes to the real power that is available to all contributors. Appointed leaders clearly have additional powers (such as status, formal authorities and privileged information). However, followers have the power to resist, to deny or to ingratiate themselves with their leaders. The struggle to take up a 'follower' role is just as much a power struggle as that to become a leader. These are important countervailing influences that are ignored by leaders at great cost to their leadership.

3 *Leadership is entirely context and situation specific*. It matters who is on the team, what the team is for and what challenges the team is facing. Those aspects, and other situational influences, matter so much that rules or recipes or handbooks do not work for leaders, and that it is rather naïve and unhelpful for organizations to ask for standard tips and advice, or 'general' leadership development programmes (Tourish, 2013).

The fact that leadership is *situational* has already famously been put forward by Hersey and Blanchard (1969); however, what we mean here is of an entirely different order. Hersey and Blanchard give circumscribed suggestions for different situations, depending on the preparedness for a task of a particular team member, which leads to somewhat formulaic, recipe-like suggestions for leaders.

In our view such suggestions are *by nature* verging on the unworkable, as a leader needs to take on board more fully the current team, tasks and context.

4 *Leadership is a social construct.* In other words, leadership is about developing meaning in work, meaning in terms of priorities, meaning for strategy, and meaning for decision making. A lot of the *meaning-making* is itself about meaning, as in 'how do we prioritize different ways of creating value for our customers?' In other words, the social constructs are partly self-referential and some of the meaning-making is at meta-level. Many of the social constructs of leadership are themselves about other social constructs. We have already noted that leadership is an ongoing struggle, or an ongoing conversation, about making meaning for the team. This struggle could be about what would make the team more effective, or it could simply be about what to do next. Essential is the fact that it is a meaning-producing process where all team members are implicated. The meaning produced is about the meaning of the work they do, whether to do more or less of it, change it, replace it, or branch out in different directions. The leadership process is a process of meaning-making for every task that the team is employed in. This is another reason why leadership is such an extraordinarily complex field.

5 *Leadership is in essence distributed not concentrated, and transactional not transformational.* Within the leadership function there is a 'market' or a 'struggle' for meaning, where offers and counteroffers, bids and counterbids are constantly exchanged between all team members. By definition this can be, for example, an open, free and fast-moving marketplace, or it can be a marketplace restricted by systems that limit free expression and exchange of opinion etc. Transformational leadership (Burns, 1978) is essentially attempting to put systems in place that work against the transactional nature of leadership, by attributing absolute or near-absolute power to an idealized leadership figure, a 'Leader' with a capital letter. This kind of leadership is in our view essentially an illusion and where it has been tried (as in sects, fascist and totalitarian regimes, and militaristic organizations) it has consistently led to dire consequences for all involved: corruption and degeneration for leaders and terror and oppression for other team or organizational members.

We are not denying that there are *inspirational* leaders, we are only saying that inspirational leaders do not operate under a *transformational* paradigm, certainly not in the long term. In other words we have noticed that truly inspirational leaders have always contributed fluidly to meaning-making, towards openness and participation. Those inspirational leaders that most would recognize, such as Gandhi, Gorbachev and Mandela, have consistently been able to be followers as well as leaders, listeners as well as active influencers, and have not needed to rely on a unique, transformational position or narrative in order to do so (Brown, 2014). So we would argue that inspirational leaders are not 'above the law' in any way; they do not transcend the definition of leadership given earlier. Quite the contrary: the transformational status attributed to great leaders and projected onto them by their followers is in our view one of the biggest issues they have to contend with. It is an issue that can make them vulnerable and impair them as leaders, particularly if they start to believe in that special status. We will look at such 'overdrive patterns' of successful leaders in detail in Part Two of this book.

6 *Leadership is relational not individual.* Perhaps the most important corollary of our chosen definition is the fact that leadership is a process *between* people more than *within* people. An act of leadership is always a communication. Therefore, leadership requires a meeting between a 'gesture' (or 'assertion') and a 'response', or more precisely, a meeting of two or more contemporaneous gestures which mutually influence one another.

Taken together with the previous point, leadership is by and of itself collaborative and communicative in nature, which means it cannot be located just in any one person at any moment of time. It is a mutual, co-creative process of intimating, of responding, of recognizing, that goes on all the time between team members, whether a leader has been designated or not, whether we pay attention to it or not. Leadership can be seen as the background to action, the ground that carries or illuminates the figure, always present, always evolving.

In the next section we will explore the essential *relationality* of leadership further, as it is not straightforward to keep in mind such 'in-between', shared processes without reverting back to individuals or processes authorized and owned by a single person or entity.

What this means for success as a leader

Now we have explored our simple definition of leadership and drawn a criterion for measurement from it, namely the organization's or team's output, we can return to measures of success for leaders.

The most important aspect of effectiveness in leadership is now easy to guess. The output of an organization is a result of the combined work of all members of that organization, who work together as a team. The best outcome will be obtained if the best people are hired for the right jobs and can focus on their own outputs as well as helping others with theirs (the latter is their contribution to 'leadership'). The best leader is therefore the one who encourages the leadership contribution from all team members and helps aggregate the various contributions in a concerted approach. It is well known that the best ideas may come from anywhere and that local experts in particular can have the best ideas, or at least the ideas that are best adapted to their local practice. It is also well known that the best decisions are taken by the widest possible congregation, as they tap into the amazing 'wisdom of crowds' (Surowiecki, 2005). Therefore the greatest effectiveness for any leader comes from facilitating and aggregating the widest potential of meaning making, direction and feedback.

On the basis of extensive research Surowiecki suggests that although for most team activities the group average is mediocre (the 'largest common denominator'), this is not true for decision making where the average group decision is in fact consistently better than a decision taken by the best member of the team. Surowiecki concludes that organizational excellence in making the best decisions together only occurs when 1) as many team members as possible are engaged, 2) when they have a diversity of opinions, 3) when they have the greatest possible independence in their thinking, 4) when they are decentralized and 5) when they have a mechanism in place (which could be just group averaging or voting) to aggregate what they come up with. This type of fluidity in generating and aggregating the team's views is precisely what leadership can do for the organization.

Tourish (2013, page 210) also argues that the greatest success factor for leaders is their ability to keep the processes of leadership *fluid*, open and dynamic. In fact, there has been direct evidence for a strong correlation between 'leadership effectiveness' and 'routine communication' which includes giving timely information and being open to upwards communication

(Luthans, Hodgetts and Rosenkrantz, 1988). For a more complete summary of these data see Chapter 11.

It is in our view essential for a leader to learn how to make their mark *without* hindering others from occupying themselves fully with the job of leadership as well. The main challenge for formal leaders is *despite* the power differentials that are there, to open up and facilitate a helpful and shared pattern of meaning-making. Only with such an interactive pattern can the leadership function be firmly rooted within the whole organization or team, and thus enhance the output of that organization.

This means in practice that leaders need to be open to a two-way conversation, they need to be able to listen to all team members (and the wider context too), and they need to allow and sustain, even to encourage, the frustrations of *critical upwards feedback*. Only in this way can they keep their leadership alive and preclude it from becoming a one-sided and therefore rather ineffectual affair. As we will see later in the book (Chapter 11), sadly, in an estimated over 50 per cent of organizations leadership has not been upheld in such a way. In other words, most leadership appears to be seriously falling short of enhancing the output of businesses. We do realize that it is a big ask of leaders to suggest they keep the leadership process fluid and open, mutual and rich in meaning-making. It means leaders must show understanding of the position and predicament of their 'followers', and how that position makes it hard to be open and critique the present arrangements (eg for fear of retaliation, out of anxiety about what others and in particular more powerful leaders may think, or from reluctance to take up such a responsibility beyond their more narrowly defined remit). It also means that leaders sustain painful and unexpected, even unreasonable, messages regarding leadership which they are wont to take overly personally as they think it is their 'job' to lead. Ultimately, if we were forced to choose between a 'strong' and a 'weak' leader, we would be biased towards the latter – just like Brown (2014), and as Aesop also seems to be in the fragment at the end of this chapter. In case of 'weak' leaders there is more of a chance that they will get out of the way when there are good ideas for leadership within the team.

Safeguarding fluidity is not the only important contribution we expect good leaders to make, but it is in our view the most essential and critical aspect of the leader's role. Other aspects in the relational domain are vital as well, and for this reason we will devote more attention to leadership talents such as the ability to care for and make meaning of feelings in a helpful way (the aspect of 'containment' in the leader's role), frustration tolerance, inspirational thinking, humility, and compassion, all in Part Three of this book.

Having spoken about the individual role of the leader and the leader's talents we need to emphasize once again that leadership does not reside in this person whatever the gravitas and dignity of the job title and personality, whatever the respect she or he is paid or the compensation he or she receives. We agree with Tourish (2013) that such respect is exaggerated in the present-day business world, and that this is actively wrecking organizations. Here is a quote from Tourish that explains it better than we could:

> Spartacus was the leader of a slave revolt in ancient Rome from 73 to
> 71 BC – a revolt that brought the empire to the brink of collapse. History
> is written by the victors. But in this case Roman sources recorded that,
> before his final battle with Crassus, Spartacus's men brought him his horse.
> He ceremoniously slaughtered it, to demonstrate that he shared their fate
> in either victory of defeat. By contrast, many leaders today make sure that
> they have Golden Parachutes. In the event of failure they emerge from the
> wreckage with enough wealth to sustain them for the rest of their lives.
> Such differentials damage relations between leaders and followers. They
> also damage organizations and societies. A step change in practice is needed.
> Leaders need to be more willing to share the spoils of victory and the pain
> of defeat with their followers.
>
> Tourish, 2013, page 213

There are only very few domains where leadership still seems to be valued realistically, such as in professional sports, in the arts and occasionally in professional medicine, where a 'manager' still earns less than a professional 'worker'. We would argue that unhelpful definitions such as the *leader is the person in charge* or *in command, the leader is responsible, that's where the buck stops,* or the *leader bears all the accountability* have historically been behind this real distortion of practice. If only corporations could bring themselves to define leadership slightly differently, slightly more realistically, they could save themselves and their shareholders a lot of money that they are presently paying out to overvalued, so-called 'transformational' leaders.

In the next section we want to explore this further and to put relational leadership more in the context of contemporary developments in psychological thinking.

FIGURE 2.1   The essence of relationality: we *are* different people in different contexts

A relational perspective on leadership

A shift in conceptualizing leadership

In recent years, we have seen a significant shift in the social and organizational sciences. There has been a movement away from the focus on the leader or the helper as a *person*, towards a focus on the *relationship* between leader and follower as a central vehicle for change. It has involved a change of emphasis from a focus on techniques and interventions, goal-setting and action-planning, towards an appreciation of and engagement with patterns of relating. This shift places relationship, to self and to others, at the heart of practice. This 'relational turn' as it is known (Mills, 2005; De Haan, 2008) has mirrored similar movements in all fields of psychological work as well as in organizational theory, sociology and the arts.

Important predecessors to relational thinking are Pirandello who passionately asked questions about the influence of relationship on character,[1] and John Bowlby who hypothesized *attachment* as a biologically-based instinct which informs other drives, with individual differences in *attachment style* related to internal models of self-in-relationship.

Why has the world seen such a profound new emphasis on the importance of relating? Firstly, there have been remarkable and synchronistic developments in the areas of 'postmodern' philosophy, neurobiology, and the study of human development. Research in these three areas has revealed an interconnectedness between human beings that was hitherto only recognized in some philosophies and spiritual traditions. Since the Renaissance and in particular the 'Age of Enlightenment', men (and women) have committed themselves to positivist, evidence-based, logical ways of understanding the world that have led to huge leaps in understanding and development but left little room for mysteries such as intuition, inter-subjectivity, and unconscious connection. This has gradually given way to a focus on difference, plurality and context. Recent discoveries in affective neuroscience have provided significant evidence (eg Rizzolatti and Craighero, 2004; Panksepp, 1998; Schore, 2003) to underscore the centrality of relatedness in human development and behaviour. Organizational thinking based on chaos and complexity theory, which recognizes how small gestures can amplify into large-scale pattern shifts, is encouraging us to think of an organization, and even a society, simply as a collection of interactive processes rather than a structure or system (Stacey, 2012). What is more, the loving relationship between mother and infant has been shown to be crucial in developing the brain and the sense of identity, while in later life, an accepting and supportive relationship can also facilitate changes in neural patterns and in our confidence and sense of self in the world (Schore, 2003; Allen, 2011; Wampold, 2001).

The findings of all these disciplines are built on a revolution in epistemology offered by feminist psychologists such as Jean Baker Miller, Joyce Fletcher and Carol Gilligan, who challenged 'the gendered nature of knowledge creation' (eg Miller, 1976 and Gilligan, 1982). They pointed out that traditional child developmental theories (eg Piaget, Erikson and Freud), all of which stressed the importance of ego strength, autonomy, and separateness, stemmed from a psychological research base that was the exclusive province of men. These feminist thinkers offered another understanding of health and maturity, which involved interdependence, cooperation, and the 'relational skills' of support and empathy. This new understanding highlighted new ways of entering relationships: not just as means to a purpose, but with a true commitment to being changed by them. This feminist perspective is similar to our underlining the importance for leaders to be open to change by 'upward feedback', which we believe to be a core ingredient for leaders' effectiveness as discussed earlier in this chapter.

The new relational focus is not only a result of these developments. It has also arisen out of a need to understand something that could not be explained or comprehended within existing psychological or leadership theories, and to respond to increasingly complex systems. Seen through this lens, the relational focus, rather than being a formally organized school or system of beliefs, can be thought of as a framework or way of thinking about the leader, the subordinates, the team, the organization – and about how leadership works. This perspective says that leader, follower and organization are intimately interlinked and that for leadership to have any impact at all the links in between would have to be impacted as well. Moreover, progress and change will occur only in the presence of links that are or become nurturing, meaningful, supportive and challenging. So what could be more helpful than focusing on the link, the connection, the *relationship* itself while it emerges and evolves?

Are we waves or particles?

The radical idea in relational psychology is that it is perhaps not 'us' having a leadership role in organizations, and that it is not 'us' who have to respond to ever greater pressures and societal changes. Rather than us taking up roles and initiating action, it is more appropriate to say that our relational environment, including the relationship networks that we are engaged in, is called upon to respond and act. When we shift, our relationships will shift. When we move, we will make a move in those relationships. All of this may hang together so much that it is our relationships we may have to change first and foremost in order to step into whatever is our response to any change. In other words, we think more about a leadership 'function' that is being carried by the team than we would think of any particular individual 'doing' the leadership for the team.

A useful way of thinking about this is the *Fourier transformation* in physics (Fourier, 1822). This transformation allows for a representation of a given function in two ways: either as a discrete unit that travels through time in a linear fashion (such as a person, a leader), or as a composite of waves that are always shared, as they are contemporaneously superimposed. Similarly, we can think about ourselves either as a discrete 'unit' going through organizational life and home life, along discrete actions and discrete meetings, from 'e-mailing time' to 'meeting time' to 'sport time' etc. Or we can think of ourselves as a 'superposition' of selves, alternate ways of being and presenting ourselves (Hermans and Kempen, 1993) where going through our daily routines, different relationships give rise to a range of resonances and self-representations. We know through the phenomenon of transference (Freud, 1905) that we tend to re-create known 'presences' with new colleagues and relationships, so these permeating presences or selves may be an altogether faithful and perhaps more helpful way of understanding our behaviour and contributions in every single moment.

Another important psychological concept, that of *overdetermination* or multi-causality (Freud, 1900), can also be brought to bear. If we are able to think of the leadership function as a multitude of different influences that are relatively stable in time, coming together to define leadership at any given moment or at any given location or relating to any given issue, then we also begin to think differently about significant events such as the launch of a new product, the derailment of a leader, the creation of a new 'leadership team', or the breakdown of a negotiation. We will then no longer attribute any of those events to a single cause, but we will look at a wider number of significant 'causes' all coming together, and all in themselves more than sufficient to explain the significant outcome.

Through our habits which are deeply ingrained we go through life repeating old relational 'wavelets' most of the time as we are engaging in similar successes, conflicts and ways of relating as before. With our context looking different every time (say, another country) or the people we interact with being different as discrete units (they have different names and identities), we deceive ourselves into thinking that we pretty much linearly move through life changing ourselves and our surroundings. On the contrary, underneath we might still be drawing from exactly the same collection of patterns and 'wavelets' of relating that we were drawing from when we were little children. Psychological research in the area of attachment does seem to confirm that we have habitual patterns of relating and that these habitual patterns are passed on to people we share our lives with and to future generations through their early attachment patterns to us (Van IJzendoorn, Juffer and Duyvesteyn, 1995).

One advantage of representing ourselves by a wavelike structure, or (in other words) of thinking about ourselves as collections of relational patterns which we don't own as they are shared and endlessly recur and recombine, is that we do not have to think about ourselves as 'going through change'. We can then think of ourselves as being essentially stable whilst being responsive or resourceful enough to bring to the fore a different aspect of ourselves, or else we could think of ourselves as stable yet exposed to all sorts of different pressures. This would create a narrative about change where aspects of ourselves are brought out, instead of a narrative where we shift, change, or resist change ourselves. In that former narrative we and those with us would essentially resonate with the new 'interference' rather than thinking of ourselves as, say, an agent or a victim of change.

If we go back to our main measure for good leadership in the previous section, *safeguarding fluidity*, two different aspects come to mind that are to do with looking after safety and insight:

1 Relational leadership entails making sure that team or organizational members can speak out and contribute with their honest views on the topic.

2 Relational leadership entails helping out with the co-creation of meaning in the moment.

Modern attachment research has shown that these two different aspects, safety and meaning, are intimately related in our 'attachment styles', ie when we feel secure we make more meaning, and when we are able to make meaning of the situation we are in, we feel more secure. More about these two different, but related aspects of leadership in the next section.

What makes us secure?

Further research in the area of attachment (Fonagy *et al*, 1991) has shown that there is probably a measurable property of our minds that is linked to secure attachment or feeling at ease with the circumstances around us, which has been called the *reflective-self function* or the *ability to mentalize*. In order to understand how this property may develop it is necessary to consider its likely genesis in early childhood development.

The reflective-self function is an operationalization of the capacity to 'mentalize' (Brown, 1977) or the capacity for 'metacognition' (Main and Goldwyn, 1990) or 'psychological mindedness' (Appelbaum, 1973; Grant, 2001). The reflective-self function measures an individual's *quality of understanding of another's intentionality*, and is measured on a 9-point Likert scale. The measure combines understanding of self and others, so it applies in equal measure to reflections on one's own and someone else's intentionality. The measure also combines 'true' understanding and 'plausible' understanding, or in other words 'accurate' and 'habitual' modes of understanding, as no measure for 'objective' or 'shared' understanding is introduced (Fonagy *et al*, 1991). Joyce McDougal (1978) indicated that in early childhood the 'mother functions as the baby's thinking system'. This notion of mothering as a containing, mirroring and reflective activity is prevalent throughout the psychoanalytical literature and lies at the root of the idea of the reflective-self function.

Reflective-self function is not the same as *empathy*, although empathetic understanding will have to be based on this capacity. Reflective-self function is more fundamental than empathy and refers to the capacity to understand what goes on within oneself or within another, whereas empathy refers to an understanding from within, the capacity to feel what another person feels, ie to become sympathetic or 'in tune' with those feelings oneself.

Reflective-self function is also not the same as *mindfulness*, although mindfulness can be seen as a capacity that reflective-self function is based on or draws from. Mindfulness is a spiritual faculty in Buddhism which amounts to an attentive awareness of the reality of things and is therefore very close to being psychologically awake ('Buddha' literally means 'he that is awoken'). Mindfulness, therefore, extends from understanding psychological facts to natural phenomena and even spiritual experience. Nevertheless, mindfulness frequently refers to one's own bodily functions, sensations, feelings, thoughts, perceptions and consciousness itself – in which case it would appear very akin to reflective-self function.

To summarize:

1 *Mindfulness* can be seen as attentive awareness of what is going on in the present moment.

2 *Reflective-self function*, within mindfulness, can be seen as being aware of what is going on in the minds of self and others, in the present moment.

3 *Empathy*, building on reflective-self function, can be seen as being aware of and sharing in states of mind as they occur to another person, in the present moment.

Thus, if leadership is all about meaning-making for teams and organizations, then there is some hard evidence that people can be more effective if they can feel more secure, and that they can be more secure if they have a better, or at least a more plausible, understanding of their own and others' intentions. The leadership function can help them to gain in that understanding.

As the ancient Delphic oracle maintained, it really is worthwhile for leaders to 'know themselves'. In other words, it is important for leaders to have *insight and the capacity to develop new insights and to make new meaning as contexts change and new challenges emerge.*

Leading relationally

Relational leadership means first and foremost making meaning within a web of relationships, whilst making use of and growing the strengths of those relationships.

When there are pressures in organizations it is well known that our brain can short-circuit all the problem-solving areas of the neocortex by triggering an 'amygdala' response (LeDoux, 1996; Goleman, 1996). This mechanism unleashes a host of biological fight, flight or freeze responses that we share with most animals and that short-circuit our neocortex, our thinking capability or conscious processing. This immediate, instinctive response to danger is highly effective; however, it does not contribute to meaning-making. Not only does this 'amygdala hijack' short-circuit reflection, it also actively impairs and distorts our reflective processes and mentalization.

Even if an outright biological threat response is not triggered then there are more subtle *defence mechanisms* that work against meaning-making. More than a century after their discovery (Freud, 1894) a host of different defences are now known, such as projection, rationalization, displacement, sublimation and acting out. Similar to the amygdala response these mechanisms work against unwelcome news such as a drop in sales or the announcement of a corporate restructuring, by suppressing the very message and commencing defensive responses such as argumentation or disloyalty. Similar again to the amygdala response these defence mechanisms preclude reflection and mentalization, because the very thing that needs to be reflected on is suppressed from the thinking process and actively but largely unconsciously resisted.

We have noticed on countless occasions that where the demands of modern business toughen up, executives often respond by short-circuiting or defensively suppressing their meaning-making abilities. As we have argued in the previous chapter, it is perhaps not possible to fully engage with the pace and complexity of change in the 21st century. However, we would argue that instead of keeping up with the pace of change, what is needed is more a *preservation* of our thinking faculties, of our powers of reflection, creativity and mentalization. This is where the leadership function in organizations is most in demand.

Once any truly existential danger is out of the way or has been reassessed as being stressful and frustrating rather than life-threatening (as it usually is), leaders in organizations, whether formally appointed or not, can help to restore meaning-making and effectiveness in their teams and wider organizations. Relational leadership tells us that this can be done in two main ways (De Haan, 2008):

1 *Nurturing the relationships* in the team, to make them safer and more open, so that they begin to contribute actively to the meaning-making process.

2 *Leading from the relationship*, in other words reflecting with others on what is going on in those relationships, right now.

We seem to be equipped with so many immediate, automatic, visceral and even cognitive processes that impair or attack thinking, particularly when we become stressed, that it has become very hard to follow the oracle's injunction ('know thyself') even on a quiet and undisturbed day. Biological survival is still imprinted onto our daily existence, in a completely disproportional way to the nature of the stresses most of us face today – at least at work. This is where therapy, sports, recreation, relaxation and support from loved ones play such a great role: bringing the modern executive back to a place where meaning-making can happen again and where the support of secure attachments and safe relationships allows us to make use of our reflective, meaning-making and mentalizing abilities.

CASE ILLUSTRATION

A real case example of how this happens may be helpful as an illustration here. A top executive we have known is faced with the responsibility of managing and leading a globally spread and disparate organization whilst finding herself facing severe physical disability and psychological trauma. Her immediate and instinctive response is to 'fight back': to change her routines in order to protect herself. There is a strong urge to take proactive action to defend against perceived 'threats' which generally come in the form of heavy workloads, external societal changes and inconsiderate demands from co-workers.

Whilst her newly directed energy and attention provides a short-term sense of relief and achievement, the overall context and underlying challenges do not change. Indeed the specific issues she has to address appear to multiply as they are stimulated in turn to respond to this new frenetic activity and intensity of response. The initial relief disappears and a new more intense pattern emerges, this time accompanied with a deepening sense of personal failure, frustration, fear and fatigue.

After consultation with friends and professionals and following guided meditation, the executive shifts her attention from response, action and defence to understanding and reflection. She genuinely begins to understand the futility of fighting for protection and profoundly recognizes the necessity of gaining new and deeper insight into the relationships and connections creating the patterns of demand and intensity that she has hitherto been locked into.

As this case illustration shows, what is often needed in modern business life is a fresh capacity of meaning-making, with much more emphasis on insight and understanding than on re-establishing safety or finding solutions. What is then needed is new focus for meaning-making, with much more emphasis on the 'in-between' people and the relational patterns that we are part of, and less emphasis on understanding what happens within ourselves and others. What is needed is a shift away from control, action and change, towards relating, mindfulness and mentalization.

Characteristics of relationship patterns

When as a leader you shift your perspective in this way from 'particles' to 'waves', you will notice other aspects of the workplace that may be important. In the following section we describe four characteristics that emerge out of a more relational perspective.

Boundaries

Boundaries are a good way of getting to the 'in-between' people, departments, or organizations. Boundaries are the places where we 'touch' each other, where our gestures are perceived and our words begin to be heard. Boundaries are not things, no one has ever pointed to a boundary as a definable physical shape nor have they succeeded in moving a boundary between people, however much force or power they applied. A boundary is a place of meeting, or an interface, or the invisible layer in between. The boundary is permeated by 'wavelets' or 'force fields' and is the place where they interact and form patterns.[2]

One of the unique properties of a boundary is that it looks different from all sides: different people will view their boundary or place of contact entirely differently. One will see potential, another a rupture, and a third a resource that contributes to their jobs. Boundaries and their (perceived) permeability are essential to what people will say and will not say in a relationship. If they have a positive experience of this interface, or in other words if they feel understood, they will approach it with trust and they will generously offer their thoughts, their work and their products. If they make a different sense of it they will be more guarded, nervous or withholding.

Leaders can be helpful in drawing attention to a boundary, as a place where one's responsibility ends and another's begins, where (mis-)understandings are born, and where job roles are defined.

CASE ILLUSTRATION

Fred is a man with a plan. He has been talking with key accounts of his business, with top managers in his company and with consultants in his industry. And he has recently achieved a clear understanding of what the future needs from his team. He also knows that the feedback from the outside world is very positive and that this plan will build on the strengths that are available in the team. To his utter amazement he does not receive any gratitude when he e-mails the plan around to his team. He only gets questions which he senses have a very critical tone to them, as if they are all saying, 'don't bother us' and 'what a hopelessly poor plan'. He cannot understand how they do not see that this plan is actually not hard to implement, is in the interests of the team itself and the colleagues individually, and will make them much more successful.

Maybe the fact that he had e-mailed it around had something to do with it, he thinks. When he starts to talk with colleagues, they are still by and large negative and critical, and he begins to see that they don't feel any ownership. He wonders aloud whether they would want full ownership of the plan. They now respond slightly more positively and they start to talk about boundaries. What Fred hadn't clarified about his plan, or set out within the plan itself, is who takes responsibility for what. He had never entered into a contract with the team around his own role and theirs, and he had not realized that they would like to feel empowered to take charge of at least some part of his brilliant plan. Team members now come with counterproposals where different individuals are responsible for different aspects. In fact, the relationship is reversed, with Fred now asked not to produce anything but only to overlook the process and ask the difficult questions.

Roles

Roles are the spaces that are delineated by boundaries. They define the potential space that a person senses within an organization, in other words they are the sum total of their boundaries for them. A work role is much more than a function, more than a job description, more than status or authority. It is the space within which people feel able to contribute, create meaning, process and participate. Outside the role, one feels uncomfortable and insecure; inside the role one is much more self-assured. A role is therefore the sum total of what we feel that we are responsible for, our unique contribution to other 'roles' and the organization as a whole. A role in any project, organization or daily activity is made up of formal descriptions, informal relational pressures, organizational demands, and individual abilities to inform and influence boundaries.

In the wavelets and fields analogy that we have used so far to illustrate the relational perspective, roles are the broad domains in which wavelets can resonate, the kinds of things a person has responsibility for or feels capable of contributing to.

It is possible to carry out a *role analysis:* in other words, to explore with a colleague his or her available roles, and the choice of roles that may be open to them (Reed, 2000). The following distinctions can be made in this respect:

- *Role biography* focuses on the person: what roles has the person played in this and in other work processes, and what experiences are associated with those roles?

- *Role history* focuses on the organization: what roles has the organization traditionally offered and nurtured?

- *Role dialogue* focuses on both: what conversation or negotiation takes place – partly unconsciously – between organization, team and person, in order to arrive at the most appropriate role interpretation?

Leaders can link their understanding of boundaries with their understanding of roles. Is this person really responsible and available to do this piece of work, and do they have the proper boundaries or interfaces to express themselves in it? The leader's own role is often called 'management discretion' or 'discretion' (see also Chapters 11 and 12).

CASE ILLUSTRATION

Gianna has been growing the bottom line of her business yet does not get new investment from her boss. She is a forthright, frank person, from Italian descent, and has let her boss know that she is not happy with how things are going. Her boss, being of Asian origin, addresses issues in a different way. He has operated much more cautiously and has been friendly with everyone without, however, fighting Gianna's battles in his senior team. So for many months, and even years, Gianna's department has remained understaffed and the conversations between her and her boss have become increasingly prickly. It was only when the two discovered some of the differences in the roles they were playing for the business that things began to ease up. They had not realized that with the same engineering background they both fulfilled entirely different requirements in the wider organization. One was an excellent mediator and kind supporter, whilst the other (Gianna) was very driven and offered a critical 'edge' to the common business. Together they could now devise a strategy for what they both wanted: more investment in their team.

Valency

Valency is a relational term indicating our propensity for responding to, and connecting with different group emotional patterns. Starting from what is defined by a job description and job remit and building on the boundaries that relational patterns in organizations have left open for a job role, valency is our own personal contribution to shifting and changing those boundaries, to forming our role in an organization. Valency is therefore our unique response to a boundary or to a role.

In the wavelets and fields analogy that we have used so far to illustrate the relational perspective, roles are the possible 'eigen functions' or 'steady states' of the wavelets, ie the characteristic shapes in which they appear or the empty spaces that they 'resonate' into and fill up.

Leaders can work with valency by imagining the team or organization as an individual that puts pressure on its members to act in a certain way. Those team members that find it hard to go along with the overwhelming tendency of the team and organization and express themselves differently, will have a valency that is picking up the pressure, taking the heat. Such an individual will then speak for the team or organization in its current position.

It is important to realize that an individual who seems to be awkward, not fitting in, not performing very well, or being scapegoated by a team, may be carrying an important valency that is actually registering something important for the team as a whole to be aware of.

CASE ILLUSTRATION

Jacques is a senior manager in a fast-moving consumer services industry and has realized that he cannot keep sales and delivery as separate departments, so he has decided to merge them. In a large open-plan office sales and delivery staff are now sitting together in little islands grouped around particular specialized services.

Jacques knows from recent meetings that the merger is not happily received and that the integration is not progressing smoothly. When he walks through the offices he notices an eerie silence and a certain 'deadness' in the air, and in the way the place is decorated, or has not been looked after. He hears about conflicts between team members. He has decided that he wants to mediate and spends many hours with each of the individual 'islands' trying to talk things through and explaining yet again why it is so important for customers that front-office and back-office now know what the other is doing. Only when he gets down to the individual irritations, the 'valencies' of what team members have picked up and what they are each individually grieving for in terms of their previous work environments, can he slowly get through to the nub of issues and begin to identify what each can bring to their 'island'. From desert islands they now slowly grow into something habitable.

Parallel process

Parallel process is where you can address the 'wavelets' or transference dynamics that team members bring to the table. If we think of organizational processes as relational and more wavelike in structure, then we can take any meeting or event as a 'measurement' of relationships that are present for the individuals or teams in other contexts.

Looking at a single meeting or event in this way begins to provide us with a clue or a perspective on other events. We can safely conclude that patterns or dynamics in the here and now are similar to patterns elsewhere. The form that a meeting or event takes becomes much more meaningful than if we see the event as discrete and unconnected with other events involving the same people. What we would surmise is that an important relational theme is addressed *in the moment*, ie right now as members of the team work together.

Leaders can link their understanding of dynamics in the moment with their understanding of dynamics elsewhere. Leaders can describe what they see right in front of them and infer similar patterns existing elsewhere. This can be a very powerful hypothesis and the observation of 'here and now' dynamics is hard to escape as the evidence is right there whilst we speak. As with any hypothesis there will be other explanations as well, given the overdetermination of relational events mentioned in the previous section, but leaders would do well to keep open the possibility that some of what they have seen reveals issues that the teams or individuals are struggling with elsewhere as well.

CASE ILLUSTRATION

Ingrid is a great ambassador for her organization. She travels to see large industrial clients and to speak with government representatives. She has also been sent out to look at potential acquisitions for other parts of the business. She knows she doesn't spend enough time inside the business and with her direct co-workers. She relies on Kevin to chair most of the meetings and to keep her department together.

Recently Kevin said to her, 'You love your freedom, don't you?' and this made her think. She realized how she had been very free, independent and self-sufficient as a child and how she had re-created some of her childhood roaming about in her work role. She decided to watch herself more and to start phoning back to the office at least once on the days that she wasn't there, and also to come in more regularly despite part of her personality railing against that. Soon enough she had an opportunity to notice some of the parallel processes she had created, through the amount of cancellations at meetings, and the hesitation from her staff in inviting her into project reviews with them.

Example of a relationship pattern

Boundaries, roles, valencies and parallel processes can all be pictured as membranes, cells, cellular functions and DNA within an organism, but this would be too simple a picture. Boundaries, roles and valencies are essentially wavelike, existing in more than three dimensions, permeating through to other parts of the organization, as they exist in the minds and therefore also in the actions of others. Boundaries between department A and B are therefore everywhere, not just in the physical or psychological space between those two groupings. The same with job roles, they are defined as much by what people think or believe about what someone should be doing as they are by the task lists, relationships and input–output patterns around an individual. These are complex concepts, yet well understood as wavelike presences in organizations. Changing the individual who fulfils the role makes an obvious difference to boundaries and valencies and to the role itself. However, it is quite common in organizations to see a successor creep back into the same limitations, expectations and contributions as their predecessor afforded – even if they never meet each other and on the surface seem entirely different individuals with entirely different remits. Boundaries, roles or valencies are not fully defined by the contributions of any one individual and are therefore persistent when individuals change, just as they may evolve whilst an individual remains in post.

We would like to offer a relatively straightforward and measurable example of valencies, the kind of relational patterns that we carry with us from an early age and that are both linked to our personality and to the messages that we have internalized from our parents.

Transactional analysis, a branch of psychotherapy that has studied 'transactions', ie relational boundary crossings, for many decades, has shown that we can model valencies as 'behavioural drivers' that we all possess to some degree. The degree to which particular behavioural drivers come to the fore in our daily interaction with others distinguishes us from our co-workers. Taibi Kahler (1975) has suggested a basic set of only five behavioural drivers that we will all recognize:[3]

- *Be perfect*: stepping in when perfection, high standards, attention to detail are called for.

- *Please others*: stepping in when care, harmony and empathy are called for.

- *Hurry up*: stepping in when short deadlines, high intensity and speed are called for.

- *Be strong*: stepping in when resilience, calm and cold logic, and reliability are called for.

- *Try hard*: stepping in when motivation, enthusiasm, and a creative, broad outlook are called for.

Once we have adopted and established a particular behavioural driver early on in our life this driver easily becomes a daily routine. One can imagine many other, more subtle valencies than these core drivers, such as taking on the role of hermit, rebel, saint, scapegoat, prima donna, fixer, victim etc. In Part Two of this book we will show how such more elaborate valencies can turn into personality overdrive patterns.

In the previous chapter we looked at the challenges which the demanding 21st-century context presents to us and our ability to adapt. We considered the limitations of our adaptability as human beings and the futility of efforts to protect ourselves against growing demands and frenetic workplace realities. In this chapter we have introduced the importance of a relational perspective, demonstrating the importance of insight, support and meaning-making.

To end this chapter here is an analogy of leadership that is some 2,600 years old, which includes an extreme example of followers getting the leaders they deserve.

The frogs who demanded a king

The frogs, annoyed with the anarchy in which they lived, sent a deputation to Zeus to ask him to give them a king. Zeus, seeing that they were but very simple creatures, threw a piece of wood into their marsh. The frogs were so alarmed by the sudden noise that they plunged into the depths of the bog. But when the piece of wood did not move, they clambered out again. They developed such contempt for this new king that they jumped on his back and crouched there.

The frogs were deeply ashamed at having such a king, so they sent a second deputation to Zeus asking him to change their monarch. For the first was too passive and did nothing.

Zeus now became impatient with them and sent down a water-serpent which seized them and ate them all up.

> It is better to be ruled by passive, worthless men who bear no spitefulness than by productive but wicked ones.

Aesop's Fable 66, 6th century BC

Summary: patterns of leadership

Leadership can be defined as the *function that is devoted to enhancing an organization's effectiveness.*

This definition has a number of implications:

- leadership and followership are two sides of the same medal, just like leadership and management: they all fit within the same function;
- leadership and power are interlinked;
- leadership is entirely context specific and contingent;
- leadership is a social construct dealing with other social constructs;
- leadership is in essence distributed not concentrated, transactional not transformational, and relational not individual.

We argue that the best single success criterion for leadership consists of *safeguarding fluidity*, ie keeping the leadership function shared, lively and robust.

Safeguarding fluidity requires a considerable amount of containment (looking after safety) and meaning-making (looking after insight). Modern psychological research has shown that these aspects are more related than was thought, through the demonstrated correlation of secure attachment and reflective-self function.

Leadership as a relational construct can be devoted to meaning-making and enhancing effectiveness between people through reflection on:

- *Boundaries*: what is the interface between departments like?
- *Roles*: how do departments shape their function for other departments?
- *Valencies*: where are departments stepping in to fulfil unmet needs?
- *Parallel processes*: what patterns do we notice that are repeated throughout the business?

We give a few basic examples of valencies, in the form of five different *behavioural drivers* that all of us partake in to a highly personal extent.

Notes

1   Take for example this quote from *Six Characters in Search of an Author*: 'The person you are with me is quite different from the person you are with somebody else. But we go on thinking we're exactly the same person for everybody, the person we think we are in our own mind and in everything we do. But this isn't the case at all!'
2   And as such boundaries are to relationships what followers are to leaders: both units are essentially the same as two sides of a medal or as a separation that connects. Taken together they transcend polarity. Other concepts expressing an interface that limits yet opens up at the same time, are containment (Bion, 1963) and metaxy (the 'in-between' that both separates and connects, first used in Plato's Symposium).
3   The best way to familiarize yourself with the 'drivers' is by completing the short questionnaire on the behavioural drivers in Appendix A of this book.

The leadership shadow

03

> *Everything that irritates us about others can lead us to an understanding of ourselves.*
>
> **CARL GUSTAV JUNG,** *MEMORIES, DREAMS, REFLECTIONS* **(1963)**

To be charged with a leadership position is an honour and distinction. It elevates you into a position of responsibility over others and puts you in a role of crucial importance for the team. You cannot obtain leadership authority unless it is given to you (unless of course you want to take things by force or by divine decree – anathema in today's big organizations); hence a promotion is felt as one of the most genuine compliments one can aspire to in the workplace. The same is true on a smaller scale for a single successful leadership 'intervention', ie an 'in the moment' position taken for leadership of the organization which is received positively.

At the same time, being honoured and set apart as a leader always opens up a rift, between the 'leader' and the 'team', between the 'meaning maker' and the recipients of meaning, or (if you wish) between the 'ruler' and the 'common people'. This rift is the essence of what we call the *leadership shadow*: leadership by nature creates a split between a gesture and a response, or between guidance and the ability to follow through. Such a rift, distance or setting apart serves to make meaning and to consider meaning: the split symbolizes and thus maintains a *relationship*, in which learning and development can take place, and action can be prepared. Any bid for leadership creates a certain tension in a relationship, which is perhaps best expressed by the image of light and darkness, figure and ground, foreground and shadow.

The Sun King chose to identify fully with the light and to create a simple stark shadow around him. 'I rule, you follow,' was the repeated injunction. His leadership was exceptionally 'strong' and unambiguous, even regarding the topic of leadership itself. In the organizations of today the picture is a lot more mixed and there is room for a dazzling array of colours, with manifold greys and shades.

Knowing about your own shadow

In order to look at how our shadow develops over time it may be useful to look first at the leadership shadow as a universal metaphor of our souls, our darker tendencies, our suppressed qualms, that appears in many myths and fairy tales from ancient Egypt and Greece. Certainly in psychological terms the correct perception of our own physical shadow takes a lot of time to evolve: Piaget has shown that the ability to recognize one's own shadow is a very difficult process, one that is only mastered at the age of eight or nine. In literature, shadows sometimes appear as negative, shady and discarded, and in other cases they appear as prized possessions. They also undergo deep transformation in the storylines. It is interesting to study how the human shadow fares in artistic imagination, if only for the rich meaning that can be extracted from it about the kinds of overdrive, hubris and shadow patterns which we can daily observe in ourselves and our leaders.

Romantic storytelling in particular has an abundance of shadow fantasies. The selling of one's shadow appears as a prelude to the Faustian pact where you sell your soul to the devil. In Chamisso's *Peter Schlemihl's Miraculous Story*, Peter sells his shadow to an admirer who praises its beauty. The sack of gold he receives turns out to be bottomless but also of little value to him in overcoming the deep shame he feels at having no shadow. Finally, at the very moment when he reneges on the sack of gold, he finds peace of mind and is able to turn his mind to productive work (botany) as well as begin his personal journey towards forgiveness. At the end of the story he concludes that, if one is to live with others, one must learn to honour first one's shadow and then one's gold, ie appreciate one's dark sides and then one's bright sides.

Strauss's opera *Die Frau Ohne Schatten* (The woman without a shadow) is also about the quest for a shadow. Here the protagonist has become the Empress of the Eastern Island despite being a spirit creature, daughter of the Lord of the Spirits, which is why she does not have a shadow. In order to bear children or even to remain in human form, she needs to find a shadow within three days. This spiritual journey will initially seduce her into a pact where she would buy the shadow from the dyer's wife, again (as in Peter Schlemihl's story) for large quantities of gold; but in the end she refuses to steal the shadow when she gets a chance. Finally, as she takes this decision at great personal risk, because of the compassion she feels for the woman who would have to live without a shadow, she is rewarded with a shadow and her future children are announced to her.

In the fairy tale *The Shadow* by Hans Christian Andersen the writer's shadow first breaks free and then gradually takes over his owner's life and begins to command him in the most Pinteresque way, to the point where finally the owner can only become the shadow's shadow – or be executed.

All these stories seem to emphasize the great perils of a life without a shadow, a life without having your shadow at your side, a life without access to your shadow's resourcefulness, insight and inspiration. This is exactly what we want to emphasize in this book, as well, for the leader and his or her shadow. Writers have recognized the importance of the splitting that goes into creating a shadow of oneself; witness the countless tales of doubles, alter egos, doppelgänger, Jekyll and Hyde, Superman, the Hulk etc.

A pertinent feature of the 'split' that leadership creates is an equivalent split within yourself. This is because, as an active leader you often have to push the 'follower' within yourself boldly to the background; an endeavour which in itself entails in some circumstances a strong-willed, single-minded and bold leadership decision. More broadly there is, in our view, a 'shadow side' of yourself that is triggered the moment you conceive of yourself as a leader, a hidden shadow that over time can become less accessible, which may have supreme implications for your effectiveness as a leader.

We would argue that stepping forward to make a leadership gesture always creates a rift within oneself: a rift between one's sunny, active, constructive or aggressive side that has the ambition to contribute, create and prove something; and one's doubting, pessimistic, needy, vulnerable and concerned side, which craves for connection with oneself and others. The shadow side is therefore part and parcel of leadership.

The essential rift and the play of light and dark accompanying this process may be very subtle. For example, you may bring a very caring side of yourself to your leadership role, bringing out your particular warmth, care, and also concern and neediness about care. What we are arguing here is that even in such cases there is bound to be a whole side of our personalities which we push down in order to make such a bid for leadership, or for following the leadership role through. In the case of a very caring, concerned, warm leader there may be a whole side of yourself to do with conflict, resentment, self-importance, that you are keeping down. We argue that such a mechanism is consistently present to some degree. In order to make the 'bid' or put forward the 'drive', other aspects have to be left behind, pushed back and discarded, somewhere in the dark of our experiences and self-experiencing.

CASE ILLUSTRATION   The bright and shadow sides of Quentin

Quentin is creator and founder and CEO of a medium-sized company (QuenCo) that has pioneered a new retail channel supported by the internet, at high margins. After six years of doubling in size and revenue every year, new entrants backed by large multinationals start to flood the market and are soon able to sell at lower prices than QuenCo. As a consequence QuenCo's sales growth declines rapidly and the board concludes that the company can only respond by reducing costs and offering discounts. This fails, however, to produce any uplift and clients are only made more aware how expensive QuenCo's services have been. Even loyal clients that have been with the company from its inception are now being lost to the competition. Also, QuenCo prided itself on the breadth of its offerings; now there is a new focus on high-margin lines which means that customers familiar with a greater diversity of products are becoming disappointed.

Quentin believes that the way out of this negative spiral is by innovating. So he becomes less available as he travels, designs and works from home trying to come up with new and radical solutions, just as he did so successfully when he founded the firm. When back for meetings he becomes openly hostile with anyone who challenges or disagrees with his approach. He presses on with more cost cutting and publicly blames the competition: their foolhardiness in slashing prices is the only problem that he wishes to see. Over time some of the senior directors in the head office start to mock his leadership style of now-you-see-him-now-you-don't. And it is not just hard to predict when Quentin will next be in the office; the way he behaves is even less predictable. For a customer-facing organization such as QuenCo that relies so heavily on its employees, its customers and their goodwill, it appears to have lost something of its soul. Hard times are approaching, making Quentin even less predictable and more explosive.

Generally it is very tempting to identify with our more 'sunny' side, the 'leadership' side of our interventions, certainly in public. So in most cases we tend to ignore the 'shadow' side of our leadership from an early stage and for as long as we can. This can go on for a sustained period whilst we continue to 'grow' our leadership presence and 'mature' in our leadership role. What the outside world sees is a healthy, mature, straightforward process of stepping into ever more senior leadership positions.

Such a stepping up and stepping into roles works very well until as a leader you happen to be wrong, and you encounter profound criticism or some other kind of questioning of your leadership contributions, thus revealing that you have something important to learn relating to your meaning-making abilities. This moment may never come (although that certainly is very unlikely) if you are in a very secure, growing and steady business or if you are very proficient at offering your particular, limited leadership contributions. However, in the present very demanding business environment, those confrontational moments of slipping up in leadership do occur, and they occur more and more often.

The moment you do need to learn or change something is the moment you need to revert to your discarded shadow: either by stepping aside, choosing 'followership' and allowing somebody who knows better to show the way, or by using some of those underdeveloped talents that you have yourself ignored for some time. At that point there is a conflict, between your pride and your passion, between your best intentions and your innermost shame, and between your 'up' and your 'down'. The side of us that is 'up' wants to stay up, win more leadership presence and influence, whilst the side that is 'down' is by now used to not getting much of a hearing. It is striking how few top leaders voluntarily listen to their own true underlying needs, and how few senior leaders voluntarily relinquish their senior position or recognize another candidate as objectively stronger than them. The side that is up prefers to forget about the side that is down, pretending that it does not exist. That is why we see so much *omnipotence* in leaders, which masks their profound feelings of *impotence*. Impotence comes along with omnipotence as a shadow side, although few leaders would acknowledge that, even to themselves. Only in their most private feelings and nightmares will there be traces of their strong feelings of impotence.

We acknowledge that is very hard to remain in contact with something that is of necessity split off in order to engage in leadership. Nevertheless, leadership being a meaning-making process *in relationships* and good leadership being all about keeping such relationships *fluid* (see Chapter 2), we argue that it is necessary for all balanced leaders to keep in contact to the greatest degree possible with their shadow sides. Some are fortunate enough to have very strong management teams, or even very strong spouses, who can keep a spotlight firmly pointed at the shadow side of the leader, but most of us are not that lucky and will have to do some of this work ourselves or with a trusted advisor.

The first thing to remember is that our unconscious is more than ready to receive discarded and 'ugly' parts of ourselves and shield them off from daily scrutiny. By absorbing those ideas, our unconscious plays a role in maintaining a rosy and bright outlook and a gratifying picture of ourselves as leaders. Moreover, our rational, conscious thinking is equally happy to keep disturbing doubts and emotions to one side, and focus on the organization's tasks at hand. Within the leadership arena, therefore, both our conscious and unconscious are profoundly *anti-relational*: both our sense of comfort and our best interests would like to get rid of this relationship with a needy, helpless, hapless, doubtful, dysfunctional, dark and gloomy shadow. One can imagine how hard it is in such circumstances to stay in tune with one's own leadership relationships.

Nevertheless we would encourage you as a leader to keep an open mind regarding this relationship, despite the pressure not to acknowledge it and to go for the bright side and the solutions, not just for future gain (as we may ultimately need the shadow's inspiration or trust at some future moment) but also primarily for keeping our own leadership function sane and functional right now, in the midst of our greatest efforts and successes. Awareness of what or who we are leading is crucial for a leader – and this 'who' and 'what' happens to be not just outside in the form of organizational colleagues but also inside in the form of a personal shadow that is not easily approached.

In this chapter we would like to explore how you can keep this awareness of your relationships alive and also acquaint yourself with your leadership shadow. We will demonstrate how you can make use of your own shadow sides to be a better, more balanced leader. First we would like to make these very general observations more practical and concrete.

The shadowing process affects different aspects of our leadership differently, creating concurrent illusions of infallibility, omnipotence and invulnerability.

For convenience we like to distinguish leadership contributions as pertaining to three different domains, or, if you wish, consisting of three different aspects:

1 *Supporting:* facilitating or enabling the team's effectiveness, enhancing the resources and competences that are available – a 'making' or 'doing' function. Leadership contributions from this domain consist of *actions* such as actively taking a position, chairing a meeting, going out on a mission for the organization or completing an action that facilitates or enhances the effectiveness of the team.

2 *Inspiring:* supplying the team with strategy and meaning-making – a 'thinking' function. Leadership contributions from this domain consist of *reflections* or *insights* such as raising a hypothesis, putting forward a strategic plan or a practical solution, arguing a decision taken or reflecting with the team on a difficult issue.

3 *Containing:* looking after or caring for the team, nurturing and providing space for processing emotions and for understanding to emerge – a 'feeling' function. Leadership contributions from this domain consist of *empathy* and *warmth* such as offering understanding and clemency, sustaining a difficult feeling, bridging a conflict and keeping a tricky issue in mind.

These functions of leadership overlap nicely with the ten 'roles' that Mintzberg (1973) found after a detailed study of a week in the work of five different CEOs:

1 *Supporting* includes the roles of *leader* (guiding, praising, promoting, evaluating), *entrepreneur* (initiating change) and *negotiator* (committing resources to the unit).

2 *Inspiring* includes the roles of *liaison* (maintaining links with the outside world), *monitor* (keeping abreast of information) and *disseminator* (passing on information).

3 *Containing* includes the roles of *figurehead* (doing ritual, ceremonial tasks), *spokesperson* (representing the unit's interests outside), *resources allocator* (nurturing with resources such as money, workers, material) and *disturbance handler* (handling crises).

Each of these domains is impacted in different ways by the leadership shadow although the underlying mechanism is the same. Whatever is supported externally is moved out of awareness internally, so sustaining a leadership position looks different from each of these three angles:

1 Offering support creates an illusion of omnipotence, as if internally we ourselves do not need support. Less assertive sides in ourselves can easily be pushed away as if we have no need to follow others.

2 Offering inspiration creates an illusion of infallibility, as if our own limitations of understanding do not exist or will not impact on our leadership contributions. We may be tempted to see ourselves exclusively as part of the solution and never as part of the issues, and may even struggle to see ourselves as part of the organization.

3 Offering containment creates an illusion of invulnerability, as if internally we ourselves do not need looking after. More vulnerable sides in ourselves can easily be pushed away as if we have no anxieties or fears.

These are just broad brushstrokes of how engaging in leadership means opening up a relationship with others and with ourselves, where a rift will exist between light and dark aspects of leadership. Essentially, the leadership shadow will be represented simultaneously outside, in the leadership function of the organization, and inside, in the leader's relationship with self, or the leader's self-experiencing. The picture is of course indescribably richer when we consider real organizations with real issues, as well as real leaders with real personalities.

As leaders, each of us feels differently inclined to contribute to these domains. Some of us are much more triggered by action (we call such leaders 'movers and shakers' in Part Two), some of us are more inclined to observe and reflect for the organization (we call such leaders 'rigorous thinkers') and still others prefer to nurture and foster growth in the organization (we call such leaders 'sensitive carers').

In addition, as leaders we will be more or less skilled at acting in each of these domains. We will have developed abilities and competencies over the years of our experience, but we may also have gaps in skills, blind spots or unexplored developmental areas. Areas of need or development which may increasingly become evident to others may remain hidden to us even when circumstances trigger patterns that on reflection may cry out for personal attention.

Such tendencies as we experience them in ourselves and in our make-up influence what sort of material we relegate into our shadows upon instigating the rift that is leadership. In this book we distinguish 11 main dynamics of driven leaders, leading to 11 different shapes of this leadership relationship, whilst admitting that such a relationship is also driven strongly by the issues, the needs and other personalities in the organization. There is usually some self-selection process going on, where the various patterns and preferences that make up a leader almost magically find the kind of organization and issues that represent a pretty good match for them. And there are plenty more dynamics that one would also describe, as shown in Chapter 9, about neurotic patterns in leaders.

Here is a summary of those personality patterns that we can all recognize because we all have developed them to some extent for ourselves. We will return to these patterns more extensively in Part Two. They are not 'types' but rather 'strands' of personality that we can recognize in each of us, developed to a greater or lesser degree.

Leadership as doing

Where assertiveness comes to the fore, doubt and vulnerability go into the 'shadow':

1 *Charming Manipulators*, whose actions may brush up against the rules and mould them to their own design. In this leadership style strict accountability may go out of the window, because their own accountability may be relegated to the 'shadow'.

2 *Playful Encouragers*, whose influence is felt mainly indirectly. In this leadership style taking full responsibility for their actions may be difficult, as their responsibility may be relegated to the 'shadow'.

3 *Glowing Gatsbys*, who influence from the front and bask in their successes. In this leadership style it may be easy for them to criticize others but harder to look at themselves in a similar way, as their humility may have been relegated to the 'shadow'.

4 *Detached Diplomats*, whose actions remain largely in their own world, disengaged and disconnected from those around them. In this leadership style it may be hard to keep the organization's issues and people in focus, as their ability to reach out may be relegated to the 'shadow'. In fact, when this pattern is highly developed, leadership interventions themselves may go under and the leader seems very absent.

Leadership as thinking

Where knowledge comes to the fore, trust goes into the 'shadow':

1 *Responsible Workaholics*, whose stamina is admirable and who can take up a vast array of leadership agendas. However, they may find it difficult to see the forest for the trees, because their ability to prioritize and make a firm stance on a controversial issue may be relegated to their 'shadow'.

2 *Impulsive Loyalists*, who are very involved but may be subject to mood swings. They may find it very hard to hear bad news about how the business is doing, because some of their tolerance and self-confidence may be relegated to their 'shadow'.

3 *Brilliant Sceptics*, who are scrupulous and alert but may focus rather more on the negatives. They may think that people are for or against them, and in particular suspect that they are against them, because their trust and safety may be relegated to their 'shadow'.

4 *Creative Daydreamers* always have fresh thinking to offer but they may try to be different just for the sake of it, or the link between their thinking and reality may be feeble.

Consequently, some of the creative thinking may not be applicable or may be plain wrong for the future, because dry realism and utility may be relegated to their 'shadow'.

Leadership as feeling

Where empathy comes to the fore, self-expression goes into the 'shadow':

1 *Virtuous Supporters*, who try to look after their people and are liked by everyone. They may find it hard to look after their own interests or assert themselves when they have something to offer, because their own personal power may be relegated to their 'shadow'.

2 *Accomplished Thespians*, who are generously offering their own feelings and ideas but may over-occupy the centre of attention. They may enjoy the limelight a little too much and become obsessed with their public image, because their natural self-affirmation may be relegated to their 'shadow'.

3 *Simmering Stalwarts*, who are reliable and ambitious yet afraid to make decisions that might involve risk. They may be concerned or

hesitant because of what other people might think or do, because their self-confidence may be relegated to their 'shadow'.

FIGURE 3.1   Our leadership shadows or 'gremlins' are varied: an inner theatre we prefer not to look at

Connections between your 'shadow' side and your 'light' side

Clearly, one would hope that leaders more often than not develop the right actions, useful ideas and genuine care for others. However, aside from these they should be interested enough in themselves to ask questions about drivers, personality patterns and what is going on in the neglected shadow of their own leadership presence. In this section we want to give some ideas for exploring and even making use of what is going on in your shadow. As we have argued before, your shadow side and your bright side are intimately connected, but drift apart upon taking up a leadership role.

There are essentially two ways to find out about your shadow. One is to be curious about what messages actually pop out from that hidden and shielded area of yourself. And the second is to follow through your leadership qualities and explore what they say about your shadow sides.

Self-analysis

The first of these approaches is very hard to do by yourself, as you are required to see what is almost imperceptible, and you have to engage in a form of 'self-analysis' that is not for the timid. The best access you can have to your own shadow side is through your dreams at night: when your 'leadership persona' falls asleep your 'shadow self' finds more of an opportunity to assert itself. If you are very alert you may also find traces of more hidden life when you are awake, such as any involuntary thoughts, concerns or mistakes that you notice within yourself. We would always recommend exploring this terrain with a qualified coach who has a background in psychoanalysis and therefore some understanding of the markers of your shadow side, and what they might have to tell you.

CASE ILLUSTRATION   Getting help

Karim was a corporate star. He had made a quick rise to the top. By 24 he had become the youngest area sales manager of a specialist pharmaceuticals business in his country. By 28 he was the youngest country manager in the region. He achieved this by beating every single sales target that he was given. The area sales teams that he led were invariably the top of the company sales league. After he took over as country manager, within two years he turned a long run of poor sales and financial results around into solid revenue and profit performance. He *drove* for results, he saw the bigger picture, and he identified what he, his team and the company should focus on to achieve success.

At a personal level, work was life. He lived and breathed business, and his perfect day was a day spent in the field motivating one of his sales team, in the office grappling with customer issues along with his colleagues, or on his own working through the numbers in the monthly management accounts to find out ways of becoming still more profitable. On the door of his office he had a sign for all to see which said: 'If you can't do it, learn how to do it NOW!'

Karim also liked to play hard. Each day invariably ended up in his favourite place, on a five-a-side football pitch kicking a ball around with his closest mates. Whilst he himself didn't drink alcohol, at the end of the game together the group would end up in a bar to celebrate the winning team. At weekends the celebrations often went on long into the night.

At the relatively youthful age of 31, and now the top-performing country manager in the company, Karim started noticing that at the end of the celebrations he found it harder and harder to switch off and go to sleep when he got home. Once or twice he got anxiety attacks in the car when driving back home after a night out. At work, his behaviour also started to be noticeably different. Increasingly he challenged his team members on the county management board to drive harder and harder to improve the margins of the company even though the business was already at the top of the company performance league. As his finance director on the team put it, 'If there's an orange, Karim will squeeze it drier than anybody else'.

Within a few months the collegiate atmosphere in senior team meetings began to turn sour. Karim would dominate the meetings and talk relentlessly, listening less and less and losing his temper if anybody appeared to contradict his demands for greater efforts.

Gradually over the next couple of years Karim's sleeping problem became acute. He found it difficult to sleep more than four or five hours a night. He was increasingly waking up feeling anxious and tired. He had stopped playing football with his mates, partly because he felt short of time (he needed to work harder in the evenings to stay on top of everything) and also because he invariably got into arguments with one or another of his friends when they went out to 'celebrate' at the end of every match. In addition he was beginning to get severe headaches, and sometimes the headaches lasted all day.

In desperation, Karim visited the company doctor, who, having prescribed some medication, enquired into the last time Karim had taken a holiday. Apart from statutory public holidays, Karim hadn't been on leave from work in the last five years. (He had always taken compensation in the form of added pay in lieu of holiday.) The company doctor firmly suggested that Karim consider taking a holiday, immediately. In addition he indicated that he would recommend, and make a note in Karim's medical reports at the next company bi-annual medical check-up, that Karim consider taking more time off and getting help from HR to reorganize some of his work and give him more executive staff to deal with some of his heavy workload. Whilst Karim thought this was an unrealistic and impractical suggestion, he respected the doctor and quite liked his HR director so he felt able to confide in him. Feeling desperate for the first time in his executive life, he arranged to have what he intended to be a brief lunchtime conversation with the HR director. The conversation ended up lasting most of the afternoon. At the end of it Karim, sceptically and rather self-consciously, agreed to get professional help with his extreme stress levels.

Core competences analysis

The second approach is much more straightforward, and can be aided by a simple model that was first proposed by Daniel Ofman (Ofman, 2002). In this approach you map the terrain around your own core competences or qualities, to find clues as to what your shadow sides might be telling you about areas where you are underdeveloped. Although this second approach is more straightforward, we would still recommend doing it with a coach or with a friend and partner who can ask you the necessary questions.

In this 'core qualities' approach to the leadership shadow you go through the following steps. First you try to identify three core qualities or competences that you bring to your leadership role at the moment. These could be contributions such as 'determination', 'creativity', 'adaptability', 'loyalty' or 'caring', just to name a few. Then you explore what happens with that quality when you go into overdrive, ie when you offer too much of that particular core competence. On the basis of concrete examples from your leadership practice, try to determine what is happening to each specific core quality when it goes into overdrive, and try to write this up in a single word.

If we take 'determination' as an example, the 'overdrive behaviour' may be 'pushiness' or it may be 'doggedness':

Determinaton ⟶ Pushiness

Next – again for each of three competences listed – try to flip this 'overdrive behaviour' into its opposite, ie what is the balancing behaviour that is being left out of, or that is lacking in your leadership style (on the assumption that such balancing competence is probably somewhere available to you, but is relegated into your shadow and thus not accessible). Again, starting from 'determination', turning into 'pushiness', the particular balancing or 'shadow competency' that may be missing is 'patience': ie, you have run out of patience or you find it hard to develop patience in demanding situations:

The fourth and last step is to inquire into the overdrive pattern of the shadow competency that you have just found. When these qualities appear in overdrive in other people, how do they look to you personally? If you are able to identify this, you will have discovered why you sent them into your 'shadow' in the first place. Again, it would be best if you could describe this overdrive behaviour in a single word. In the example of 'patience' this might appear in other people as 'stoicism', or 'passivity', or even 'laziness':

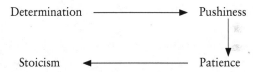

What you have mapped so far is a core personal quadrant, linked up with one of your core competences in your leadership role. Ofman (2002) called this your 'core quadrant' (Figure 3.2), and used the following labels for the four qualities/drivers that you have mapped: 'core quality', 'pitfall' (for overdrive), 'challenge' (for shadow competency) and 'allergy' (for overdrive of the shadow competency).

FIGURE 3.2 A core quadrant (Ofman, 2002)

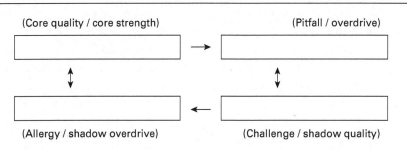

The interesting corollary of this core quadrant is that your shadow, as explored in this way, does not only hold shadow competences that may balance your own core leadership contributions, but also clarifies for you the traits that you find irritating in other people.

When other people remind you of the aspects of yourself that you have neatly packaged away in your unconscious or shadow then this opens up your shadow in an inconvenient, unpleasant way. Not only are you reminded of something that you have once chosen to disregard and suppress, but you also witness somebody unashamedly living that very same trait. This leads to a feeling of outrage, often mingled with envy: a very powerful sensation that by its sheer acuteness reveals itself to be linked with your own shadow.

Now this gives you a new way to explore your own shadow. Just think about the person at work who irritates or annoys or offends you the most at this very moment. Then try to write down the quality of that person that irritates you so much, in one single word (eg sluggishness). Next try to see that particular quality as an overdrive condition of another quality that is in fact positive (in the example, this could be, 'consideration', 'care', 'levelheadedness', or many others, depending on the particular person and your irritation).

Another creative option would be to carry out the same exercise with an irritating TV personality, or a particularly irritating politician, or even a family member. You will find that if you honestly and carefully follow through on the steps described above you will reveal something about your own hidden shadow.

There are other ways of doing this that go beyond Ofman's original work yet follow the same basic plan. You could for example think of a colleague that you rely on for certain actions, such as your 'right-hand person' or perhaps another member of the team who sorts things out for you. In many cases such a person has particular valencies (see Chapter 2) that make them 'carry' a part of your shadow for you and you can ask yourself, what is it that I have left entirely to this person to do? What competence of mine has been expressed only through this person, and has been left undeveloped by myself? What have I projected into this person? From that shadow competence you can again build up the core quadrant as above.

Development of your leadership shadow over time

Now we have explored the rifts that make leadership into a relational practice and that are the origin of leadership shadows, we can go back to the leadership journeys that we mentioned in Chapter 1.

We have observed on many occasions that the journeys of leaders can be described in terms of several interlocking cycles or processes. We have already spoken about a shadow side to leadership which over time can become less and less accessible. Now we want to explore some common dynamics in leaders that we have observed.

In the first place there are clear *virtuous cycles* associated with leadership, at least on the surface. Leadership interventions build on each other and grow the effectiveness of a team over time. Leaders notice that they can help out and build their contributions over time. These 'leadership cycles' help to create self-belief and a positive identity as a leader, but this does not happen without paying a certain price (Petriglieri and Stein, 2012). Through identification with the positive, helpful image of leadership other less helpful parts of the personality continue to be split off, and others in the organization may reinforce this process. This makes one's leadership style and identity more and more outspoken and increasingly similar to one of the overdrive patterns that we have signalled. In this way an ongoing presence in an organization's leadership arena can grow various forms of hubris or overreaching.

Other cycles that move along with the development of leadership presence are *cycles of recovery* and re-energizing, which keep a leader in good shape; however, they are usually not powerful enough to reintegrate the various bits of the leadership identity that have been relegated to the leadership shadow.

Another stream of ongoing activity is essentially *transferential* in nature, where leaders tend to recreate domains of their lives and careers where they encounter similar yet highly personal issues. We all carry around an 'inner theatre' (Kets de Vries, 2006) of intimate relationships which we have struggled with and which we tend to repeat.

Finally, there are *cycles of learning* where shadow sides of leaders can be reintegrated, albeit through very onerous, hard work. About this fourth cluster of leadership dynamics, Jung wrote that in most people a real confrontation with their own shadow does not take place ever, as it is usually defended against so vigorously (Jung, 1952). Jung called the process of meeting, acquainting yourself with and progressing alongside your own shadow an *individuation process*, a process through which you finally become a more rounded individual. We think this holds a lot of truth when it comes to the darkest, neediest, remotest corners of our mind, but in business the picture today is less black and white. In our view there are manifold 'lesser shadows', that are pushed out with every leadership intervention, and that can be met and returned to without too much difficulty. The process is, however, essentially the same as the one described by Jung. We will give some examples below.

We can all easily deceive ourselves into thinking that we have come through an individuation process or that we have become mature and rounded leaders, yet in most cases this is a rather comfortable illusion and does not conform to the truth.

These first two detailed chapters on the topic of leadership (Chapters 2 and 3) will be progressed further in Part Three where we will incorporate more research findings on the effectiveness of leaders. Let us therefore summarize what we have found already in terms of *effective leadership*. If you go along with the definitions in Chapter 2 and the psychological material in this chapter, a number of heuristics for good leadership follow, such as these:

1 It is crucial for leaders to keep the process of leading fluid, and in particular to be *open to (sometimes painful) upwards feedback from within the organization.*

2 It is no less essential for leaders to keep their practice healthy and balanced, and in particular to be *open to (sometimes painful) upwards feedback from their own shadows.*

3 To remain open to both types of feedback (from within and from outside) it is important for leaders to be as *relational* as they can be by:

   – nurturing their relationships, ie leading not in the abstract and not just indirectly, but *here and now with colleagues*, so as to be genuine;

   – making meaning of the moment in relationship, ie *addressing the parallel process* and how it shapes leadership issues in the here and now.

4 Finally, in order to foster the openness and liveliness that they need for the points above, we would say that leaders need to engage in active and honest (self-)reflection.

In Part Two of this book, we return to our examination of how ambitious executives behave and relate to their challenging contexts. We continue this examination by first looking at the recurring patterns of behaviour which tough and focused executives develop and how these behaviours can be effective or ineffective in certain relational contexts. In particular we present these 'behavioural cameos' as patterns of behaviour typical of tough and focused executives we have met, the aim being to show common ways of behaving and relating and the shifts in behaviour that occur when executives respond to challenges – in the place of (and in the absence of) developing new insight and meaning-making.

We specifically look at how the successful and ambitious leaders we have encountered in business behave when facing challenges in their environment or with their relationships. We see them developing behavioural overdrive patterns, and ask ourselves why and how this happens. How do these over-drive patterns in turn affect their relationships and environments? When do such overdrive patterns begin to turn into unhelpful ones, and how can leaders avoid this? And under such vicious conditions of overdrive, how can they still transform their agency so as to reconnect with their best insights and genuine stability?

By first presenting these patterns as being 'owned' by individual men and women, we heighten their accessibility. However, we emphasize that this is an explanatory device only. Reality is thankfully more complex and resource-ful than that – involving multiplicities of relationships and behavioural patterns – and is demonstrated in a variety of ways in different circum-stances. After initially introducing these patterns as belonging to individual men and women, we want to move to a more realistic relationship and multi-stakeholder perspective. We hope to show that by understanding our-selves and the multiplicity of patterns that we have the ability and potential to present, we gain an insight into our being and relatedness that has the potential to give more strength, stability and resilience.

To end this chapter here is an analogy of leadership that is some 2,600 years old, which underlines the importance of knowing yourself as a leader and in particular knowing your own shadow.

The two carrying-pouches

Once upon a time, when Prometheus created men, he hung from them two carrying-pouches. One of these contained the deficiencies of other people and was hung in front. The other contained our own faults, which he suspended behind us. The result of this was that men could see directly down into the pouch containing other people's failings, but were unable to see their own.

One can apply this fable to the muddle-headed person who, blind to his own faults, meddles with those of others which do not concern him at all.

Aesop's Fable 303, 6th century BC

Summary: the leadership shadow

In this chapter we have studied the process of taking up a leadership role and have identified what lies at the core of every leader's attempts to achieve effectiveness for the team: a 'rift' between leader and team, between this way and other ways forward, and between the leader's own leadership persona and his or her shadow.

As leaders 'shine their light' on the effectiveness of the organization, they cannot help but split off other areas which become their own leadership shadows.

The rifts and shadows that always accompany leadership remind us of the essentially 'relational' nature of leadership. Our relational definition of leadership presupposes a link between areas of light and darkness, between leader and team, and between the leader and the leadership shadow.

We suggest three styles of leadership that each cast their own distinct shadow:

- the *supporting* function, where leadership expresses itself as 'doing' and assertiveness comes to the fore, whilst doubt and vulnerability go into the shadow;

- the *inspiring* function, where leadership expresses itself as 'thinking' and knowledge comes to the fore, whilst trust and safety go into the shadow;

- the *containing* function, where leadership expresses itself as 'feeling' and empathy comes to the fore, whilst self-expression and power go into the shadow.

As every leader participates selectively in those three functions, unique aspects of their personality are asserted whilst other aspects are relegated to their personal shadows. The only way to take these aspects back and work with them is through either:

- self-analysis, picking up hints from under the surface and mostly aided by executive coaching; or

- working through what irritates you about others in order to understand your own shadow – Ofman's core-qualities model can help you do this.

The journeys of leaders are influenced by interlocking virtuous cycles, recovery cycles, cycles of transference and hubristic cycles. Through individuation processes the rifts of leadership can be gradually healed.

At this stage of the book we can conclude that all leaders can become more effective by:

- driving for (sometimes painful) upwards feedback from within the organization;

- driving for (sometimes painful) upwards feedback from their own shadows;

- working relationally by nurturing their relationships and addressing the parallel process here and now;

- engaging in active, meaningful and honest (self-)reflection.

How you thrive as a leader: do-it-yourself

The story of yourself as a leader

We believe that in order to remain driven whilst regulating overdrive patterns, it is important for you as a leader to regularly stand still and reflect on your leadership. Hence, at the end of every part of this book we have written a practical chapter that is essentially an invitation to reflect. Such reflection is, in our view, the only way the quality of your leadership will grow and improve. Reflection is also essential for your own preparedness, openness and thoughtfulness in working with others in the organization.

Obviously the story of you as a leader, as a contributor to the leadership function in your organization(s), started a long time ago. In this chapter we would like to invite you to explore some of your own core patterns as a leader more deeply by making contact with those formative years and experiences.

Your family background

Make a drawing of your family structure, with the previous two generations and all the other people that were around in your family or in the house for substantial periods (ie for many years) when you were young. In the drawing try to represent closeness and distance between family members as you remember them or see them now:

FORM 4.1

Family structure

Then *ask yourself the following questions about your drawing.* We would like you to think about how various leadership *functions* and *issues* were taken up in that very early 'family business' that you were part of. Make some notes or a mindmap of who was (mostly) looking after which leadership functions:

FORM 4.2

How were responsibilities shared/divided in this family?
How were decisions taken?
Who was leading on which topic in this family?

Lessons from the family

Then *ask yourself what those formative years in that family structure taught you*:

FORM 4.3

What have you become really good at relationally?
What have you become really bad at relationally?

Transference to the workplace

Now try to look at the idea of 'transference' in how you are embedded in your present work environment. *Which of those relationships between yourself and the other family members are you still playing out or working with:*

FORM 4.4

Are you still competitive with some core colleagues on the team as you once were with your sister? Do you see repetition in the broad area of 'rivalry'?
Are you still vainly looking for support from your boss as you once did from your father? Do you see repetition in the broad area of 'disappointment with others'?
Do you still wish you could run back to your mother's cup of tea at the end of a frenetic work day? Do you see repetition in the broad area of 'seeking support'?

These were only generic examples. We would now like you to *list some highly specific ones, where you feel you are in a relationship at work that feels like one of the relationships 'back then' at home:*

FORM 4.5

Write down at least five such possible parallels between your family of origin and your closest work relationships.	1.
	2.
	3.
	4.
	5.
Then try to find a recent 'event' at work related to leadership that brought out one of those five parallels.	
How was your own role at that event influenced by the leadership patterns in your family of origin?	

Identify conflict

Here is a more 'advanced' request, a difficult reflective task. Look again at the event that resonated with one of the parallels between work now and family then. For this event, *try to formulate a core underlying 'unresolved conflict' in your life by finishing this sentence:*

FORM 4.6

I realize now, by looking at this event again and exploring a parallel between how I handled myself at that event and some of my early family dynamics, that there might be an underlying conflict or tension that I am experiencing between ...
... and ...

You can think of a conflict between the leadership demanded by the event and the particular experience or driver that you offer to the event.

If this does not work for the event selected above, try another event. In particular, events where you are in doubt or critical about your own contribution may teach you something about hidden conflicts within yourself.

Explore what drives you as a leader

Your own drivers

Complete the drivers' questionnaire in Appendix A1 of this book, if you haven't done so yet. *Then, explore the following:*

FORM 4.7

For every driver that scored above 75, try to find a recent work-related example of where this valency played a role, in the sense that the driver influenced your contribution.	Driver 1: Example:
	Driver 2: Example:
	Driver 3: Example:
For each of these strong drivers explore how your personal way of being driven influenced your relationship with at least one colleague or direct report.	Driver 1: Influence:
	Driver 2: Influence:
	Driver 3: Influence:

Your colleagues' drivers

Try to guess the drivers of four key people around you, people you work with on a daily basis. From your experience of working with them, *give them two of the drivers from the drivers' questionnaire* (be perfect, please others, hurry up, be strong, try hard). Then for each of them, *look at the mutual influence of those strongest drivers and yours*:

- Do these drivers play into each other constructively?
- Do they oppose one another and lead to friction?
- Do they inspire you?
- Do they exhaust you?

FORM 4.8

Key colleague	Colleagues' drivers	My strongest drivers	Mutual influence
1	1	1	
	2	2	
2	1	1	
	2	2	
3	1	1	
	2	2	
4	1	1	
	2	2	

Explore a critical relationship at work

You can choose either a relationship that you feel is not settled, or which could be improved. Or you can choose a relationship where you feel you are 'complementary' to your colleague, where your personalities seem to be really different. It could be a leader–follower relationship. In any case it would be good to choose a relationship that is relevant for you at the moment and that you would consider sub-optimal, ie confusing, painful, critical, and/or imbued with friction.

First, *make a 'core qualities' quadrant for yourself* (Figure 4.1), as it pertains to this particular relationship (see page 67 in Chapter 3 for an example based on the quality 'determination'). What is your core strength that you bring to this relationship? On the basis of that core quality try to map your own 'overdrive' (pitfall), 'irritation' (allergy) and 'blind spot' (challenge).

FIGURE 4.1 The core qualities quadrant for your chosen relationship

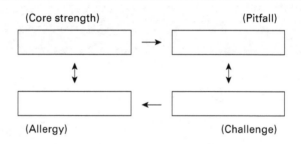

Then *make a double quadrant with the other person that you have chosen* (Figure 4.2). If, for the 'allergy' in your own core qualities quadrant you have chosen something about them that really irritates you, then by definition that is their 'pitfall' in working with you. So you can make your 'allergy' and their 'pitfall' identical.

In Figure 4.3 is an example of how all of this hangs together, starting from the same example around 'determination' that we used in Chapter 3.

How would you be able to take something from your own double quadrant (Figure 4.2) that you could learn in terms of your challenge? Try to write a short story about how the complementary 'core strengths' above, from you and your colleague, could work together more productively. What needs to be said between you and your colleague for that to happen?

How could this new way of working together contribute more generally to your 'leadership agenda'?

FIGURE 4.2   The double core quadrant

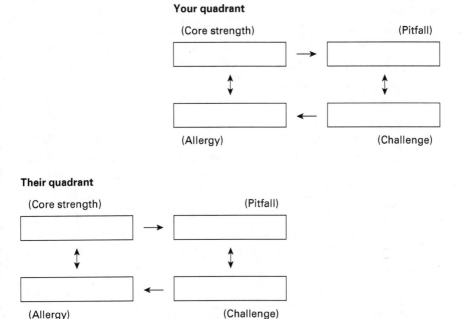

FIGURE 4.3   A completed double core quadrant

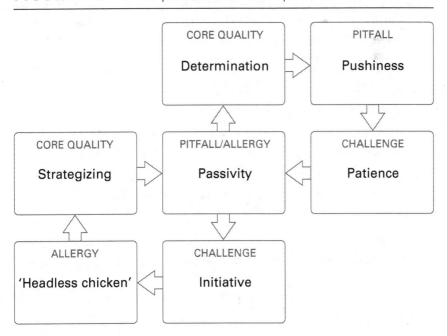

What you have reflected on in this chapter can make a real difference to your leadership practice, if only because you may become more conscious of your automatic routines, decisions and difficulties. Tracking down patterns in your own make-up and your life's history can be very useful and can bring an understanding of yourself and of your frailties as a leader. You can begin to spot things in advance, appreciate where others are coming from, or even smile about the curious and highly personal pickles you are getting yourself into.

It can be even more liberating to share some of this work with a trusted advisor or executive coach. So if you work with someone that you trust with all of this information and who is relatively independent – ie not employed by your company, not someone from your intimate friends or your spouse – then we would highly recommend telling that person your findings from this chapter. Then after you have gone through your notes try to listen to them as openly as you can whilst they make their own sense of all of this rich material.

Summary: how you thrive as a leader

This chapter has helped you to explore your background, roles and relationships as a leader and helped you to see what is not easy to detect: some of the underlying, hidden forces that propel you into a leadership role (or not) and that propel you within that role as well, through your *behavioural* drivers and *valencies*. You have been invited to:

- review the prevailing leadership dynamics in your family of origin;
- inquire into potential transference patterns which you take from one leader–report relationship to the next;
- determine some of the core behavioural drivers that inform patterns in how you take up and contribute to work and leadership;
- look into the potential consequences of having these particular informing drivers, in the form of personal vulnerabilities.

Finally you have been invited to use some of what you have learned about yourself by mapping a single relationship at work, in the form of a 'double quadrant' based on one of your core qualities.

PART TWO
The way leaders come to grief

Introduction:
the importance
of leading oneself

> *It is an observation no less just than common, that there is no stronger test of a man's real character than power and authority, exciting as they do every passion, and discovering every latent vice.*
>
> **PLUTARCH (*LIVES*, CA AD 100)**

Plutarch is right in commenting that leadership, just like parenthood, will 'excite every passion': stir up all our emotions, the loftiest as well as the basest. It is not just the responsibility that we feel for others and for the impact we have on their life, which sparks off these emotions. In equal amounts we become the recipient of the expectations and projections from those that we lead, as well as those that we are accountable to. More often than not our direct colleagues will burden us with the frailties and feelings that they struggle to handle themselves, in the hope that we will take care of them particularly in this arena: the management of their own insecurities and passions. The test of character that the quote speaks about is not just the handling of our own emotions; more than that it is the handling of the emotions that permeate our immediate world, swaying us, our direct colleagues and also the wider organization.

The stirring up of emotion, plus the excitement of the position that we find ourselves in, carries the risk of us reverting to the 'default' way of handling issues as we always do under stress. This default position seems to be unique to each one of us and is very much linked to early experience and the way our personalities were formed when we were very young. Some of us suspect that others might not hold to their commitments, and hence become suspicious (paranoid) leaders. Others deal with high emotion by disowning it and reverting to a cold and controlled, sublimely calm place of their own, and hence become cut-off (schizoid) leaders. Still others become emotional themselves and let their emotions lead them in a vain attempt to rid themselves of all the stress and projections, and hence become moody (borderline) leaders. Others prefer to duck their responsibility and recoil into a position of ignoring genuine demands on leadership, sidestepping the issues of the day, and hence become disingenuous (passive–aggressive) leaders.

As this part of the book will attempt to demonstrate, there is a very rich palette of ways in which we can be led by the stresses that come with an exposed and responsible position. These ways are situationally determined, contingent on the strength of emotion and one's own ability to handle some of it by oneself, but they are also determined by the way our personalities were formed, probably very early in our lives.

Obviously, we would not advocate being overly led by those emotions and pressures that any leadership role stirs up. Best is always to manage those emotions within ourselves, build our own 'reflective-self function' and make our attachment to the leadership role and its demands as secure as possible (see Chapter 2). We will return to the themes of building up resilience, knowing ourselves and strengthening a secure base for our leadership contributions in Chapter 14. However, we also recognize that really all of this 'dealing with emotion' is predominantly an illusion and leadership *will* continue to stir up emotions and open up every latent vice, just as Plutarch argued. For that reason it is perhaps more important to recognize our own automatic responses to stress, our own personality patterns when we go into overdrive, and that is what the next five chapters are devoted to.

We agree with Plutarch's suggestion that leadership is primarily a *test* of our character, a touchstone of our handling of emotions and projections. Leadership brings out less helpful 'overdrive' patterns but it is up to the leader how to respond to them. In this regard the first task of a leader is *leading oneself*, making sure that our passions don't lead us astray, that our vices don't get us into trouble. Essentially, leading oneself means that we aim to handle the emotions that are stirred up by the leadership function, that we try to countenance the projections that will be directed at us, without renouncing the valuable information that emotions and projections contain, the former about our own state and vulnerabilities, and the latter about our co-workers' issues and struggles. Leading oneself seems a balancing act where we do allow ourselves to be stirred up and our passions to be excited, so that we can reap from all those excitations valuable information about the state of affairs; yet do not allow ourselves to succumb to the grip of such emotions, to go into overdrive and to derail. Leading oneself means maintaining this very precarious balance.

In the next chapter, Chapter 5, we will look at this cross between leadership and derailment, drive and overdrive, which characterizes every responsible leadership role. Having succinctly mapped the territory in Chapter 5, we will endeavour in Chapters 6 to 8 to describe the most common personality patterns of leaders, at the same time highly individual to a leader and also recognizable by all. These are patterns we all possess; however, the way they come to the fore is individually determined, as well as determined by degrees of stress and projection. Chapter 9 summarizes those patterns once more, sketching various features of the *neurotic leader*, the leader who is battling to keep his or her personality patterns down and yet experiences plentiful reminders in terms of stress and projection, reminders of what it means to be a leader on a daily basis. Chapter 9 also gives an overview of the quantitative research findings in terms of leaders' personality patterns and how they impact on the effectiveness of their contributions. Finally, in Chapter 10 we offer help in reflecting on your own leadership overdrive patterns by inviting you to ask yourself questions that we believe are relevant for your personal journey as a leader and your own ability to handle yourself as a leader.

What makes top leaders tick?

> *A skilful commander is not overbearing.*
> *A skilful fighter does not become angry.*
> *A skilful conqueror does not compete with people.*
> *One who is skilful in using men puts himself below them.*
> *This is called the virtue of not-competing.*
> *This is called the strength to use men.*
>
> **LAO-TZU (CA 600 BC)**

FIGURE 5.1   What makes a leader tick?

This chapter sets the stage for looking at what makes senior executives tick and contribute, as well as transgress and derail. In other words, it looks at the positive side of leaders as well as their dark side. The characteristic behaviour patterns of top leaders are the focus of this part of the book. With the help of some well-known real-life case examples out of the public domain, background information on the recurring characteristics of business leaders, and psychological regularities within such patterns that underpin character, you are invited to think about your own patterns of contributing towards your role. Thus we hope to stimulate an awareness that may steer you in deciding when such patterns are helpful, constructive and productive and when they are becoming unhelpful, problematic and counterproductive.

Over the last 20 years we have had the privilege of working with some very smart, tough, focused and resilient executives. The unifying characteristic of these diverse individuals is that they were in demanding roles, carrying out large amounts of work under intense time pressures and facing tough relational challenges. Most have been ambitious, smart and driven. This chapter looks at the various ways in which senior leaders are driven, and how those very ways can drive them overboard as well.

As their coaches we have often been surprised and challenged by the straightforward way in which they have related to us. Many have been willing to give us first-hand insight into the work and relational challenges they face. We have found our interactions with them rich and illuminating. We have learned with them as we have coached them. Together we have gained a deeper appreciation of the demanding circumstances of executive roles today. We have consequently become more understanding of, and empathetic about, the relational complications many of them face in their daily efforts to meet their pressing work schedules and business demands. We understand more and more why they are so driven whilst we keep doubting whether this 'drivenness' is the best answer to the challenges that they face.

We have experienced them as demanding a lot of themselves and of others working alongside them, including us. We have seen them continually taxing themselves mentally and physically: squeezing out every last drop of resilience that their bodies and minds could muster.

We see them work hard and play even harder. Some exercise little and eat poorly. Meetings may be tense and frequently interrupted. Lunches are quick and smartphones continue to vibrate throughout some of the reflective work that we are trying to do with them. Even when relaxed and in convivial mood, conversations may still have a terse, slightly unpredictable edge to them. It is as if the challenges they carry press unrelentingly and directly into every conversation and onto every relationship.

More often than not, we experience them at their relational best. They have a capacity to be engaging, encouraging, effective and driven with us and presumably many others. Occasionally the veneer of well-polished leadership interaction may crack and fall away. On these occasions we experience them as anxious and self-doubting, feeling slightly inadequate and helpless in a changing world with unforgiving demands.

As a result we have now dedicated a significant amount of time and effort to helping tough, focused and very smart people to relate and work with bodily, self, interpersonal and environmental awareness. In some cases our concern has been specifically and overtly to help them to 'relate' better. At other times relational challenges have emerged out of addressing a significant 'business' issue that they were facing. It is clear to us that 'how well I as an executive relate to others' is a central concern that is critical to the ability to manage complex organizational issues in the multinational, multifaceted organizations that increasingly characterize our modern business world.

Effectiveness through being focused and tough

As you would expect, working on a relevant and personal issue with such smart and focused professionals is as challenging an experience as it is rich in insight. We find that as coaches we cannot be outside the conversations that we are engaged in. We are inevitably drawn into and pressed to contend with the convoluted interpersonal dynamics that accompany the activities of the highly committed and driven professionals that we are coaching. We have to face and learn about our own relational vulnerabilities, we have to address our own interpersonal issues, and we have to do so 'on the spur of the moment'.

Ambitious executives usually have a highly developed sense of focus and determination that enables them to remain motivated and productive through situations of great ambiguity or conflict. This 'focus' and 'toughness' demonstrates a remarkable resolve, and enables them to turn their attention swiftly and determinedly to other things that demand attention, without losing their sense of proportionality and ability to balance (sometimes contradictory) short-term achievements within an overall direction or desired long-term outcome.

More often than not the leaders we have met use this 'tough, focused, and driven attention' incredibly aptly and skilfully. At their best they come across as vibrant and productive with high qualities of attention and presence. This means that they can remain open to possibility and development even as they make tough decisions regarding pressing business issues. Good focus allows them to be incredibly stretched personally and professionally and still have the capacity to function effectively.

However, while being incredibly productive, focused and driven, these leaders also acquire rather obstinate traits, labouring unremittingly with full commitment. They acquire a habit of stepping up even when not being immediately rewarded: conviction and firmness in maintaining a sense of optimism despite being constantly knocked back by contrary events or disappointments as initiatives get thwarted.

This commitment and focus also reveals their tremendous resilience at a more personal level. The executives are able positively to remain detached from unhelpful feedback and criticism. They are able to live with discomfort, doubt or contradiction and to endure the messiness of mixed positive and negative feelings and responses. Consequently these focused executives may come across as being quite deaf to feedback and resistant to change.

Overdrive leading to relational myopia and ineffectiveness

Anyone working with top executives will become aware of occasions when the tough focus appears to go beyond the effective and leads to unhelpful behavioural features which put strains on relationships (Furnham, 2010).

We notice that under certain circumstances patterns of relating come to the forefront in executives' behaviour that are uncharacteristic of the way we habitually experience them. It appears that when pushed beyond a certain edge or under certain contextual and interpersonal circumstances, we are all drawn into a kind of 'overdrive' that is characterized by contradictory and unhelpful interactions. In these circumstances we have repeatedly observed the 'tough focus' turn into 'relational myopia'. When drawn into this space, executives lead their organizations in ways that are short-sighted and that work against their own positive intentions and ultimate well-being. They turn the considerable strengths that were previously evident in their work into ineffective interactions that expend much mental and physical energy. As a result they achieve little progress towards mutually shared goals.

Thus, faced with certain pressing challenges, these 'tough executives' demonstrate patterns that are relationally problematic. The positive manifestations of 'tough focus' become overcooked and adopt unhelpful and ultimately unproductive patterns of reticence, stubbornness or frenetic activity. Instead of being open to possibility and ambiguity, and willing to engage in continuous and creative conversations with themselves and others, these executives instead become seriously unhelpful, obstinate, resentful, inarticulate or intense. They become a caricature of themselves. They go into 'overdrive'.

Relational effectiveness coming under strain

Relational effectiveness matters because we live in a complex, fast-changing and uncertain world. Specifically, executives leading the more complex and pacesetting organizations that shape our public and commercial worlds are required to act quickly and with conviction, without having recourse to sufficient information. The 21st-century executive world is not a place for equivocal wimps. Executives are expected to be decisive. Problems are seen as requiring deliberate and intelligent attention. Consequently leaders are developed and encouraged to be tough and to prevail in adversity. This presents them with the personal and psychological challenge of navigating an uncertain world of contradictory demands mixed in with their own doubts and sense of personal inadequacy.

The ability to remain productive within this environment is a key requirement for success at individual, organizational and societal levels. For those engaged with complex problems of business and society, relational effectiveness is not an optional extra, it is a requirement.

At the top of the business hierarchy relationships need to remain effective through even the most challenging of personal and contextual circumstances. Often executives discover this when they are working across organizational boundaries and during significant change and ambiguity. Superior relational effectiveness is critical for senior executives working at the frontline of their organization. Typically such executives find themselves answerable to a board and chief executive, and feel responsible for ensuring that the organization is meeting its external obligations to shareholders, owners and other stakeholders. Such executives often feel 'caught' between the reality and demands of their numerous stakeholder needs, their contextual environment, the requirements of their role within the organization, and the commitments and goals of the organization from the perspectives of their supervisors or shareholders.

We have found that senior executives' relationships may typically go into overdrive and myopia when placed in situations where there is this persisting stretch and challenge with high stakes. Typically these are circumstances of changing roles or new challenges. For example:

1 *When an executive is promoted into a new role that has challenges that they have not faced before.* In this instance the executive has to raise his or her game quickly and take on new ways of working and behaving that need to be seen (by them and by others) to be productive. Often promotion to the new role is accompanied with an expanded scope of responsibility. In the case of frontline externally oriented roles, this expanded scope will often be a combination of internal leadership responsibilities as well as external customer or other stakeholder relational responsibilities. The newly promoted executive has to master the requirements of the role quickly, meet demands of subordinates, attend to external pressures and show up at meetings and organizational conferences. Consequently the executive has no choice but to behave in a 'tough' way and to be 'oblivious' to anything else that is a distraction to their main mission.

2 *When a role that an executive is comfortable in and used to unexpectedly takes on a new character.* Internal or external changes may create new and unexpected demands on the executive. The executive suddenly notices expectations to engage in a different way or to achieve more stretching and different outcomes. In this circumstance the executive finds that their previously well-organized and settled way of working is turned upside down. They suddenly find that their boss, their subordinates, and their external

interlocutors are all demanding responses and behaviours that were not previously required. Consequently the executive has to 'toughen up again', become much more focused, and pay much greater attention to working differently in order to have an improved chance of achieving the new outcomes and the enhanced standards of performance that are now expected. In this case too, the executive changes the way they relate to those around them, and may be experienced by others as becoming suddenly disengaged, unfathomable or politicized.

3 *When an executive finds him- or herself in a new role that has not existed before.* This is possibly the most demanding of the three scenarios. In this instance, the executive has to simultaneously create a new focus and purpose for the emerging and therefore ill-defined role, and deal with many demands and pressures, without precedent, role history or guidance from a predecessor. The executive has to work out, for him- or herself and with limited support, what, in this cacophony of activities and requirements, they have to pay attention to first, and what they should risk leaving for later, or even ignore. Again in this process the executives often find themselves relating in a tough and urgent way, carefully dedicating their energy to the most important issues and relationships, whilst moving away from issues and requests that seem distracting or just not a priority.

In addition to these scenarios, executives may obviously feel themselves under pressure when their circumstances and support networks outside work become challenging. This may be due to relationship difficulties, illness or bereavement. Under such circumstances executives may find themselves experiencing disruptions originating from their lives away from work but affecting their sense of stability and effectiveness in work and outside of work.

There is accumulating evidence in the literature that overdrive patterns are much more common and increasingly visible in higher levels of leadership. On reviewing recent research, Kaiser, LeBreton and Hogan (2014) show that whilst about a quarter of a sample of 6,774 managers of all levels had at least one dark-side trait sufficiently elevated to be considered a performance risk, by contrast across three samples, and including 378 senior executives, a much higher percentage (98 per cent) had at least one risk factor. In other words, virtually every upper-level manager is at some risk of performance problems related to his or her dark side, which raises the importance of self-development for them.

Three real-world cases

We have summarized below three real-world cases illustrating experiences that are quite common in organizational executives' lives. In each of these cases, circumstances create conditions in which executives push (or are pushed) forward, drive hard and are then seen to overreach themselves and to overshoot. Success, derailment, failure and recovery become inevitable concomitants of their undertaking. It is our firm view that if they are to succeed in their present and future endeavours, all hard-driving executives have to learn to contend with these experiences.

The BBC 2012 leadership debacle

After a keenly anticipated leadership selection process, the BBC announced on 4 July 2012 that the new director-general chosen to succeed the erudite Mark Thompson as the chief executive and editor-in-chief was going to be the well-groomed BBC insider, George Entwistle. In the press releases and reports that followed Entwistle was hailed by the current chairman and former director-general alike as being an exceptional leader and a brilliant catch for the BBC top job. Amongst the qualities highlighted were Entwistle's creativity, leadership, formidable track record as a programme maker, intuitive understanding of public sector broadcasting, passion for the BBC, and clear vision of how the BBC can 'harness the creativity and commitment to staff...'.[1]

George Entwistle took up his appointment as Director-General on 17 September 2012. And within 54 days, on 11 November of the same year, he was forced to resign. In so doing he had infamously become the shortest-lived director-general in the BBC's history. In what amounted to a public verbal flailing and shaming, Entwistle had faced a series of episodes where his leadership effectiveness had been challenged, ridiculed and questioned internally by his own staff and externally by the media and politicians.[2] By the time he left his post MPs were being quoted in print questioning his lack of curiosity. Apparently most damagingly, his performance in a BBC Radio 4 *Today* programme interview with John Humphreys was being cited as revealing his lack of awareness and attentiveness. The *Today* programme particularly questioned why he, as editor-in-chief, had no awareness or up-to-date knowledge of significant developments relating to the highly scrutinized *Newsnight* report about Jimmy Savile's transgressions, which had not been broadcast.

Even after being forced to resign, Entwistle's sad tale stayed in the headlines with his formerly supportive boss being forced repeatedly to defend the £450,000 pay-out agreed as part of Entwistle's contractual severance arrangements.

The HBOS merger calamity

In 2001 the Halifax Building Society and Bank of Scotland, two highly revered British financial institutions, one with over 150 years of mortgage lending in England and the other with 300 years of respected banking traditions in Scotland, merged to form HBOS, a new financial services organization. On formation, the new entity was capitalized at over £30 billion and over the next six years was to grow to a market capitalization of over £40 billion.[3] The growth represented a new strategic thrust that relied on a combination of growth in the mortgage book, increased corporate and foreign lending, and heavy reliance on wholesale-market capital funding. In addition to the change in strategic business model a new leadership was put in charge to drive the new focus on growth. The leadership team comprising a non-executive chairman, chief executive, and head of lending, collectively presided over a change in focus and culture that was later to be seen as being inappropriate to the challenges that the new banking entity was to face.[4]

Within six years the head of corporate lending had been fined and banned by the Financial Services Authority; the non-executive chairman was admitting that 'with the benefit of hindsight the bank did become exposed to excessive levels of risk, particularly in the housing markets and corporate division'; a parliamentary finance commission was noting that 'senior risk managers lacked the authority to damp the dominant sales culture of the bank'; and in addition it was noted that 'the chief executive during the period was not a career banker'. Collectively the leadership had presided over the collapse of one of Britain's largest companies, the largest bankruptcy in UK corporate history, resulting in £40 billion being wiped off the capital that 3 million shareholders had invested and in 40,000 jobs lost. The HBOS name was to disappear as the bank was to be merged into the Lloyds banking group.[5]

However, the saga continued to ramble on – at personal and corporate levels. For example, in April 2013 Sir James Crosby, former CEO of HBOS, asked for his knighthood to be removed, issued a public apology and reportedly agreed to forego a significant proportion of his £580,000-a-year pension. This led to additional pressure on Sir James's successor, Andy Hornby, and former chairman, Lord Stevenson, to make a similar public gesture.[6] In September of the same year it was reported that the Whitehall committee responsible had accepted Sir James's forfeiture request.

The Olympus governance scandal

In April 2011 Michael Woodford became the first European to become the CEO of Japanese camera maker Olympus, well known for its leadership in digital recording technology and innovation. By the end of 2011 Woodford had been sacked. In a subsequent commentary in the *Wall Street Journal* he wrote:

> I was president and CEO of Olympus Corporation when the financial scandal broke last year, after I had exposed a massive fraud of approaching $2 billion which has subsequently become known as Japan's Enron. Less than a month after I had been forced to leave the company, Olympus's share price had dropped by a staggering 81.5 per cent compared to the day before my dismissal. In monetary terms this represented a fall in market value of over $7 billion, and in witnessing the meltdown of this iconic Nikkei-listed company the business world was aghast.[7]

What had followed his initial challenge to the Japanese board had been a series of accusatory counterclaims that now reads as a well-documented saga of corporate acrimony, machination and recrimination. In his detailed report *Inside the Olympus scandal*, Woodford (2012) notes how his lifelong career in Olympus (he joined at the age of 16 and climbed his way to the very top) had not prepared him for the battle he was to face in persuading first the Olympus board and then external shareholders of the apparent financial fraud that was taking place within the business. In a saga that culminated in former Olympus chairman Tsuyoshi Kikukawa pleading guilty to charges of falsifying accounts to cover up losses of $1.7 billion, Woodford was finally vindicated – but only after an intense and extended period of denial, stonewalling and catcalling. Woodford admitted to being under tremendous personal and emotional stress. He reported facing severe threats to his marriage and even receiving security advice from the British police.

Woodford subsequently sued Olympus and was awarded £10 million for unfair dismissal. The personal and organizational lessons however are still unfolding. The *Independent* newspaper commented in an article reporting on Woodford's victory that, 'The scandal has revived calls for more outside scrutiny of its boardrooms, but failed to trigger sweeping corporate governance reforms in Japan similar to those introduced a decade ago in the wake of US scandals such as Enron and WorldCom.'[8]

These real cases illustrate experiences that are surprisingly common in executives' lives. Circumstances create conditions in which executives are propelled forward, take responsibility as they are wont to, and are then seen to overstretch themselves. If they are to survive or succeed in these and future endeavours these hard-driving executives have to learn to master such conditions.

More specifically the cases described above highlight three important points:

1 Firstly, they show that the crises executives face often result from a combination of challenging changes in role and/or context. Hence executives may unwittingly be presented with a mix of leadership needs – which taken together they are not well suited to respond to effectively.

2 Secondly, while executives can and do 'rise to the occasion', and there are instances when executives are successful in providing the leadership needed to resolve the situation effectively, it is also evident that success is not guaranteed. Executives' *qualities* may be inappropriate for the episode being faced. In relying on their tried and tested strengths they may still overshoot into overdrive (hubris) and find that what they are offering is inadequate, inappropriate or insufficient. Faced with failure or disappointment they may feel forced to retreat into introspective ineffectiveness (hurt).

3 Thirdly, it is clear that effective recovery is possible. Some executives may reconnect with their new realities in ways that enable them to find resources within and around them to recover. In doing so they may discover a grounding process of reflection and insight (humility). This leads to real learning. However, many other executives will remain stuck in confusion, hurt and grandiose fantasies. They may remain unable to deal with the new realities and associated personal and organizational implications.

In summary, relational overdrive and relational myopia often occur amongst the most experienced and most capable executives on whom an organization relies. It occurs in organizations that are pacesetting and at the front end of driving change or setting the pace within their market sector. It occurs in periods of rapid change when an organization's survival or ability to compete is dependent on innovation and rapid adaptation to challenging new realities. Our experience is that overdrive can emerge amongst executives from every kind of organizational and cultural background. It can be demonstrated in all sectors of industries, whether rapidly expanding, disrupted as a result of deregulation or revitalized by new market entrants. The three real-world case examples above of widely reported incidents are only illustrations of the widespread and natural occurrence of organizational and leadership experiences of overdrive and myopia.

An intuitive and psychological description of relational overdrive and myopia

In the remainder of this part, the next five chapters, we outline a descriptive typology of helpful and unhelpful patterns of tough leadership. This typology is based on our observations of executives from different sectors and roles over many years. The psychological descriptions are based on clinical traits that have been described by psychiatrists over many decades and can be found in medical manuals. In particular, the 11 distinct patterns that we have chosen to elaborate on in the next three chapters, were drawn from the *American Diagnostic and Statistical Manual* (DSM-5) (American Psychiatric Association, 2013) and can also be found in *The International Classification of Diseases and Related Heath Problems* (ICD-10). These 11 patterns are by no means mutually exclusive but they give a broad overview of the possibilities of going into overdrive.

For executives and senior leaders the remaining chapters of Part Two are intended as an intuitive and experience-based *metaphorical* description of patterns of behaviour that may stimulate you as a leader to reflect on your own patterns of behaviour. You may recognize in these descriptions patterns you see in your own (or your peers', subordinates' or bosses') circumstances and in so doing stimulate an awareness that may steer you in deciding when such patterns are helpful, constructive and productive and when they are becoming unhelpful, problematic and counterproductive.

If you are reading this as a coach or consultant, the descriptions may be a window through which you can acknowledge the challenges and circumstances your executive clients face. As a coach you can think about the typology as an instrument for studying how non-problematic and ostensibly healthy relationships may be transformed into less helpful and problematic ones, often simply by increasing the pressure. The descriptions are therefore best used as a stimulus for reflection, a possible route to greater insight, by executives, coaches, or between executives and coaches who work together to make sense of a challenging context.

In this part of the book we will elaborate on distinct ways of going into 'relational overdrive', of the phenomenon where habitual modes of relating break down to myopic and ineffectual contributions at work. We will introduce 11 characters which are caricatures but at the same time recognizable figures inhabiting the executive wings of many an organization. We will endeavour to demonstrate that going into overdrive makes these personalities border on known personality disturbances in medical diagnosis. We will also link some of their overdrives with known behavioural drivers (Kahler, 1975; and see Chapter 2) going overboard.

At the outset we want to emphasize that we hold the idea of a personality 'type', 'character' or 'caricature' lightly:

- Firstly, it can be argued that there are as many types as there are people in this world.

- Secondly, a contrary argument can be made, namely that all these so-called types can be found contained within a single person, even within every single person.

- Thirdly, it is the relational matrix around us that brings out the type we become, so organizational 'types' may very easily change when they change jobs, or when there is a merger or a different composition of working teams. And conversely, hiring a fresh leader into a stable workforce may bring out traits that are primed in that workplace, such as traits of the previous person holding that job.

- Fourthly, in any typology of personality, traits of one type can easily be mixed with traits of another, to create ever new, unique types. As long as we do not know whether character is built up from fundamental building blocks and which building blocks these might be, we can endlessly combine the many character traits and descriptors that have been proposed in an ever expanding literature.

So, writing in terms of personality types is fraught with difficulties and we are convinced we could have chosen different types and permutations to make the same points as we are making. We have chosen these particular *patterns* instead, because they have a long history in psychiatric literature and because they each have been well researched. Over the past two decades they have even been operationalized as a psychometric instrument for leaders in organizations, in the form of the Hogan Development Survey (HDS, Hogan and Hogan, 1997), so that every executive or coach who reads this book can undertake a personal positioning exercise on the same 11 patterns.

This is why we keep the descriptions fairly loose and will introduce other traits in the real-life case vignettes that we use.

The structure of each of the next three chapters is as follows. For each pattern under discussion we present:

1 The executive 'pattern' in full bloom.

2 The executive 'pattern' in overdrive – in the thralls of hubris, myopia or unmanageable pressure.

3 A brief analysis of the executive 'pattern' with the help of the DSM-5 (American Psychiatric Association, 2013) personality disorders, Paul Ware's work on behavioural drivers (Ware, 1983), and Daniel Ofman's work on core personal qualities (Ofman, 2002).

4 How to overcome this particular pattern: an exploration of how others can work with the particular pattern or how a workable 'challenge' can be formulated for the executive, and what sacrifices they may need to make when they are 'in the grip', 'in overdrive' or 'myopic' in this particular way and want to reverse their fortunes.

5 A real case study of an executive that we have met in our practice, where we have disguised potentially identifying details.

In the final chapters of Part Two we look at some other 'neurotic patterns' of leaders that can be found in the literature (Chapter 9) and we offer help in recognizing, exploring and reflecting upon your own dominant patterns as a leader (Chapter 10).

In our analysis of how overdrive can be overcome, we are influenced by a long tradition, going back to the Greek tragedies and further back to the Egyptians, where it was held that the overdrive situation creates a form of internal burden which grows with how much the individual transgresses the natural order (ie how extreme are the aberrations of the personality patterns) and also with time. In Egyptian mythology, hubristic accounts were settled soon after death: the goddess Ma'at (the divinity of truth, balance, order, law, morality and justice) weighed up the heart (which was believed to contain the soul) of the deceased against her ostrich feather. Only an unburdened heart, light as a feather, can reach the 'paradise' of afterlife. A heart which proved unworthy was devoured by the goddess Ammit and its owner condemned to remain in the underworld. In this tradition, to get rid of such a burden a process of catharsis (cleansing or purging) needs to be undertaken, so the work of overcoming this condition may be very protracted and may feel like a sacrifice.

The experience of catharsis is one which demands all of our resources and all resilience available, including outside resources like friends and professional support. One of the most surprising yet powerful resources that executives can muster in overcoming their overdrive, comes precisely from those people with whom they are having most difficulty. Their most troubling frustrations and irritations when in overdrive can and will become their most helpful allies, when they are successfully moving beyond these patterns of derailment or overdrive. It is on this empirical yet uncanny principle that the model of 'core qualities' (Ofman, 2002) is based. We will be drawing heavily on this model to illustrate the challenges of the executive when trying to pull back from an overdrive situation.

We have given the 11 patterns of leadership personality informal names. You will recognize yourself and others frequently in these patterns; we are all driven by them as well as nurturing them to some degree. They tend to come out at different times and can be seen in many shades of intensity, from the slightly neurotic to the full-blown deranged. Table 5.1 names them:

TABLE 5.1   Names of leadership personality patterns

Personality patterns:		
A. Movers and shakers	1. The Charming Manipulator	
	2. The Playful Encourager	
	3. The Glowing Gatsby	
	4. The Detached Diplomat	
B. Rigorous thinkers	5. The Responsible Workaholic	
	6. The Impulsive Loyalist	
	7. The Brilliant Sceptic	
	8. The Creative Daydreamer	
C. Sensitive carers	9. The Virtuous Supporter	
	10. The Accomplished Thespian	
	11. The Simmering Stalwart	

Dotlich and Cairo (2003) have given a very helpful short summary of the accompanying overdrive patterns which we have adapted into the following short summary of the 11 patterns.

Overdrives of the 'movers and shakers'

- *Antisocial* patterns linked with the Charming Manipulator: you believe the rules are made to be broken. Do you find it hard to be held accountable for your actions?

- *Passive–aggressive* patterns linked with the Playful Encourager: what you say is not what you really believe. Do you find it hard to take responsibility for your views and actions?

- *Narcissistic* pattern linked with the Glowing Gatsby: you think that you're right, and everyone else is wrong. Do you as a leader often think that others are wrong and not up to their jobs?

- *Schizoid* patterns linked with the Detached Diplomat: you're disengaged and disconnected. Do you often distance yourself from the everyday running of the business?

Overdrives of the 'rigorous thinkers'

- *Obsessive–compulsive* patterns linked with the Responsible Workaholic: you get the little things right and the big things wrong. Do you often fret about minutiae whilst losing focus on the big picture?

- *Borderline* patterns linked with the Impulsive Loyalist: you're subject to mood swings. Do you find it very hard to hear bad news about how the business is going?

- *Paranoid* patterns linked with the Brilliant Sceptic: you focus on the negatives. Do you often think that people are for or against you, and in particular against you?

- *Schizotypal* patterns linked with the Creative Daydreamer: you try to be different just for the sake of it. Is your picture of the future often proven wrong?

Overdrives of the 'sensitive carers'

- *Dependent* patterns linked with the Virtuous Supporter: you try to win the popularity contest. Are you looking after everyone and trying to make them all feel happy?

- *Histrionic* patterns linked with the Accomplished Thespian: you need to be the centre of attention. Are you obsessed with your public image?

- *Avoidant* patterns linked with the Simmering Stalwart: you're afraid to make decisions. Are you concerned or hesitant because of what other people might think or do?

We believe none of these patterns is gender specific and they can all be expressed by both men and women. Hence we have made half of the descriptions female and the other half male, randomly.

Again, we are choosing these patterns in particular because they have a long history in psychiatry and psychotherapy and because they have been operationalized for leaders and the general population (Hogan and Hogan, 1997). Finally, we were encouraged by recent research that shows that there are some convincing indications that for a group of 704 US army cadets over the course of a four-year leadership-development programme the very same 'subclinical traits' have been important moderators of their performance (Harms, Spain and Hannah, 2011). In Chapter 9 we give a short summary of what was found in this study and in other similar studies.

The next three chapters may seem somewhat repetitive in design and style, and on first reading it may be difficult to remember all the various overdrive patterns. One way of accelerating your reading is to commence with only the summaries at the end of the sections, and only read the full section when you notice something interesting or relevant in a particular summary. Another way of taking in this wide-ranging information is to start with your own drivers, which you have summarized in Chapter 4. With the help of Table 9.1 in Chapter 9 you can find overdrive patterns that you are more likely to engage in on the basis of your driver patterns (the drivers are listed in the column 'Working Style' of Table 9.1).

Summary: what makes top leaders tick?

Tough executives work hard and are extremely driven. They are often engaging, encouraging, and able to relate effectively with a variety of people with diverse styles and needs. They are usually on a relatively healthy cycle leading to success and the rewards of success.

However, occasionally the veneer of well-polished leadership interaction may crack and fall away. On these occasions leaders experience precisely those characteristics that are not very 'leader-like', such as anxiety, self-doubt or despondency. They may feel inadequate and helpless in a changing world with unforgiving demands. This is very much the flip side of the leadership medal. Precisely what is sacrificed or discarded to achieve or display success, plays up and comes back to haunt the leader.

Top executives work hard and play even harder. Some exercise little and eat poorly. Meetings may be tense and frequently interrupted. Even when relaxed and in convivial mood, conversations may still have a terse, slightly unpredictable edge to them.

The challenges of a top leader press unrelentingly and directly into every conversation and onto every relationship. They are exhausting to them as well as to their direct reports.

In many cases the main concern is for executives to relate better in times of stress and to somehow process and work with their high demands, suspicions, fears and exhaustions, so that they can keep offering a balanced and constructive approach to those colleagues and clients who need them and whom they need in order to fulfil their role.

Times that bring out such 'overdrive' patterns are in particular:

- when leaders are promoted into a new role;
- when existing roles take on a new character;
- when leaders have to scope out a role that has not existed before;
- when leaders' personal circumstances profoundly change or become challenging.

In the following chapters we intend to show some classic patterns of derailment that have been described, and we offer help to discover where you, the reader, might fit into those patterns.

A recurring theme will be how on the one hand ambition and drive can open up healthy cycles full of production, reward and success but at the same time can also go into overdrive or derailment which is when vicious cycles force leaders to pay a high price for their ambition.

We show how derailment is just the flip side of the medal of success and will therefore always accompany success: what is sacrificed or discarded in order to achieve does carry on playing a role in the background, a role that is bound to come to the fore when circumstances allow.

Notes

1 George Entwistle's biography can be found in the BBC Media Centre:
   http://www.bbc.co.uk/aboutthebbc/insidethebbc/managementstructure/
   biographies/entwistle_george/. See, for example, speeches given by
   Mark Thompson during his time as DG of the BBC: http://www.bbc.co.uk/
   aboutthebbc/insidethebbc/howwework/speeches/2008/thompson_mark_faith.

html. Details of press releases can be found in the BBC Media Centre: http://www.bbc.co.uk/bbctrust/news/press_releases/2012/dg_appointment.html

2   For example: the BBC's own news website reported that 'Mr Entwistle's resignation came after he was criticized for his performance during an interview on the BBC's Radio 4 *Today* programme on Saturday 10 November, in which he admitted he had not read a newspaper article revealing the case of mistaken identity involving Lord McAlpine, and that he had not seen the *Newsnight* broadcast when it aired on 2 November as he "was out".' http://www.bbc.co.uk/news/uk-20284124. The *Evening Standard* reported Lord Patten, then BBC Trust chairman, as saying after Entwistle's resignation: 'With the benefit of hindsight, we chose the wrong one. But we chose him from a very distinguished field; it was the choice of the whole of the Trust. It was unanimous.' He stressed there was a 'terrible paradox' because Entwistle was selected 'precisely because he identified very clearly the management failings in the BBC which needed to be tackled – silo mentality, internecine warfare between different parts of the BBC, the fact that it doesn't operate sufficiently as a team, the leaking.' But the former director-general was 'actually destroyed by those very management failings' and by being implicated in the original furore over *Newsnight* ditching a programme into sex claims against Jimmy Savile. http://www.standard.co.uk/news/politics/we-chose-the-wrong-man-in-george-entwistle-to-run-the-bbc-admits-lord-patten-8427251.html.

3   See parliamentary commission on banking standards transcript: http://www.publications.parliament.uk/pa/jt201213/jtselect/jtpcbs/c705-vi/c70501.htm

4   For a full account of the HBOS story *see Hubris: How HBOS Wrecked the Best Bank in Britain*, R Perman, Berlinn Ltd.

5   See summary of HBOS history 2001–2009: http://www.lloydsbankinggroup.com/about_us/company_heritage/HBOS_Heritage/hbos.asp

6   Reported in various papers 9 April 2013. For example, see *Financial Times* 9 April 2013

7   See WSJ blog: http://blogs.wsj.com/speakeasy/2012/12/04/seven-keys-to-being-a-successful-whistleblower/

8   See *Independent* newspaper report: http://www.independent.co.uk/news/business/news/victory-for-woodford-as-olympus-bosses-face-jail-8175972.html

The 'movers and shakers'

> *I'm selfish, impatient and a little insecure. I make mistakes, I am out of control and at times hard to handle. But if you can't handle me at my worst, then you sure as hell don't deserve me at my best.*
>
> **MARILYN MONROE (1926–1962)**

FIGURE 6.1   Four 'movers and shakers'

Introduction

This chapter describes four 'overdrive' patterns in leaders, which are related to the leader's patterns that focus on action (the first three cases) or paradoxically and actively withdrawing from (productive) action as in the fourth case:

1 The first pattern of leadership – which we have linked to *antisocial* characteristics – moves to charm and dazzle you and to engineer a very impressive performance.

2 The second pattern of leadership – which we have linked to *passive–aggressive* characteristics – moves to encourage others and find encouragement, being both sensitive to motivation and reluctant to act when not motivated.

3 The third pattern of leadership – which we have linked to *narcissistic* characteristics – moves to propel him- or herself forward into a glorious future, impressing everyone around them.

4 The fourth pattern of leadership – which we have linked to *schizoid* characteristics – distinguishes him- or herself by not being moved in those occasions where other people would be: their main characteristic is a stoic, tough or detached form of 'non-movement'.

What the four leadership patterns in this section have in common is that they all give primacy to 'behaving' above 'thinking' and 'feeling', hence they can be approached and worked with most straightforwardly through addressing behaviours and actions, employing to-do lists, specific goals, and practising new forms of action.

Thus, the overdrive patterns underpinning the 'movers and shakers' in this chapter are all linked with the first of these three domains or functions of the leadership process:

1 *Supporting*: facilitating or enabling the team's effectiveness, enhancing the resources and competences that are available – a making or doing function.

2 *Inspiring*: supplying the team with strategy and meaning making – a thinking function.

3 *Containing*: looking after or caring for the team, nurturing and providing space for processing emotions and for understanding to emerge – a feeling function.

The supporting function is giving primacy to behaviour and action, which you will recognize in the four leadership patterns outlined in this chapter.

Antisocial patterns in leaders

So, in the interests of survival, they trained themselves to be agreeing machines instead of thinking machines. All their minds had to do was to discover what other people were thinking, and then they thought that, too.

Kurt Vonnegut, *Breakfast of Champions* (1973)

A leader with antisocial patterns to the fore: The Charming Manipulator

The Charming Manipulator is an astute politician and diplomat in any circumstance, whether immersed in an ongoing challenge or in opening up new terrain. He really thrives in new and challenging contexts, turning out amazing managerial performances year after year. Just like the Glowing Gatsby (see page 127) and the Accomplished Thespian (see Chapter 8), the Charming Manipulator thoroughly enjoys turning out superior performances and being seen as a great business success story. Moreover, he is fun to be with, spontaneous, flexible even if somewhat impulsive.

Any organization, public or private, will get excessive amounts of work done by the Charming Manipulator. The Charming Manipulator is keen to please, to charm and to over-deliver, whilst remaining entrepreneurial, selfless and optimistic at the same time. He is adventurous and thrives on taking great risk to achieve extraordinary success. As an executive he really wants to be 'in demand' and to surround himself with teams of hardworking collaborators, who, with all his intensity, charm and self-belief, may turn into teams of 'followers' or 'flatterers'. The Charming Manipulator thrives on positive feedback and always has new plans and projects up his very long sleeve.

Those who work with him will experience him as dedicated, resourceful, persuasive, creative, and occasionally somewhat full of himself. A lot of weight can be put profitably on his shoulders, and he will not be fazed or ruffled by massive change or huge challenge. He will always find allies, inspire and motivate peers and direct-reports, or anyone who has been bogged down by the change. If necessary he will rewrite history in his own mind to retain and grow hope and belief in the future.

Here is what happens when a leader's antisocial patterns go into overdrive:

The Unscrupulous Schemer

When pressures become too great or excessive risk-taking gets the Charming Manipulator into trouble, he will initially withdraw, become impatient, rethink his strategy, and may come out with new plans of a less wholesome nature. If things have gone wrong he may not find remorse within himself and may be disinterested in learning from his mistakes.

His manipulative side may take over and he will at the same time become excessively charming. He will loosen his identification with the company and may at times work at cross-purposes and scheme actively against others.

The Charming Manipulator becomes a skilled 'advocate', defending storylines that are by themselves questionable but which suit his own games and machinations. He may continue to engage others brilliantly, so his following may remain strong, with all the more damaging consequences for the fulfilment of his role and the larger organization.

Consequently he increasingly becomes a loose cannon or a fifth column by himself, and principles of loyalty and ethics may be less and less respected. Internally he may withdraw in his own world of mortification, wounded feelings and self-defence, carrying grudges against all those he believes are taking bad news out on him or covertly working against his strategies and ideas.

In extreme circumstances the Charming Manipulator may have run-ins with the organizational hierarchy and may even have brushes with the law or contravene regulations. This may lead to the creation of a corrupted business unit. Even worse, he may be able to actively *dictate* the law within his part of the business and in the process turn into a kind of 'fat spider in the web': irreplaceable, threatening, and squeezing out large amounts of energy and money from the system.

FIGURE 6.2   The bright and shadow sides of the Charming
Manipulator

Analysis

The Charming Manipulator can be recognized as the 'antisocial' personality
adaptation and was also described by Paul Ware (1983). In terms of working
style his main drivers are 'be strong' and 'please others' (Kahler, 1975; and
see Chapter 2).

Ways to support this individual are usually through his 'behaving' styles: being actively engaged and assertive with him, and then 'thinking' about the real meaning of his actions (usually in large part born of shame, resentment or envy).

The best approach towards the Charming Manipulator is therefore through his 'behaving' styles or the actively supportive leadership domain (which is his 'open door' in terms of Ware's 1986 model): from there he may be open to 'think' again about what he is doing (Ware's 'target door'). The third leadership domain, that of 'feeling', may be hardest to reach and unavailable (Ware's 'trap door').

With the help of one of his greatest strengths, charm, we can think about how he may get into trouble. His natural charm and the success he experiences with influencing and winning over others can easily lead to creating a following and working with his many relationships in a manipulative way. Charm may descend into flattery or the propensity to motivate others to give more than they would otherwise mean to or would want to do. Charm may turn into manipulation and the charmer overreaches. At this point the strength becomes a 'pitfall' and this executive goes into overdrive.

From the pitfall it is usually relatively easy to see the challenge, as it is the natural opposite of the pitfall. In this case the challenge would be 'level-headedness' or common-sense realism. Another way of finding the challenge is to ask ourselves what we find most irritating in other people. In the case of the Charming Manipulator this may be 'criticism' born out of common sense, or 'righteousness'. This is the 'allergy' area of the successful charmer, the area where he easily becomes deflated, or annoyed, or frustrated (Figure 6.3).

FIGURE 6.3   The core quadrant of the Charming Manipulator

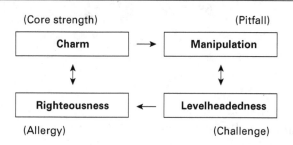

The sense one gets in the presence of this kind of leader is that one has to feel charmed and excited in his presence. We pick up an element of entitlement and indulgence, and hence a relatively strong claim on us to indulge, flatter or be amused. Freedom and excitement seem strong themes, and seem forever unfulfilled. When the pattern is strongly developed we may suspect some form of deception and an expectation of 'getting away with it'. We may feel as if we are some kind of 'utility' in the life of the Charming Manipulator which makes us feel rather empty and perhaps resentful. In order not to harbour suspicious or risky qualities such as fondness, trustworthiness and the capacity for generosity, a Charming Manipulator may be projecting these onto us. All those sensations or feelings that are rare or even unattainable for the Charming Manipulator himself come to reside with us and we start to feel we want to help out, adore and admire this person. If the same person is placed over us and holds some power over us, we may experience an expectation to get away with things and to be able to use our loyalty for personal gain, or we may feel drawn into becoming an accomplice in unholy schemes and machinations.

In working with this executive we first need to be aware of what is projected onto us and not allow ourselves to be seduced into being overly entertained. We may then help him think about what he can learn from those that irritate him the most, and what sort of challenge he can realistically set himself. If he can balance his charm with realism, and with a common-sense approach to others, he may avoid going into overdrive whilst continuing to draw on his core strengths. He can give himself permission to be modest, vulnerable, and even to be led by others. In this way his 'antisocial' tendencies become more balanced without there being any pressure to 'fix' them or give them up.

In practice, this can be a great sacrifice for those that have developed extreme forms of manipulation or recklessness, and who command large organizations or crowds of followers. It can feel very exposing to depend less on this crowd and to admit mistakes, or to admit not knowing.

CASE VIGNETTE 1   The Charming Manipulator

People say they feel Francesca's presence even before they meet her. Her influence goes before her. Her name is repeated, her jokes are retold and her behaviour recounted, often with fondness, sometimes with irritation but rarely without some kind of closing question mark. Having been appointed customer service and internal sales team leader of a demoralized and overworked team of a small building products and services firm in Tuscany, Italy, Francesca's appointment somehow coincided with the transformation of this group of rather despondent individuals into an exciting, motivated and effective team of dedicated customer service and sales co-workers.

In the six months since Francesca was appointed team leader, customer complaints are down, working hours are up, sick leave and absences are down; in addition customer satisfaction and repeat orders are going through the roof. Customers talk very fondly of the changes in the business. Many know Francesca well enough to call her directly and to use her first name and a number of them have been known to send thank you cards and small gifts of appreciation to Francesca and other members of the customer service team.

Francesca's success seems to derive from a powerful mix of focus and engagement. People say she always knows what she wants and that she 'never lets go until you are happy doing what she wants you to do for her'. She flatters, cajoles, pushes, pleads, pulls, bribes, smiles and pouts. She offers enticements as well as more threatening consequences. She works hard to get what she wants and to make you feel you are in the possession of something very special. If you cannot do it today tomorrow will do. Team members say that if she can offer it to you, she will; they add: 'Just remember to collect before being taken in again'.

Occasionally things go wrong. Customer orders are not delivered on time. The weather disrupts the convoys of building vans; or the picking lists in the warehouses get mixed up leading to the wrong packages being put together and sent to the wrong customers. Then Francesca steps in. She takes the customer's criticisms on behalf of the team. She never blames the staff and she offers to get things fixed quickly. Customers simply love it and the team are grateful. All are left happy and feeling the weight of Francesca's influence.

Her reputation with production has not been building up as much as with her clients. They say Francesca always overpromises and never gives clients a realistic account of what the firm can deliver and what it cannot. Moreover, production leaders often feel they are blamed for mistakes that were actually made in the sales team, and that their style and delivery has sometimes been ridiculed in front of clients. There was one incident where an entire delivery for one important customer was redirected to another new customer who had been on the phone that very morning. The former customer was extremely unhappy and had to be told all sorts of untrue stories to explain in some acceptable way that their expected delivery was actually going to come two weeks later. Moreover, the production department had to bend over backwards and be forced into extended overtime work to make the new delivery date a possibility. Francesca just brushed off the complaints. In a subsequent review meeting with the production department she simply pointed at the fact that the customer was happy and the positive effect on the bottom line for that month. There was a lot of irritation in the meeting that Francesca did not seem to notice.

CASE VIGNETTE 2   Refaat El-Sayed

Here is a real-life case description for this personality taken from Manfred Kets de Vries' *Reflections on Character and Leadership*:

An interesting example of how elements of imposture can affect a business enterprise has been the case of Refaat El-Sayed, the disgraced former chairman of Fermenta, a Swedish biotechnology firm. Before his fall, this Egyptian immigrant was able to dazzle the Swedish financial and industrial establishment, the media, and the public at large. El-Sayed became a folk hero to the man on the street because of his unpretentious lifestyle and his indifference to the trappings of wealth, despite having become the richest man in Sweden. He would be photographed in his small apartment in a suburb of Stockholm drinking Coca-Cola and eating pizza or be seen playing soccer with an amateur league.

Because of his activities he became the inspiration and pride of Sweden's large immigrant population. In 1985 he was voted 'Swede of the Year' by Swedish television. Unfortunately, what initially looked like a storm in a media teacup – the revelation that he had never, as he had alleged, held a doctorate – turned into a full-fledged scandal when an increasing number of irregularities were revealed. Fermenta stock, once the darling of the investment community (having reached an incredible price/earnings ratio of 56), plummeted more than 90 per cent in one year, damaging many individuals and Swedish institutions.

Kets de Vries, 2008, page 92

The antisocial personality pattern was already recognized more than two thousand years ago, when someone added the following parable to Aesop's corpus inspired by his or her personal experience of commercial life.

The scorpion and the frog

A scorpion met a frog on a river bank and requested a lift across the river on his back. The frog refused stating that, how would he be sure that the scorpion would not sting him. The scorpion responded that, as they would be in the river, if he stung the frog, he would die too. The frog agreed and took the scorpion on his back and they started crossing the river.

In the middle of the river, the scorpion stung the frog. The frog got paralysed due to the venom in the sting and started drowning. The frog just asked one question, 'Why?'

To this the scorpion replied, 'Because it is in my nature...'.

Apocryphal, related to Aesop's Fable 82, 6th century BC

Summary: antisocial patterns in leaders

- This antisocial pattern of leadership will normally only come out when several factors conspire to bring it out: a natural inclination, high ambition or high stress, uncertainty and ambiguity, and a degree of over-specialization with high commitment to a particular challenge.

- Clinically, the pattern is characterized by high levels of charm, flattery and seduction, combined with a diminished sense of boundaries, responsibility, and accountability. When caution and level-headedness are thrown to the wind, the pattern may become manipulative and undermining.

- Behavioural drivers that often go together with this particular pattern in leaders are tendencies to 'be strong' and to 'please others'.

- A first connection with this leader may be made through her overflowing communication. Any initial meeting will be lively and full of actions, exhortations to action, requests to change tack, and plans for the future. The challenge is to help her to move on to thinking about all those actions, and to reflect more quietly regarding what all this is about.

- The antisocial leader is not very open about emotion, and often not very introspective regarding emotion either, so feelings will largely remain a no-go area for anyone working with this pattern of leadership.

Passive–aggressive patterns in leaders

And why is it, thought Lara, that my fate is to see everything and take it all so much to heart?

Boris Pasternak, *Doctor Zhivago* (1957)

A leader with passive–aggressive patterns to the fore: The Playful Encourager

The Playful Encourager is typically present in new roles within well-established and understood circumstances. She is usually an executive who has come up through the ranks and has experienced how the organization has developed and responded to new challenges. She will have been successful and recognized for a long time and will have a record of achievement that is unquestionable. She is able to keep her cool and not to take things too seriously, being naturally aware of boundaries and responsibilities. Even if she knows how to work very hard, she will not take work home and respects 'down-time', holidays and family life.

In a new role the Playful Encourager focuses her energy in enabling and helping others to step up and address challenges she easily recognizes and apparently understands. She manages her business very autonomously. She relates pleasantly and with confidence based on the recognition and goodwill she already has. She relies on her longstanding knowledge of the organization, on her excellent connections, and is open and attentive to the needs of others.

At her best the Playful Encourager is a confident, straight-talking stalwart who is happy to work with and through others – without putting excessive demands on them – and to encourage teams and whole organizations to build on successes and to utilize strengths that exist and have a proven track record.

Here is what happens when a leader's passive–aggressive patterns go into overdrive.

The Elusive Resister

The Playful Encourager becomes the Elusive Resister when her focus and drive for present results become detached from the realities of those that she is encouraging to achieve those results. Because she relies tremendously on her own knowledge and connections, she becomes frustrated when her encouragement does not appear to deliver the outcomes in others that she expects for herself. She puts off and gets irritated by tasks that she does not like doing, and may seem stubborn when pushed for results. She becomes pushy rather than encouraging and resentful rather than direct and dependable.

To those in her environment she becomes less predictable, as she will sometimes go along with and sometimes resist the same suggestions. She will show elusive resistance, not letting anyone know of her private misgivings, but acting them out in less committed and half-hearted implementation. Or she will only support bosses who have earned her trust, and avoid those who have not.

At her most challenged the Elusive Resister uses tricks of manipulation and intimidation to make others work towards her own goals – or blames them behind their backs when they don't. In addition she uses her longstanding knowledge of the organization and wide-ranging connections to browbeat and bully others into the actions that she believes are right for the organization.

She is therefore experienced as difficult, irritable, untrustworthy, self-absorbed, stubborn and tormenting.

FIGURE 6.4   The bright and shadow sides of the Playful Encourager

Analysis

The Playful Encourager can be recognized as the 'passive–aggressive' personality adaptation and was also described by Ware (1983). In terms of working style, her main drivers are 'try hard' and 'be strong' (Kahler, 1975; and see Chapter 2).

Ways to support this individual are in the first instance through her 'behaving' styles: looking at her actions, their consequences, showing empathic understanding for her vulnerability and defensiveness, and then 'thinking' about what other actions she could adopt.

The best approach towards the Playful Encourager is therefore through her 'behaving' styles or her tendency to be ambivalent in her support (which is her 'open door' in terms of Ware's 1986 model); from there she may be open to 'feeling' why her support is so equivocal (Ware's 'target door'). The third leadership domain, that of 'thinking', may be hardest to reach and unavailable (Ware's 'trap door').

With the help of one of her greatest strengths, sensitivity, we can think about how she may be getting into trouble. Her thin skin, selfless encouragement of others and the forthrightness of her contribution can develop into oversensitiveness and intimidation of those she previously encouraged. Sensitivity may thus descend into petulance or even bullying. She becomes wedded to her own picture of the world and her own expectations of others. At this point the strength becomes a 'pitfall' and this executive goes into overdrive.

From the pitfall it is usually relatively easy to see the challenge, as it is the natural opposite of the pitfall. In this case the challenge would be 'tolerance' of others and their different ideas. Another way of finding the challenge is to ask oneself what we find most irritating in other people. In the case of the Playful Encourager this may be people who become more insistent and take an active leadership stance towards them. This is the 'allergy' area of the successful encourager, the area where she easily becomes deflated, or annoyed, or frustrated (Figure 6.5, Ofman, 2002).

FIGURE 6.5   The core quadrant of the Playful Encourager

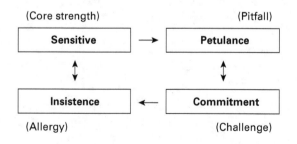

The sense you get in the presence of this kind of leader is a slight shiftiness and awkwardness, as if you cannot be sure if the person is fully with you or not. You get the impression that there may be some critical part hidden under the friendly exterior. You pick up an element of unease, frustration and an unfulfilled need for safety, agreement or self-expression. The leader's own hopes and dreams seem strong interests, and they seem forever unfulfilled. When the pattern is strongly developed we notice this person as being privately resentful and somehow subversive. The Playful Encourager resents being disturbed or interrupted, but this resentment is not expressed directly – rather by means of procrastination or excuses. In order not to harbour difficult feelings such as annoyance, irritation or gratitude, they may be projected onto us when we meet a Playful Encourager. All those sensations or feelings that are troubling or even unattainable for the Playful Encourager herself come to reside with us. If the same person is placed over us and holds some power over us, we may suffer impatience, volatility or annoyance about our work and a tendency to say one thing but do another.

In working with this executive we first need to be aware of what is projected onto us and not allow ourselves to be seduced into being overly irritated. We may then help her discover what she can learn from those that have been irritating her, and what sort of challenge she can realistically set herself. If she can balance the encouragement with acceptance and tolerance of the views of others, she may avoid going into overdrive whilst continuing to draw on her core strengths. She can then perhaps either surrender to the prevailing dominant views and powers around her or even better, actively work on her commitment to this new agenda that she has been resisting so far. In this way her 'passive–aggressive' tendencies became more balanced without there being any pressure to 'fix' them or give them up.

In practice, this can be a great sacrifice for those that have developed extreme forms of resentment, procrastination or intimidation. It can feel like an existential defeat to have to admit to having been ambivalent and undermining, and to accept a side of yourself which, far from being encouraging, digs your heels deeply in the sand.

CASE VIGNETTE   The Enlightened Encourager

Ruben is the new vice-chancellor of a university and he has hit upon hard times. State funding is being withdrawn whilst fee income has not come up sufficiently to make up for holes in the various budgets. Ruben has come through the academic ranks and he was a professor of civil law with a specialty in mediation. He is strongly committed from the outset to engineer a fair process where deans and heads of departments can decide amongst themselves where money is going to be saved by letting go of academic disciplines or qualifications.

Ruben sets up a small steering group with one internal and one external process consultant, and starts to send out personal invitations asking key figures within the university to join the steering group. Gradually he works towards a 12-person-strong strategy group of insiders: key professors and decision makers. He undertakes a personal conversation with each one of them, genuinely inspiring them with the importance and responsibility of their new role on the strategy group. The strategy group then comes together for some 15 sessions of half-a-day each, usually facilitated by the external process consultant or by Ruben as the chair of the group. Discussions in the group are initially very engaging. The professors use their creativity to generate ambitious and challenging future scenarios, and then reason back from those to the present day to arrive at new priorities for fund-raising and academic excellence. A lot of effort is also spent on agreeing on the terms and values that should underpin the decision-making process. The professors comment both during meetings and during lunches and breaks that in the strategy group they feel genuinely committed. They say they are working together better than ever before.

Gradually and irrevocably, from the open and free discussions and the excellent desktop research, the stark contours of the decisions to be made become increasingly clear. A very bold decision will have to be made for the future of this university. Whether the decision entails slicing budgets in 'salami fashion' across all faculties, or giving up important centres of excellence with in some cases hundreds of years of history, or alternatively forcing faculties to slim down and merge together, everyone can easily recognize that the consequences are going to be momentous. It also becomes gradually clear that, from some of the options that are on the table, three members of the strategy group are standing to lose personally along with their departments.. These group members are becoming increasingly defensive. Now, as 'crunch' time is approaching the discussions become ever more tactical and the round-about monologues of the three team members ever longer and emptier. Ruben has given up chairing the meetings as he feels he can no longer be sufficiently independent, so he is leaving the facilitation more and more to the external consultant.

After a few meetings which bring no new information and no decisions of any purport, the consultant adopts a firmer stance and plays back the obvious fact that a decision is being avoided. Ruben is called upon by most of the strategy group to force through a decision, whilst its members also begin working along entrenched 'fault lines' with three or four subgroups aligning with alternative, mutually exclusive scenarios. The atmosphere and the openness are in no way reminiscent of how the group started to do its work. There are now primarily subgroup meetings of vice-chancellor and consultant with individuals or with pairs of professors, whilst meetings of the strategy group become longer with more and more ambitious targets. All seems to be to no avail, and Ruben starts to look unhappy and frustrated in the meetings, sweating visibly as occasionally his own personal preferences come through in his body language. He is clearly fighting back the unspoken invitation from within the group to take a decision for all, and he becomes increasingly uncomfortable.

After several more unproductive meetings Ruben announces that he wants to work more with the unions and student bodies, whom they have not involved until this point. Although he claims the strategy group will have a future role, his attendance wanes and when he is present he seems to show less interest. In his progress meetings with the consultant he starts to speak more about other interests, or asks abstract questions about the 'process' in general. Other members of the strategy group also withdraw their interest and participation, and before long the whole group is a thing of the past. The important decisions for the university are still open and rarely mentioned in the meetings. At this point the deficit over the previous year is reported, which turns out to be much higher than for previous years and the press and central government wade in with their views. After a brief review by a committee the board and all the deans are asked to step down and make way for an executive committee of outsiders, who are asked to clean up the finances in the shortest possible time span, which they manage to do. Ruben cuts a slightly petulant, passive figure, seems entirely unaffected but nevertheless spends a lot of time brooding and holding grudges. He now returns to his chair in the Faculty of Law where it takes him a good few years before he has new academic inspiration or appetite for another leadership position.

This passive–aggressive personality pattern was already recognized more than two thousand years ago, when Aesop discovered a very peculiar pattern of dealing with loss and disappointment, which we now call 'rationalization' and which feeds into the passive–aggressive personality pattern.

The fox and the bunch of grapes

A famished fox, seeing some bunches of grapes hanging from a vine which had grown in a tree, wanted to take some, but could not reach them. So he went away saying to himself: 'Those are unripe'.

Aesop's Fable 32, 6th century BC

Summary: passive–aggressive patterns in leaders

- This passive–aggressive pattern of leadership will normally only come out when several factors conspire to bring it out: natural inclination, high stress levels, uncertainty and ambiguity, and a degree of over-specialization with high commitment to a particular challenge.

- Clinically, the pattern is characterized by high levels of resistance, procrastination and resentment, combined with an inability, or insufficient opportunity, to express or work through these resistances. When disappointments mount and personal influence diminishes, this leader may become difficult, irritable, self-absorbed and unyielding.

- Behavioural drivers that often go together with this particular pattern in leaders are tendencies to 'try hard' and 'be strong'.

- A first connection with this leader can be made through ambivalent or resistant behaviour, which invites either a similarly ambivalent response or else a challenge. Rather than allowing tit-for-tat, an endless cycle of resistances and counter-resistances, withdrawal and counter-withdrawal, it is advisable to break this pattern by asking about the leader's feelings.

- The passive–aggressive leader is often well aware of his underlying critical feelings or grievances. It is possible from that perspective to be aware of the futility of passive aggression as a means of expressing or dealing with those feelings. Thoughtful reflection is more hidden and sometimes harder to access, and is therefore often the 'closed door' of this leader.

Narcissistic patterns in leaders

There is nothing which power cannot believe of itself, when it is praised as equal to the gods.

Juvenal (*ca* AD 100)

A leader with narcissistic patterns to the fore: The Glowing Gatsby

When she enters a room she usually gets noticed. Not just because of her striking beauty. It is also the way in which she carries her physique, as if in truth she rises above all others in the room. Add to that her crisp coiffure, the immaculate way she dresses, the bright piercing eyes, and all ingredients for a 'head-turning' entrance are complete. People routinely assume that she might be the most senior person in the room.

This 'glowing' greatness routinely takes on major challenges and turn-around projects, which she claims with conviction and holds with lightness. Whether in new and challenging surroundings or in mature, political hierarchies, she tends to perform extremely well and surpass expectations. She not only seems to be in complete control of her portfolio, she also readily has an 'improvement plan' or innovative ideas to offer. Within a very short period she manages to warm others to her style, is capable of rapidly recruiting a few good people to collaborate more closely with and for getting things done through delegation. With her positive outlook she finds it easy to motivate others.

She always seems to be ready for her next promotion. People are impressed by the way she seems to handle her responsibilities lightly yet as if in full command, and by the way she knows her own limits and is able to delegate.

The Glowing Gatsby is energetic, assertive and bold, with the ability to 'sell' the fruits of her own creativity. There may occasionally be minor incidents where she may come across as too demanding or intolerant to critical views. Despite the occasional 'prima donna' behaviour where she fusses about personal things that look rather unimportant to others, her peers and stakeholders usually agree that this Glowing Gatsby is an asset for the company.

Here is what happens when a leader's narcissistic patterns go into overdrive.

The Superior Being

Her confidence, social skills and abilities push a Glowing Gatsby towards the highest ranks in her organization and the summit of her abilities. Her confidence, proactivity and relationship-building keep her in the limelight and at the apex of the local hierarchy.

When at the apex she might find it hard to really learn from experience as she finds it hard to admit mistakes and listen to advice. When important criticism or disappointing results do come through she may find it hard to cope with them. At such a point a really grandiose sense of self-importance and entitlement may surface, which may lead her to estrange herself from her peers and superiors with her unnecessarily arrogant or intimidating attitudes.

Now this great performer can transform into a rather superior being who becomes aloof, petty or absent, unable to forgive, unable to learn, and on the look-out for other opportunities or other people whom she thinks (rightly) will view her in a more positive way.

Within herself she may hold grudges indefinitely, which propels her onto a mission to prove her detractors wrong through new successes. On the back of her new success she may get into new trouble, new critical or envious feedback, and may then descend into the next cycle, with even more grudges and more exasperation.

At her worst she becomes superior and quiet, and may develop psychosomatic complaints such as headaches. She may oscillate in the time span of just half an hour from 'proud' and 'all-powerful', to 'devastated', 'powerless' and 'destitute'. She is unable to help herself in the same way that she had been able to genuinely help others who had been low or lacking motivation in the past.

FIGURE 6.6   The bright and shadow sides of the Glowing Gatsby

Analysis

The Glowing Gatsby can be recognized as the 'narcissistic' personality adaptation (see also the *Diagnostic and Statistical Manual*, American Psychiatric Association, 2013). In terms of working style her main and overriding drivers are to 'be perfect' and 'be strong' (Kahler, 1975; and see Chapter 2).

Ways to begin to support this individual are usually through her 'behaviour' styles: the Glowing Gatsby passionately wants to perform sublimely and to be (seen to be) special. If a colleague manages to win the trust of the Glowing Gatsby and will be seen by her as supportive and loyal, they can look together at some of the behavioural patterns that cause difficulties, such as perceived arrogance, self-promotion, claiming credit, being opinionated and demanding, and finally her competitiveness and sensitivity to criticism.

The best approach towards the Glowing Gatsby is therefore through her 'behaving' styles or her performance as a supportive leader (which is her 'open door' in terms of Ware's 1986 model); from there she may be open to 'feeling' around her sensitivities (Ware's 'target door'). The third leadership domain, that of 'thinking', may be hardest to reach and unavailable (Ware's 'trap door').

Narcissistic personality adaptations can grow acute after a slight or criticism. Overreaction to such a *narcissistic injury* can grow to remarkable proportions. We can study the effects of narcissistic injuries in some of the greatest plays ever written, such as Sophocles' *Philoctetes* and Ibsen's *John Gabriel Borkman*. In *John Gabriel Borkman* we can see how Borkman's existence is still incapacitated eight years after his release from his prison sentence after he was found using his position as a bank manager to speculate with his investors' money. From the start of the play it is clear that he has never come to terms with the self-image of a crook or a prisoner. Similarly, that classic paragon of impotent rage, Philoctetes, only very gradually overcomes the personal slights and injuries of having been tricked and left behind by Odysseus and the Greek army 10 years before the start of the play. No matter how much sense and reason his friends try to talk to him, at the end he can only overcome his injured obstinacy through the divine intervention of his godlike personal hero, Heracles.

Interestingly, it is also possible to develop undoubtedly narcissistic patterns whilst resisting personal praise and honours. We can encounter narcissists spurred on by a sense of superiority and criticism of self and others. Such a person can be obsessed with 'being perfect' to such an extent that no one will ever come near his ideal. Nowhere is such a narcissistic pattern better described than in the character of Coriolanus in Shakespeare's eponymous tragedy: the proud man who abhors praise and flattery, yet is utterly committed to winning the highest honours. His dislike of praise can be seen as an expression of his deep personal pride, whilst at a deeper level his entire sense of self and survival seems to rely on a self-image of complete self-sufficiency. His vulnerability, neediness, dependency on others and humility are all entirely replaced with his sublime self-sufficiency. All he really cares about, therefore, is his own self-image. Tolerance of praise might imply that his self-confidence would be affected by others' opinions of him which would diminish it.

By considering two of her greatest strengths, self-confidence and displaying greatness, we can think about how the Glowing Gatsby may be getting into trouble. Her ease and certainty combined with high self-regard may be perceived by others as selfishness or arrogance. A confident and balanced contribution may thus descend into a grandiose sense of self-importance and entitlement. She loses her sense of reality and becomes self-infatuated. At this point her great strength becomes a 'pitfall' and she goes into overdrive.

From the pitfall it is usually relatively easy to see the challenge, as it is the natural opposite of the pitfall. In this case the challenge would be 'humility', a sense of service and comradeship with others. Another way of finding the challenge is to ask oneself what we find most irritating in other people. In the case of the Glowing Gatsby this may be disinterest or not being noticed, which may lead to a real 'narcissistic injury'. This is, with outright criticism, the 'allergy' area of the Glowing Gatsby, the area where she easily becomes annoyed, touchy, manipulative, defensive or out of touch. She may rebalance her over-sensitivity to criticism or disinterest by a superior stance which puts even more distance between herself and others.

Figure 6.7 (Ofman, 2002) presents the full picture of a Glowing Gatsby going into overdrive:

FIGURE 6.7   The core qualities quadrant of the Glowing Gatsby

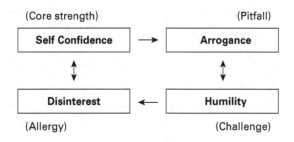

The sense one gets in the presence of this kind of leader is that of feeling inferior and somehow 'ordinary', as if one has very little to bring to the table. We pick up a lot of self-confidence, as if this person deserves all the favours, praise and recognition that they are getting, and actually more too. Self-promotion and entitlement seem strong themes, and seem forever unfulfilled. When the pattern is strongly developed we also notice a habit of winning petty games, sarcasm, one-upmanship and playing the 'wise guy'. The Glowing Gatsby is extremely alert to potential favours and praise but also to hints of disregard or rejection. In order not to harbour difficult feelings such as vulnerability, inferiority or envy, they may be projected onto us when we meet a Glowing Gatsby. All those sensations or feelings that are troubling or even unattainable for the Glowing Gatsby herself then come to reside with us. If the same person is placed over us and holds some power over us, we may receive grandiose disinterest in what we do and experience a brusque and intimidating, or rather a superior and callous style of leadership.

Rosenfeld (1964) helpfully distinguishes two types of narcissists: those that are 'thin-skinned', sulking, fragile, hypochondriac and extremely sensitive to criticism; and those that are 'thick-skinned', insensitive, self-obsessed, superior and in need of being admired.

In working with such an executive we first need to be aware of what is projected onto us and not allow ourselves to be overly self-conscious or intimi-dated. We may then help her think about what she can learn from those that irritate her most, and what little grain of truth the criticism may hold for her, even if it's tiny. If she can balance her confident and energetic performance with a genuine openness to feedback and criticism, she may avoid going into overdrive whilst continuing to draw on her core strengths. This requires real humility and a curiosity about what others may have to offer. It is the art of looking for a charitable interpretation of one's colleagues' contributions, without begrudging them their wisdom or helpfulness. In this way her 'narcissistic' tendencies become more balanced without there being any pressure to 'fix' them or give them up.

In practice, this can be a great sacrifice for those who feel/believe that they have already travelled very far along the path towards personal success. To them, recognizing that one has shortcomings and that others may have something good, even 'superior', to offer can feel like a failure, or like a premonition of impending, crushing disaster.

CASE VIGNETTE 1   Theodore the aristocrat

Theo always sports a gloss and a tan as if he had just spent the morning weightlifting on a tropical island. He walks into his senior management team meetings with the ease of a professional footballer turning up to kick a ball around with his non-professional mates. As soon as he's in, has sat down and looked around to take in all the facial expressions around the table, he chooses a few passionate words to capture the moment and lift the mood. Then he comes up with an idea that immediately sounds exactly right as to what needs to happen. He follows this up by offering to lead its implementation as well. Everyone relaxes, animosity is being buried, and a flow of ideas from others commences as well. The meeting ends on a high and everyone agrees that it has delivered more than they expected.

Several people want to stay behind with Theo, to be noticed or to get his view on a development that they have noticed. Theo gracefully agrees to stay around in order to take in the positive feedback and give direction where needed. During the next meeting Theo casually mentions that the initiative has made excellent progress and all the planned actions have been implemented. He also warmly acknowledges and briefly thanks several of his co-workers.

However, sometimes Theo is said to have 'lost it'. Nobody reports experiencing this first-hand but some team members talk of his 'explosions'. Most often it seems that explosions happen when Theo, after very carefully and persistently helping to resolve a difficult situation does not receive the appreciation and acknowledgement that normally follows his trouble-shooting activities. And in these circumstances team members say he has been known to launch into long complaints, to become disparaging and defensive, and even to put the phone down on a critical colleague and to storm out of the building in frustration and anger. The erratic, unexpected explosions leave everybody guessing and unsure. At times Theo has left the team members behind to pick up the pieces. On returning several hours later or even the next day, Theo appears completely oblivious to the past episode (or its possible effects on the team) and is back to his charming and appreciative ways. He appears focused and energetic again and carries on with his work. Relieved and happy to have him back on board, nobody mentions the episode. As one team member said when some rumour was mentioned of problems that had occurred: 'Explosion? What explosion?'

Surprisingly, there is now a sense that after two years Theo's time with the company is running out. This is partly because with his limited experience in the sector, there isn't another promotion that he can be realistically offered. However, it is also because he seems to have lost some of his magic; as he entirely refuses to see that his business is not exactly the success that he and others had predicted. Some of his peers are now holding him to his predictions from last year, and he clearly doesn't like it. He blames political developments in Russia, the sudden departure of crucial board members, and a general downturn in the market that others do not really see. Theo no longer sees eye to eye with one other colleague in the executive committee. He is convinced that this colleague has unfairly accused him of letting costs run out of control in his business. They have had words about this in the middle of meetings, and Theo has refused to give in. In the end they have agreed to disagree and are no longer on speaking terms.

After the incident with the direct colleague Theo starts to miss meetings and seems absent-minded when he is there, and then one day he is suddenly and completely back at the table, with all his eloquence, arguing all the little points, emanating his brilliance, and yet announcing at the end of the meeting that he is going to take up a role in an entirely different sector and that he wants to thank everyone for 'a great experience' here.

After just a matter of months signs are that he is doing very well at his next company, and that in fact he is shortlisted for a promotion. His new colleagues say they are amazed at how quickly he understood the new sector he is working in. Just like his old colleagues in this organization. And just like his colleagues of the past, in the five different sectors and the three different management functions that he has collected in short succession on his CV.

CASE VIGNETTE 2   Carlton S 'Carly' Fiorina

An additional real-life case description for this broad pattern can be found in the following Kaiser and Hogan article:

> A recent example of this is the failed merger of computer manufacturers Hewlett-Packard and Compaq. The deal was orchestrated by Carly Fiorina, who was hired because the board thought they needed a CEO with a big

ego (and rock-star status) to change the corporate culture. Her constant self-promotion and inability to attend to day-to-day operations caused a dramatic drop in HP stock value.

Kaiser and Hogan, 2007

The narcissistic personality pattern was already associated with the 'peacock' some 2,600 years ago, when Aesop described the following interchange between two distinguished birds.

The peacock and the crane

The peacock was making fun of the crane and criticizing his colour.

'I am dressed in gold and purple,' he said. 'You wear nothing beautiful on your wings.'

'But I,' replied the crane, 'sing near to the stars and I mount up to the heights of heaven. You, like the cockerels, can only mount the hens down below.'

Fine feathers don't make fine birds.

Aesop's Fable 333, 6th century BC

Summary: narcissistic patterns in leaders

- This narcissistic pattern of leadership will normally only come out when several factors conspire to bring it out: natural inclination, high stress levels, uncertainty and ambiguity, and a degree of over-specialization with high commitment to a particular challenge.
- Clinically, the pattern is characterized by a leader being unusually confident, self-absorbed and sensitive to criticism, combined with a sustained period of extraordinary success. When checks and balances fail on this pattern and disappointments are avoided over long periods, this leader may become arrogant, superficial, bruised, petulant, self-gratifying or petty-minded.

- Behavioural drivers that often go together with this particular pattern in leaders are tendencies to 'be perfect' and 'be strong'.

- A first connection with this leader can be made through performance and behaviour, either through a compliment or through a challenge. This pattern of leadership will be keen on any feedback regarding how they come across, and a lively reflection may ensue.

- From this dialogue it may be possible to speak about the feelings that have led to such strong reactions, of being injured, superior etc. A narcissistic leader is prone to wear his or her feelings on the sleeve. More objective, detached reflection is much harder to access and bring to good use.

Schizoid patterns in leaders

The higher we rise, the more isolated we become; all elevations are cold.
Stanislas de Boufflers, *Le libre arbitre* (1808)

A leader with schizoid patterns to the fore: The Detached Diplomat

The Detached Diplomat can be sent on any mission. He will think and act autonomously and take full responsibility. He is independent and resilient. He combines the gifts of frankness and diplomacy, and will know how to merge in with any group or culture without attracting attention.

This 'diplomat' is admired for being a strong person and an independent mind, and for being able to handle pressure and criticism extremely well. He is often chosen for tough missions, where bold action and robustness are required.

The Detached Diplomat is very well able to lead on his own, lead from the front and from an isolated position, such as in turn-around scenarios. He can be relied upon for rare character strength and an ability to absorb contretemps, conflict and criticism, which has no parallels. He is not afraid to take unpopular decisions and to take full responsibility for them, even when they come under criticism. He is also not afraid to criticize others full-on and not mince his words whilst remaining a paragon of calmness.

Here is what happens when a leader's schizoid patterns go into overdrive.

The Bruising Bastion

The Detached Diplomat can do wondrous things in very tough environments, but he may pay a big price. His direct and blunt style and his limited attention for, or even understanding of, other people's feelings and thoughts, means that isolation is a distinct possibility. On top of this, with his sharp tongue and real lack of sensitivity, he may annoy and even bruise other leaders.

In certain high-pressure situations, rather than being emotionally affected, the Detached Diplomat will be prone to withdrawal and to cutting short a debate or interaction. This diplomat may move out of reach even of friends and supporters, and those that could actually further his agenda. He may become a Bruising Bastion unto himself, serenely imperturbable but also utterly devoid of impact or influence.

All of this will make it really hard for the 'bastion' to learn from tough experiences and to process some of the impact he has on others. It is not unusual to find a Detached Diplomat going into mission after mission, interim post after interim post, achieving substantial impact and profile at the beginning but then diminishing in influence. A fizzling-out of the 'change initiative' and a strange isolation may result, which the diplomat himself understands least of all. He is then left – again – with puzzling questions and a lack of perspective.

Analysis

The Detached Diplomat can be recognized as the 'schizoid' personality adaptation (see the *Diagnostic and Statistical Manual*, American Psychiatric Association, 2013). Ware (1983) also describes him as the 'schizoid' personality. In terms of working style, his main and overriding driver is to 'be strong' (Kahler, 1975; and see Chapter 2).

Ways to begin to support this individual are through his 'behaviour' styles or rather through his *lack* of behaviour. He seems unperturbed, withdrawn

FIGURE 6.8   The bright and shadow sides of Detached Diplomat

or passive. If a colleague is able to reach him in his passivity and tough-mindedness, then that would be the point to start: the immobility, the detachment, the simple fact that going on like this will deliver... nothing.

Next, through exploring the 'thinking' behind his (lack of) action he may realize that his reservations are not helping him to stay engaged. The

Detached Diplomat can then handle and process very forceful feedback and is likely to respond positively in wanting to think about his temperament. Unfortunately there may be periods when he is not open to conversation, coaching or self-reflection at all, in particular at times of high pressure. Otherwise, if a coach is able to hold up a mirror that this character recognizes, he will be able to work with this view of himself independently, and in such a way that he may temper some of his bluntness, harshness or detachment. Rigorously paying attention to his impact on others, helped by observations from a friendly companion, does help to temper his style and uses his strength and autonomy to develop more constructive interactional patterns.

The best approach towards the Detached Diplomat is therefore through his 'behaving' styles or his detached stance towards his role (which is his 'open door' in terms of Ware's 1986 model); from there he may be open to 'thinking' about the consequences of his aloofness or toughness (Ware's 'target door'). The third leadership domain, that of 'feeling', may be hardest to reach and unavailable (Ware's trap door').

With the help of one of his greatest strengths, tough-mindedness, we can think about how he may be getting into trouble. Excessive toughness can lead to detaching himself from others and to a propensity to offend or bruise others, even if the Detached Diplomat himself may not have noticed.

From the pitfall it is usually relatively easy to see the challenge, as it is the natural opposite of the pitfall. In this case the challenge would to be to relate more positively, to actually connect more fully with others. Another way of finding the challenge is to ask oneself what we find most irritating in other people. In the case of the Detached Diplomat this may be intimacy and closeness. When others come really close to him, confide in him or ask personal questions, he feels uncomfortable. This is the 'allergy' area of the Detached Diplomat, the situation he will try to withdraw from and wait until it blows over (Figure 6.9, Ofman, 2002).

The sense one gets in the presence of this kind of leader is that one has to stay at a distance and not engage too much. The overriding impression is of a leader withdrawing from the battlefield. Whether tough and independent or aloof and detached, this person seems to be in a world of his own, with a limited need for others. When the pattern is strongly developed we notice a lack of emotion and passion, and this can strike us as chilling, lifeless or exasperating to be with. It is as if simple humanity is lost and the leader

FIGURE 6.9   The core qualities quadrant of the Detached Diplomat

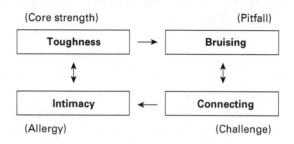

has become a sublime stoic or equally a cold computing machine. What is projected onto us is precisely what is missing: emotionality, vulnerability, possibly also anxiety and fear – all sensations that are rare or even unattainable for the Detached Diplomat himself. If the same person is placed over us and holds some power over us, we may feel rather unsupported and isolated, alone with our own feelings of (for example) inadequacy and anxiety.

Kets de Vries (2008) describes the prevalence of *alexithymic* personalities in business. Alexithymia is a personality adaptation where emotional awareness, social attachment and interpersonal relating are markedly impaired. The literal meaning of the Greek term, coined by Sifneos (1973), is a lack of words for the 'thymos', the seat of mood and emotion. The alexithymic engages in concrete, pragmatic, aloof thinking and suffers from a lack of feeling and imagination. Alexithymia may well be at the root of the schizoid overdrive patterns, as well as the schizotypal patterns outlined on pages 170–78.

In working with this executive we first need to be aware of what is projected onto us and not allow ourselves to be seduced into being overly sensitive or emotional. We may then help him think about what he can learn from those that irritate him the most (the allergy area of the core quadrants), and what sort of challenge he can realistically set himself. If he can balance the fearlessness with a genuine trust in his colleagues, he may avoid going into overdrive. He may then be able to continue drawing on his core strengths even in times of adversity. He will find that his context is actually safe enough to show his feelings, to be anxious or occasionally not to know what to do. In this way his 'schizoid' tendencies become more balanced without there being any pressure to 'fix' them or give them up.

In practice, this can be a great sacrifice for those that have developed extreme forms of detachment and resilience. For the Detached Diplomat to really connect with others means that he enters the unknown, which will make him feel immensely exposed. It means exposing himself to feelings, expectations and intimacy, which may provoke a lot of anxiety.

CASE VIGNETTE 1   The top adviser

Professor Armstrong is well known in the ministry and in his university, for his brilliance and confidence. He is essentially always right, to great precision, when it comes to his expert advice. At the same time he is essentially always wrong and off the mark when it comes to any other topic outside his specialty area, although he delivers his opinions in other fields with exactly the same aplomb and conviction, often completely oblivious of the destabilizing effect he is having on the recipient(s). When a plumber is working at his house, he will know exactly how the man should do his work. He is prone to offer similarly forthright advice when a question of politics comes up, or when someone has questions about child rearing.

In his university he has acquired a reputation for being unmanageable but also for being unsackable, because of his eminent contributions to his field and his friends in many a top university. After years of stand-offs with management they are relieved to send him on early retirement whilst allowing him to keep his secretary, room, personal library and junior scientific staff. This turns out to be an arrangement that works well for decades, and turns out to be extremely affordable as no salary has to be paid for ongoing services of great distinction. So an unorthodox solution was found that would barely have been feasible outside a university context.

At the ministry they once made the mistake of asking him to lead a committee which would report to parliament. The committee turned out to be split from the outset, with opposing scientific fractions unable to find common ground, and debates being fought out in the national press. Replacing all the enemies of Professor Armstrong with loyal academics from different universities proved to be no solution at all. Within one meeting of the new committee the scientists found grounds for fundamental disagreement and they spent the rest of their time together bickering. The committee never reported to parliament, only Armstrong with two close friends did, and undeniably the advice that parliament received was of the usual eminent standard.

The most amusing thing anyone could do was interview Professor Armstrong on leadership or management. As with his opinions on other academics, he would never mince his words, and demonstrated with great precision that all the managers that he ever got to know were rare cases of utmost incompetence. He would be unable to name even one example of even a mediocre leader, let alone someone who could cut the mustard. When asked, he could analyse in the minutest detail where each manager had taken the wrong turn and had begun derailing, in his view. By contrast he would describe himself as a visionary, supportive leader, and name one of his PhD students as an example of someone he had served very well. True, his PhD students did come through with excellent marks; however, when asked about the support they had received in the department, they would invariably name others than Professor Armstrong. When asked specifically about their professor they would say he was brilliant, witty, eccentric and rather aloof. He was frequently described as someone who in times when real help was needed, or when some crisis occurred, had been entirely absent. They described his responses as enigmatic and obfuscating, where he would, for example, quote 15th-century sources, offer Baron von Münchhausen as a helpful example of how his PhD student might pull himself up by the bootstraps, or would just be off on sabbaticals and conferences for many months in a row.

CASE VIGNETTE 2   Philip J Purcell

This is a real-life case description for this personality taken from Kaiser and Hogan's 2007 article.

> Purcell began his career with the McKinsey consulting group. He did some early work with Dean Witter, a retail brokerage firm. He was popular with senior management at Dean Witter and became CEO in the late 1970s. In 1997, he orchestrated a merger with Morgan Stanley, a merchant banking firm, in a move that was widely criticized on the grounds of poor culture fit. According to the New York Times (June 16th, 2005), as a CEO, Purcell was '... ruthless, autocratic, and remote. He had no tolerance for dissent or even argument. He pushed away strong executives and surrounded himself with yes-men and -women. He demanded loyalty to himself over the organization. He played power games...', had little contact with the rank and file, and stayed in his office to plot strategy. 'He belittled the investment bankers [at

Morgan Stanley]. Executives learned that it was pointless to argue with Purcell about anything – all it did was make him mad and he didn't even pretend to be listening.' Disgusted Morgan Stanley executives began leaving in droves, and Purcell used their departures as a chance to give their jobs to people who were loyal to him. Former Morgan Stanley executives, infuriated by the way they had been treated, created enough shareholder agitation that the Morgan Stanley board fired Purcell the week of June 13th, 2005, but only after the stock had suffered tremendous losses and the company had lost some of the most talented investment bankers in the United States.

Kaiser and Hogan, 2007

Some empathy for the schizoid personality pattern was already expressed some 2,600 years ago, when Aesop distilled this fable from his experiences in public life.

The travellers and the plane tree

One summer, in the heat of the midday sun, two weary travellers stretched out under the shady branches of a plane tree to rest.

Looking up into the tree, they agreed:

'Here is a tree that is sterile and useless to man.'

The plane tree answered:

'Ungrateful wretches, at the very same time that you are enjoying my benefits you accuse me of being sterile and useless.'

Some people are like this: some are so unlucky that even though they are good to their neighbours, they can't make them believe in their benevolence.

Aesop's Fable 257, 6th century BC

Summary: schizoid patterns in leaders

- This schizoid pattern of leadership will normally only come out when several factors conspire to bring it out: natural inclination, high stress levels, uncertainty and ambiguity, and a degree of over-specialization with high commitment to a particular challenge.

- Clinically, the pattern is characterized by a leader being unusually withdrawn, serene and reserved, combined with a diminished capacity to read or relate to others. When isolation increases and becomes sustained over long periods, this leader may become bruised, bruising or harsh, detached and cut-off from his or her environment. Surprisingly, there may not be a lot of sadness in this 'splendid isolation', rather a form of self-sufficiency.

- Behavioural drivers that often go together with this particular pattern in leaders are tendencies to 'be strong' and to be even stronger than that.

- A first connection with this leader can be made through his or her actions, which are often striking by their absence. By allowing some form of connection to emerge the leader is drawn in and his or her presence becomes gradually livelier. At that point this leader can be brought back from his derailment, as he or she can be shown the consequences of their absenteeism. By thinking about the price that is being paid for not engaging, something may shift in the patterns of behaving – and in the patterns of thinking as well – whilst throughout, feelings may remain at a very long distance, deeply buried under a more formal, reserved or detached outlook.

The 'rigorous thinkers'

FIGURE 7.1 Four 'rigorous thinkers'

Introduction

This chapter describes four 'overdrive' patterns in leaders, which are related to the leader's cognitive style or way of thinking:

1 The first pattern of leadership – which we have linked to 'obsessive–compulsive' characteristics – ruminates about his every action and doggedly carries it out with rich detail and self-monitoring.

2 The second pattern of leadership – which we have linked to 'borderline' characteristics – ruminates in a more excited way, vacillating between optimism and pessimism.

3 The third pattern of leadership – which we have linked to 'paranoid' characteristics – is a critical thinker, full of suspicions about other people's motives.

4 The fourth pattern of leadership – which we have linked to 'schizotypal' characteristics – is a creative thinker with endless supplies of great ideas that, however, rarely get executed.

What these four leadership patterns have in common is that they all give primacy to 'thinking' above 'behaving' and 'feeling'; hence they can be approached and worked with most straightforwardly through thought, cognition, deliberation, consideration, insight and the like.

The overdrive patterns underpinning the 'Rigorous Thinkers' in this chapter are all linked with the second of these three domains or functions of the leadership process:

1 *Supporting*: facilitating or enabling the team's effectiveness, enhancing the resources and competences that are available – a making or doing function.

2 *Inspiring*: supplying the team with strategy and meaning-making – a thinking function.

3 *Containing*: looking after or caring for the team, nurturing and providing space for processing emotions and for understanding to emerge – a feeling function.

The inspiring function is giving primacy to thinking, visioning and strategy, which you will recognize in the four leadership patterns in the next chapters.

Obsessive–compulsive patterns in leaders

My passions were all gathered together like fingers that made a fist. Drive is considered aggression today; I knew it then as purpose.

Bette Davis (1908–1989)

A leader with obsessive–compulsive patterns to the fore: The Responsible Workaholic

The Responsible Workaholic delivers a consistently high standard of work both in stable environments and in a new role with new challenges. Like the Creative Daydreamer (see page 170) she is willing to take on assignments with uncharted demands and an unclear role. Unlike the Creative Daydreamer, however, she responds to the challenge with more presence. Instead of nurturing others and nurturing initiatives, she brings instead her own energy and attention to creating solutions. She suggests rigorous solutions and initiates new activities. She corrals others into action and coordinates activities to try and make progress.

In a new and challenging role she takes personal responsibility for creating a new tapestry of reality for the team and the organization. She assigns roles to people and expects them to play their part within her grand design. Some of those who work for her experience her as enormously energetic and involved. Others see her as an 'anxious overachiever', always worried about how she can do more and if she hasn't forgotten anything or reneged on any promises she has made. She is seen as competently defining, directing and controlling every possible aspect, in order to create success out of an unclear or ill-defined situation.

At her best the Responsible Workaholic is a great source of vision, focus and energy. She is trustworthy and conscientious, consistently over-delivers, inspires teams, stimulates aspiration, encourages achievement, and attends to detail. She perseveres and motivates by example, showing how her direct reports and indeed entire organizations may rise to the challenge and can avoid being bogged down or disillusioned by uncertainty and lack of direction.

Here is what happens when a leader's obsessive–compulsive patterns go into overdrive.

The Troublesome Princeling

The Responsible Workaholic becomes the Troublesome Princeling when she loses the confidence and support of those she relies on in the visionary tapestries that she is weaving.

In this circumstance her tremendous energy and experience are seen as being devoted to control and double-checking, rather than to activities that are a real benefit in her organization. She becomes fussy and gets caught up in irrelevant details. She becomes slow and reluctant to share the fruits of her work. She may become controlling and inflexible.

The Troublesome Princeling's unhelpful overdrive is mostly triggered when there are unusual risks or when her creative ideas are not taken on board and actively supported by others internally and externally. She will then find herself increasingly making more and more suggestions and creating more and more elaborate proposals that others pay less and less attention to. Consequently she is experienced as a maverick, brilliant but self-obsessed, and lacking in realism, pragmatism and detachment.

At her most challenged she finds it impossible to delegate or even to identify priorities, and she gets obsessed with unrealistic standards. Her behaviour is seen as controlling, inflexible and unhelpful and her princely position is only tolerated because of her prior accomplishments or because she keeps putting in enormous time and effort.

FIGURE 7.2   The bright and shadow sides of the Responsible Workaholic

Analysis

The Responsible Workaholic can be recognized as the 'obsessive–compulsive' personality adaptation and was also described by Ware (1983). In terms of working style her main drivers are 'be perfect' laced with 'be strong' or 'try harder' (Kahler, 1975; and see Chapter 2).

Ways to begin to support this individual are through her 'thinking' styles: ruminating together with her on what she is doing, and then 'feeling' about what is really going on at a more personal level. Only through experiencing real trust and safety in the relationship, and through gradually increasing self-awareness, will the controlling workaholic become a responsible and prioritizing workaholic again.

The best approach towards the Responsible Workaholic is therefore through her 'thinking' styles, her attention to detail or her on-going rumination (which is her 'open door' in terms of Ware's 1986 model); from there she may be open to 'feeling' about what is really going on for her personally (Ware's 'target door'). The third leadership domain, that of 'behaving', may be hardest to reach (Ware's 'trap door').

With the help of one of her greatest strengths, energy, we can think about how she may be getting into trouble. Her endless commitment and selfless contribution to her work develop into a controlling or self-obsessed stance which then leads to overbearing, meticulous and troublesome behaviour. Energy may thus descend into control and anxiety. She becomes absorbed in her own contributions and in particular in the detail of her work, losing sight of the wider picture and of how she is perceived by her colleagues. At this point the strength becomes a 'pitfall' and this executive goes into overdrive.

From the pitfall it is usually relatively easy to see the challenge, as it is the natural opposite of the pitfall. In this case the challenge would be letting go of her tendency to control. Another way of finding the challenge is to ask oneself what we find most irritating in other people. In the case of the Responsible Workaholic this may be easy-going or procrastinating colleagues, who do not take things seriously and do not put in the required effort. This is the 'allergy' area of the successful workaholic, the area where she easily becomes deflated, or annoyed, or frustrated (Figure 7.3, Ofman, 2002).

The sense one gets in the presence of this kind of leader is of being in the presence of efficiency, conscientiousness and hard work. We pick up underlying elements of frustration and fear, which are the expression of unfulfilled needs to control. The ensemble of unfulfilled needs places a rather strong claim

FIGURE 7.3 The core qualities quadrant of the Responsible Workaholic

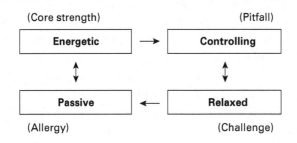

on us to adjust, adapt and shape up in terms of clarity and micromanagement. Control and rigour seem to be strong themes, yet seem forever unfulfilled. When the pattern is strongly developed we feel stonewalled and in the presence of something that is extremely hard to please or get right. The Responsible Workaholic is extremely alert to tasks, duties and obligations. What is projected onto us is all manner of independent thinking and authority, and an expectation to sort it all out for her – all sensations that are rare and unattainable for the Responsible Workaholic herself. If the same person is placed over us and holds some power over us, we may feel micromanaged and uninspired, which may escalate to a feeling of being undervalued or criticized unfairly and harshly.

In working with this executive we first need to be aware of what is projected onto us and not allow ourselves to be seduced into being overly directive and authoritarian. We may then help her think about what she can learn from those that irritate her the most, and what sort of challenge she can realistically set herself. If she can balance the energy with a sense of letting go whilst maintaining the connection with others, she may avoid going into overdrive. She may then be able to continue drawing on her core strengths even in times of adversity. She may be able to say to herself that it is okay to make mistakes or to forget deliverables, okay to be human and to have frailties, okay to be frustrated and angry. She herself and others will forgive her if she struggles to deliver the full hundred per cent to the second digit, yet they will be less forgiving if she starts to become controlling or 'red-penning' other people's work. If she can just relax and chill out a little, she may even learn to adapt to changes and value complementary qualities in others. In this way her 'obsessive–compulsive' tendencies become more balanced without there being any pressure to 'fix' them or give them up.

In practice, this can be a great sacrifice for those who have developed extreme forms of obsessive and controlling behaviour. As so often with a real and personal challenge, it may be easy to realize in principle that control is standing in the way of effectiveness. However, this conclusion is also very hard in practice for the Responsible Workaholic. It may feel immensely threatening to *not* check something, to *not* respond to an e-mail or to under-deliver. This may feel as if life itself is threatened, as if she may lose her job or her sense of achievement, as she cannot imagine that people will be tolerant of mistakes. Neither can she imagine that others may not, like her, be continuously checking and overachieving.

CASE VIGNETTE 1   The Responsible Workaholic

Timothy is the head of one of the juridical departments of a global investment bank. His job is to check the contracts or investment vehicles that investment bankers propose against the local laws. This means that he and his department act like the 'conscience' of the bank. The work of his small team is mainly operational (writing contracts) but also evaluative (assessing contracts) and regulatory (safeguarding legality). The same department has helped the bank come through the 2008 banking crisis nearly unscathed, as they did not allow derivatives within the bank, seeing them as too risky.

Moreover, he spends a lot of time promoting his staff and pleasing others including family members. In his 'midlife crisis' he realizes that he wants to rise above this, grow up, and leave his irritable bowel syndrome behind him.

Timothy feels he is a 'gatekeeper', both for the technical contracts and for the reputation of the bank. Routinely he needs the whole weekend, including a long Saturday in which he does very little apart from sleeping, shopping and sitting on the couch staring in front of him, to overcome the stress that he has accumulated by Friday. In other words, he uses the whole weekend to calm himself down. During the previous end-of-year review he told his boss how he feels more like a piñata than a senior manager, regarding the way the investment bankers treat him. Increasingly, he senses that his boss is reluctant to help him out in these conflicts and in the larger political system. Rather than empathizing with his pressures, his boss is increasingly talking about his shortcomings in his department's 'delivery' as distinct from his superior technical knowledge. As a consequence Timothy tries to improve his delivery style and communication. Increasingly, he suspects that his perceived flaws in 'delivery' are used by his boss to defer a promotion that would otherwise be due. During his next end-of-year performance conversation he wants to 'wipe delivery off the table' at the very outset and his thoughts circle around all sorts of ways of doing that. One is to object to the term 'delivery' and to point out that to his knowledge in fact he over-delivers on his targets.

In his performance review, despite a large number of detailed arguments he remains unable to convince his boss that something needs to give. Through sheer hard and meticulous work he is unable to reach a boss who looks more at presentation and communication, and the only option that he feels remains open to him is to look for yet another employer.

CASE VIGNETTE 2   Douglas Ivester

Here is a real-life case description for this personality taken from Kaiser and Hogan's 2007 article:

> Consider also the case of Douglas Ivester, the former CEO of Coca-Cola. The board believed that Ivester would be the ideal CEO of Coca-Cola because he grew up in the company and had been both CFO and COO. But his extraordinary attention to detail, which was key to his earlier success, proved to be lethal in the CEO role. Ivester was unable to focus on the bigger picture and strategic issues, and the board was forced to request his resignation in 1999, not quite two years into the job.

Kaiser and Hogan, 2007

The dire consequences of not being able to set priorities as one is submerged in the minute details which are so characteristic of the obsessive–compulsive personality pattern were highlighted beautifully by Aesop some 2,600 years ago in this little fable.

The boy and the filberts

A boy put his hand into a pitcher full of filberts. He grasped as many as he could possibly hold, but when he tried to pull out his hand, he was prevented from doing so by the neck of the pitcher. Unwilling to lose his filberts, and yet unable to withdraw his hand, he burst into tears and bitterly lamented his disappointment. A bystander said to him, 'Be satisfied with half the quantity, and you will readily draw out your hand.'

Do not attempt too much at once.

Apocryphal Aesop Fable, 6th century BC

Summary: obsessive–compulsive patterns in leaders

- This obsessive–compulsive pattern of leadership will normally only come out when several factors conspire to bring it out: natural inclination, high stress levels, uncertainty and ambiguity, and a degree of over-specialization with high commitment to a particular challenge.

- Clinically, the pattern is characterized by a leader being unusually meticulous, precise and controlling, combined with a repetitive style of work, eg double- and triple-checking on projects. When anxiety levels increase further, this leader may become agitated, fussy and self-obsessed.

- Behavioural drivers that often go together with this particular pattern in leaders are tendencies to 'be perfect', sometimes combined with 'be strong' or 'try harder'.

- A first connection with this leader can be made through making contact with the ongoing deliberations and reflections. In fact, it is almost unavoidable to make contact with this rather detailed, occasionally repetitive, tortuous thinking process. This thinking process, and the accompanying meticulous and controlling behaviour, is defensive in nature, so it is essential to inquire into the emotions lying underneath. What is this leader suppressing, what does he not dare to say to his colleagues and bosses? Once those emotions have been unearthed and can be processed, the obsessive patterns of leadership gradually lose purpose and can be allowed to return to a lesser, more balanced intensity.

Borderline patterns in leaders

There are only two ways to live your life. One is as though nothing is a miracle. The other is as though everything is a miracle.

Albert Einstein (1879–1955)

A leader with borderline patterns to the fore: The Impulsive Loyalist

The Impulsive Loyalist can often be found in a role that he knows well, because he has high loyalty and is reluctant to change his conditions. In the face of challenges this executive draws on his internal sense of confidence, his energy and his knowledge of what is needed. He quietly and independently employs this solid experience to choose what he should attend to and how he should go about doing it. He is passionate about his projects and his work relationships.

In relationships he is therefore experienced as being knowledgeable, committed, passionate, well-informed, quick-witted and as someone who can helpfully provide clear direction and navigation based on a solid experience. He wears his heart on his sleeve and can talk passionately about his work and colleagues. He usually has high expectations of those around him.

Because of his highly developed sense of self-confidence and rightness, he engenders amongst others corresponding confidence in the chosen directions and initiatives. He strengthens those around him to take action in projects which might otherwise be considered risky or inappropriately developed.

At his best the Impulsive Loyalist is a valuable resource particularly for less experienced and committed teams that run the risk of becoming rudderless when faced with uncharted and demanding requirements.

Here is what happens when a leader's borderline patterns go into overdrive.

The Self-Righteous Recluse

The Impulsive Loyalist becomes the Self-Righteous Recluse when his focus on what he knows and what he believes is right takes centre stage to the exclusion of engaging and working with others to help them to overcome the challenges they are now facing.

Instead of bringing his great understanding and knowledge to the service of others who may be less experienced and independent-minded than he is, he instead focuses on faults and failures, criticizing their inability to understand the issues and to deal with them adequately. His strong loyalist streak makes it difficult for him to come down off his high horse and to help others use his well-founded criticism constructively.

The Impulsive Loyalist's helpful resolve and insight is typically tripped over into being unhelpful when he feels that his ideas and suggestions are not respected and his superior knowledge is not being put to proper use. In new challenging circumstances he may find that his superior experience is being ignored by people who appear to him to be less understanding of what the situation needs. The Impulsive Loyalist is, however, unable to communicate how he can be helpful and will instead become irritated, bruising and destructive in his communications. He will then come across as moody and volatile, as if splitting his loyalties: alternating his commitment with his disappointment in others.

Under these circumstances he is consequently experienced as being disenchanted and negative, destructively critical and unwilling to roll up his sleeves and get involved. He is therefore relegated (metaphorically and sometimes even physically) to his office, and left muttering under his breath – becoming more and more self-righteously reclusive. At his worst he may become entirely unpredictable for others and highly emotional to the point of aggressive.

FIGURE 7.4   The bright and shadow sides of the Impulsive Loyalist

Analysis

The Impulsive Loyalist can be recognized as the 'borderline' personality adaptation (see the *Diagnostic and Statistical Manual*, American Psychiatric Association, 2013). In terms of working style his main drivers are 'be perfect' and 'hurry up' (Kahler, 1975; and see Chapter 2). A borderline pattern usually has a low capacity for tolerating anxiety or controlling impulses, and can become emotionally unstable under duress. His thinking may drift off to daydreaming when reality testing is called for. Moreover, his reflections have a propensity for 'splitting', ie mental representations of others become fragmented and charged as either 'good' or 'bad'.

Ways to support this individual are usually through his 'thinking' styles: helping him to understand the consequences of his actions and to understand what other people may be thinking. The Impulsive Loyalist is usually not very good at reading other people, including himself, which is why he may come across as erratic and unpredictable. Once he is engaged in thinking about his situation and his actions, he can then also be engaged in thinking about his behaviour in a non-threatening way. Through considering thoughts and behaviours, feelings will grow and mature.

The best approach towards the Impulsive Loyalist is therefore through his 'thinking' styles, helping him understand the consequences of his actions and moods (which is his 'open door' in terms of Ware's 1986 model); from there he may be open to 'behaving' differently and devising better strategies for action (Ware's 'target door'). The third leadership domain, that of 'feeling', may be hardest to reach (Ware's 'trap door').

With the help of one of his greatest strengths, his capacity for being passionately loyal, we can think about how he may be getting into trouble. His tendency to be right and passionate, and to insist on 'being right', may develop into becoming impulsive and impatient with others. When a loyal knowledge base and commitment become a guide for leadership without consideration for interpersonal sensitivities, this strength descends into an obstacle for collaboration. At this point the strength becomes a 'pitfall' and this executive goes into overdrive.

From the pitfall it is usually relatively easy to see the challenge, as it is the natural opposite of the pitfall. In this case the challenge would be constancy and dedication. Another way of finding the challenge is to ask oneself what we find most irritating in other people. In the case of the Impulsive Loyalist the most annoying colleagues may be those who are plain and ordinary, people who do not seem committed and attach less importance to the relationship than he does. This is the 'allergy' area of the Impulsive Loyalist, the area where he easily becomes deflated, or annoyed, or frustrated (Figure 7.5, Ofman, 2002).

FIGURE 7.5   The core qualities quadrant of the Impulsive Loyalist

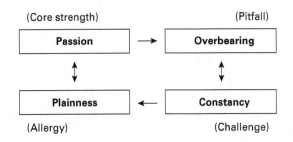

The sense one gets in the presence of this kind of leader is that one has to hold back, as if one needs to wear velvet gloves in his presence. We pick up an element of (potential) rejection and unfulfilled needs of belonging, and from these a rather strong claim on us to include, make up or atone. Acceptance and belonging seem to be strong themes, and seem forever unfulfilled. When the pattern is strongly developed we feel at the same time a need for belonging and an expectation to be rejected. The Impulsive Loyalist is extremely alert to signs of potential rejection. What is projected onto us is security, stability, serenity, and the power to reject – all sensations that are rare or even unattainable for the Impulsive Loyalist himself. If the same person is placed over us and holds some power over us, we may also feel great trepidation in anticipation of a possible temper tantrum, an explosion over minor issues or general moodiness which may extend to a feeling of intimation and bullying.

In working with this executive we first need to be aware of what is projected onto us and not allow ourselves to be seduced into being overly robust. In a gentle way we may then help him think about what he can learn from those that irritate him the most, and what sort of challenge he can realistically set himself. If he can balance the passion and strident loyalty with high regard and maturity towards others, he may avoid going into overdrive whilst continuing to draw on his core strengths. As a senior executive he has to learn that passion and enthusiasm is not all, but that strength of relationships, mutual appreciation and quality of collaboration count as much. In this way his 'borderline' tendencies become more balanced without there being any pressure to 'fix' them or give them up.

In practice, this can be a great sacrifice for those that have strayed far into impulsive and volatile behaviour. It can only be done if he can consistently control his moods and his irritation with others. For that it is not just necessary for him to be disciplined about controlling emotions. He also needs to understand why he is doing it. For that he needs to build understanding of the people he works with and he needs to have a philosophical approach to the collaboration, which is very hard for him to maintain. Little incidents may set him off again. Or his passion may lead him into flights of fancy and overblown ideas and expectations. Or he may be discouraged by contretemps or lack of recognition. Any of these swings of temper or vicissitudes of life can lead back to impulsivity if he is not able to 'maintain his cool' consistently and with conviction.

CASE VIGNETTE 1   The Impulsive Loyalist

Madeleine is a very successful strategy consultant. She always over-delivers on her assignments. Clients are generally extremely satisfied with her services and recommend her work spontaneously to others, so that she is in high demand. Yet she is rarely satisfied with or even confident about what she delivers. She complains of feeling depressed and says she often 'rebels against herself'. Some of the most torturing thoughts she inflicts on herself are around the 'academic' side of her profession, around publications or further academic development. Often she asks herself the question, why don't I come out and courageously accept that I am not that academically motivated? Exploring this further she confesses that she often promises to contribute to articles, to organize academic networking activities, or to produce elaborate summaries with models and background information. But then she finds herself at home with a lot of specially reserved time at hand and no progress – boxed into a real 'writer's block'. Energy 'leaks' away from her days at home, or dissipates the moment she picks up a book or opens a new document on her computer. She has reflected on these issues and she has engaged in personal counselling. Yet the issues are barely getting resolved, particularly now that she is promoted to ever more challenging and responsible work. The pain of her demands on herself only exacerbates and she asks herself in frustration, 'Am I always the very last priority in my life?'

Others around her have become slightly cautious in giving her advice. This is partly due to the fact that they have already given their advice and very little seems to change. But also this is due to the somewhat 'moody' responses Madeleine gives to the advice – as if it is not good enough, as if they are somehow to blame for her predicament.

The scant logic and barely hidden wish for some kind of relief through violence within the outbursts prompted by a borderline personality pattern were acutely exposed by Aesop, who had seen them in the courts some 2,600 years ago.

The wolf and the lamb

A wolf saw a lamb drinking at a stream and wanted to devise a suitable pretext for devouring it. So, although he was himself upstream, he accused the lamb of muddying the water and preventing him from drinking. The lamb replied that he only drank with the tip of his tongue and that, besides, being downstream he couldn't muddy the water upstream. The wolf's stratagem having collapsed, he replied:

'But last year you insulted my father.'

'I wasn't even born then,' replied the lamb.

So the wolf resumed:

'Whatever you say to justify yourself, I will eat you all the same.'

This fable shows that when some people decide upon doing harm, the fairest defence has no effect whatever.

Aesop's Fable 221, 6th century BC

Summary: borderline patterns in leaders

- This borderline pattern of leadership will normally only come out when several factors conspire to bring it out: natural inclination, high stress levels, uncertainty and ambiguity, and a degree of over-specialization with high commitment to a particular challenge.

- Clinically, the pattern is characterized by a leader being unusually passionate, impulsive, and staunchly loyal. When pressure increases and emotions flare up, this leader may become highly emotional or cantankerous, to the point of becoming volatile and moody. There is also a risk of a highly partisan style of leadership, splitting 'those that are with me' from 'those that are against me'. These splits may suffer sudden changes with erratically found new loyalties.

- Behavioural drivers that often go together with this particular pattern in leaders are tendencies to 'be perfect' and 'try harder'.

- A first connection with this leader can be made through his or her impulsive thinking. If the borderliner experiences enough safety to inquire into his or her own thinking patterns, he will relax further and may become able to think about his or her actions in a more detached way.

- Genuine feelings are much less accessible, and this type is leader is often not very well able to feel his or her way through the world, nor be very understanding of their own emotions.

Paranoid patterns in leaders

It is a miserable state of mind, to have few things to desire and many things to fear: and yet that commonly is the case of Kings.

Francis Bacon, *Essays, Essay XIX: Of Empire* (1597)

A leader with paranoid patterns to the fore: The Brilliant Sceptic

The Brilliant Sceptic is an admired character, who combines thorough and compassionate thinking with reliability and loyalty, and an ability to be tough, daring, frank and robust. She holds her own in any organization, and contributes from an abundance of talent and brilliant delivery. She is very insightful about organizational dynamics, politics and people in the organization. She will rise through the ranks in a very quick way, as she is universally appreciated and recognized as someone who has something to say, who doesn't hold back, and finds solutions to knotty issues. Moreover, the Brilliant Sceptic is an astute and alert contributor, whose contributions are highly effective.

One of her main strengths, beside the ability to grasp issues and understand people, is her capacity to know which issues to attend to and how to invest her energy best. She will always aim for the highest-impact contribution, for the crux of the matter, and for the elephant in the room. Quicker than most other people she will see through the web of details and arguments, and pick out the wood from the trees. When she speaks others listen with care and respect, and they don't know what they admire most: the depth of understanding or the fearlessness of her arguments.

At her best, the Brilliant Sceptic's contribution is sheer brilliance! It is also intensely humbling as she can remain self-effacing during the highest of achievements. She will not only give the impression of being on top of things, but that is her reality as well. She will delegate and support others while she monitors consistently and thoroughly any changes, bottlenecks or weak links that need to be taken into account. When needed she will not be afraid to let those that are responsible know that there is something they need to attend to.

Here is what happens when a leader's paranoid patterns go into overdrive.

The Suspicious Neurotic

Privately, even in the best of times, the Brilliant Sceptic is not what she seems. She is constantly scrutinizing herself and others for any errors or weaknesses, and she is privately much more anxious than she gives off. When tensions increase she may do overtime with double-checking other people's motives, and she may imagine all sorts of failings and disasters. This is precisely why she is so brilliant, loyal and humble at the same time: her immense suspicion and sensitivity help her to see a problem long before others do.

Under still more tension or under criticism she may imagine much worse scenarios than are realistic, and her nightly nightmares may take over her waking life. A Brilliant Sceptic appears to be little bothered by criticism or tensions, but in fact the opposite is true. She takes criticism extremely personally and adds insult to injury. She may envisage secret plots, she may be fearful of the envy of her colleagues, and she may persist in thinking that her 'bank' will go under. It takes no time for her to become argumentative with any suspected parties. This happens even when there appears to be very little evidence of perfidy or wrongdoing.

As a consequence the Brilliant Sceptic could start spying on her own employees, or become anxiously fearful of unrealistic dangers. She remains greatly sensitized to signs of betrayal or manipulation so that under pressure she almost 'expects' to be mistreated. She may even become a plotter herself, in order to retaliate and counter insurgencies that are in fact mainly imaginary.

FIGURE 7.6   The bright and shadow sides of the Brilliant Sceptic

Analysis

The Brilliant Sceptic can be recognized as the 'paranoid' personality adaptation and was also described by Ware (1983). In terms of working style her main drivers are 'be perfect' and 'be strong' (Kahler, 1975; and see Chapter 2).

Ways to begin to support this individual are usually through her 'thinking' styles: looking at the realism of her concerns and in some cases just pointing out to her that she is probably being paranoid. Her strong passion for true understanding stands in support of such reflection, so that just looking fearlessly at her anxieties and suspicions might be enough. On the other hand it is very likely that there will be some mistrust about such 'coaching conversations' as well, which might make her less forthcoming in sharing anxieties with you. In that case the veneer of Brilliant Sceptic stays in place and there is no real contact with her underlying issues. It is very important for the Brilliant Sceptic to find the setting for these conversations sufficiently safe and engaging, so that her paranoid fears and worries can be spoken about. When such a dialogue about her paranoid worries is possible, underlying 'feelings' will surface soon enough and this experience can teach her that it can be safe to show her feelings so that she can be less concerned. Her paranoid behaviour will then usually change soon enough because she has acquired some understanding about it. She will then be ready to think through why she always needs to be so mistrusting and sceptical.

The best approach towards the Brilliant Sceptic is therefore through her 'thinking' styles, thinking about the realism of her concerns and misgivings (which is her 'open door' in terms of Ware's 1986 model); from there she may be open to 'feeling' and experiencing a greater safety than before (Ware's 'target door'). The third leadership domain, that of 'behaving', may be hardest to reach (Ware's 'trap door').

With the help of one of her greatest strengths, alertness, we can think about how she may be getting into trouble. Her commitment to leave no stone unturned in her quest to acquire a full understanding of any issues or risks can easily make her overly suspicious. Loyal and acute alertness and frankness may thus descend into suspicion and spite. At this point the strength becomes a 'pitfall' and this executive goes into overdrive.

From the pitfall it is usually relatively easy to see the challenge, as it is the natural opposite of the pitfall. In this case the challenge would be to fully

FIGURE 7.7   The core qualities quadrant of the Brilliant Sceptic

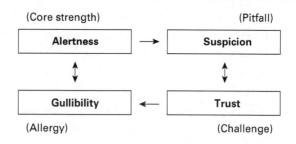

trust others and her environment. Another way of finding the challenge is to ask oneself what we find most irritating in other people. In the case of the Brilliant Sceptic this may be the sense of being gullible or protective of the trust of others, or perhaps of being naïve and over-trusting. When people are naïve and easily deceived she may give up on them or even on herself. This is the 'allergy' area of the successful Brilliant Sceptic, the area where she easily becomes deflated, or annoyed, or frustrated (Figure 7.7, Ofman, 2002).

The sense we get in the presence of this kind of leader is that the world is a dangerous place, full of people who will trick or deceive them. We pick up signs of (potential) betrayal and get the impression that if there is betrayal or deception this person will instantly respond and retaliate, even if only by accusation or counter accusation. Justice and fairness seem strong themes, and seem forever unfulfilled. When the pattern is strongly developed we note great stubbornness and a tendency to 'litigate' at the minutest cause for grievance. We sense a lifestyle fuelled by grievance, or even an addiction to turning the tables and putting suspicions to the test. Or else there can be a cynicism which says that 'litigating won't work either, nobody can be trusted and everyone is already biased against the right cause'. There is a constant sense of wrongdoing and betrayal. What is projected onto us is self-doubt and puzzlement, even naiveté – all sensations that are rare or even unattainable for the Brilliant Sceptic herself. If the same person is placed over us and holds some power over us, we may also feel unsafe and alert, as if we are constantly mistrusted and spied upon.

In working with this executive we first need to be aware of what is projected onto us and not allow ourselves to be seduced into being overly worried or naïve. We may then help her think about what she can learn from those that irritate her the most, and what sort of challenge she can realistically set herself. If she can balance the alertness with a genuine trust in her colleagues, she may avoid going into overdrive. She may then be able to continue drawing on her core strengths even in times of adversity. She will find that her context can actually be safe enough for her to be optimistic, trust and show her feelings. In this way her 'paranoid' tendencies become more balanced without there being any pressure to 'fix' them or give them up.

In practice, this can be a great sacrifice for those that have developed extreme forms of paranoid thinking and behaviour. For the Brilliant Sceptic to give up paranoia means to thoroughly relax, to stop being so vigilant and on guard. She will have little experience of letting her guard down in the workplace, and to do so will feel intensely anxiety-provoking or profoundly deflating. It may feel like she doesn't care any more about her work. Nevertheless, she can only begin to trust others by allowing them to trust her, and by being genuinely open and vulnerable in their presence.

CASE VIGNETTE 1   The Brilliant Sceptic

Petra has just turned 50 and is looking forward to her new role as CEO of a small UK-based charity dedicated to helping young single men in crisis. Petra was not looking for the job. However, after 25 years working in corporate HR for a large chemicals firm, she knows that even after reaching the level of senior vice-president she still has much to offer and feels too energetic to retire now. She wants to contribute where it still matters and she can make a difference.

In corporate HR she had become renowned for not beating around the bush. She analysed problems ruthlessly, gave clear, frank and some would say brutally honest feedback to all around her, and executed agreed plans with unsentimental efficiency and unerring determination. Her subordinates quickly learned that she had a low tolerance for: poor thinking; needless argumentation; lateness; excuses for lack of delivery; dishonesty; and lack of determination. She loved nothing better than being challenged to take hold of a complex multifaceted highly political HR issue with a variety of political or operational implications. She would then dissect and assess the issue, boil it down to the key strategic considerations, and highlight the risks and opportunities, before proceeding to create a series of possible action scenarios always with a clear rationale and recommendations attached. Petra's 'solutions' (as her pronouncements had come to be known) were almost always flawlessly thought out, well presented and ready for implementation. In reaching them she appeared to have challenged and checked every detail, and questioned every possibility, having dismissed every illogical, ill-advised or misplaced assumption.

Along the way she encouraged the brilliant whilst inevitably bruising egos of the not so brilliant. She exposed charlatans and cajoled and challenged peers, subordinates and superiors to take action and focus on what would actually make an impact. As senior VP, her own focus remained solely on improving HR performance and capability.

After 25 years of success and effectiveness, however, Petra now feels she is exhausted and just needs a break. Although she is under no pressure from anyone to give up her job, the constant drive she feels she needs to bring to the role is not as strong as she believes it needs to be – in order to stay ahead. She feels that if she could find something new and different, she could keep on top of things. However, she is aware that some of the new and younger executives in HR feel she is too challenging. She felt hurt when this first came to her attention. She can appreciate their point of view but sees no way of directly addressing it, given the need to keep up the performance of the department and to continue to drive the business forward. She also feels that the younger HR executives are not ready to step forward to offer any practical solutions to their grumblings. She is concerned one or other of her direct reports has been spreading rumours about her leaving.

Faced with these concerns and having analysed her options she feels that resigning from her role and leaving the business is possibly the best option. Leaving 'while on top' may be just what is needed for her, her HR department and the business. The opportunity to engage her energies in this new challenge with a tiny and highly relevant charity seems very attractive. Once again she feels she could really make a difference.

The spirals of suspicion ignited by a paranoid personality pattern which may make us less safe despite their emphasis on safety were already mapped by Aesop some 2,600 years ago.

The bird-catcher and the asp

A bird-catcher took his snare and birdlime and went out to do some hunting. He spotted a thrush on a tall tree and decided to try and catch it. So, having arranged his sticky twigs one on top of the other, he concentrated his attention upwards. While he was gazing thus he didn't see that he had trodden on a sleeping asp, which turned on him and bit him. The fowler, knowing that he was mortally wounded, said to himself:

'How unfortunate I am! I wanted to catch my prey and I did not see that I myself would become Death's prey.'

This is how, when we plot against our fellow creatures, we are the first to fall into calamity.

Aesop's Fable 137, 6th century BC

Summary: paranoid patterns in leaders

- This paranoid pattern of leadership will normally only come out when several factors conspire to bring it out: natural inclination, high stress levels, uncertainty and ambiguity, and a degree of over-specialization with high commitment to a particular challenge.

- Clinically, the pattern is characterized by a leader being unusually suspicious, cautious, and alert. This leader can be a good reader of other people's motives, but on becoming increasingly distrustful and having his or her worst suspicions confirmed, this leader may become highly fearful, spying on and even plotting against others – whilst feeling increasingly betrayed and in danger.

- Behavioural drivers that often go together with this particular pattern in leaders are tendencies to 'be perfect' and 'try harder'.

- A first connection with this leader can be made through his or her alert thinking patterns, psychological insight and suspicions. Some of this sharp thinking is defensive in nature, so underlying anxieties and emotions may be opened up. Much harder to access is the rather less connected behaviour – unless of course cautious thinking has gone so far as to result in real paranoid behaviour. Even then it might be more straightforward to talk about the thoughts first, then the underlying emotions, and only then the secretive or suspicious actions.

Schizotypal patterns in leaders

Fashion does not have to prove that it is serious. It is the proof that intelligent frivolity can be something creative and positive.

Karl Lagerfeld (b 1933)

A leader with schizotypal patterns to the fore: The Creative Daydreamer

The Creative Daydreamer is found in situations where there are new challenges and circumstances and where the executive is facing a new role that has hitherto not existed. He thrives in circumstances where he is not able to draw on well-known routines of previous knowledge to be of support to other people. Consequently the Creative Daydreamer focuses attention on encouraging new activity and new initiative. In these situations of innovation and transformation he is experienced as being hands-on in the way he leads and works.

He is a colourful personality with an eccentric taste, original ways of dressing and behaving, and always something unexpected and interesting to say. He contributes by stretching the imagination, with the help of different and even weird ideas, unexpected links and metaphors, and out-of-the-box solutions.

In his new role and challenging circumstances he seeks out particular 'green shoots' that he can defend and nourish. He makes very independent decisions and can stand up to criticism. He is seen as a champion for ideas and as a protector of innovation. He will work in an anti-bureaucratic way to ensure that the way the system works does not stifle creativity. Those who work with him will experience him as fun, dependable, helpful, flexible and robust. They will also experience him as attentive yet reserved, or even unaware of social cues, and generally supportive.

At his best the Creative Daydreamer courageously and brilliantly helps the new organization explore new possibilities. He ensures that lack of knowledge of the fast changes in operating requirements and new emerging rules do not become a reason to incapacitate a team or an organization.

Here is what happens when a leader's schizotypal patterns go into overdrive.

The Absent Professor

The Creative Daydreamer becomes the Absent Professor when his attention to new initiatives and new ideas is focused away from his team and organization. When not nurtured or responded to from within the organization he may get carried away towards unpractical solutions or hobbyism. At unpredictable moments an emotional cooling and detachment can set in and he stops being aware of the needs of those he works with.

His pattern of shifting into overdrive is often triggered when ideas and initiatives from colleagues and internal sources are poor and insufficient to deal with the challenges that are being faced. The Absent Professor may then get bored, humorous or even flippant. As a leader he will feel tempted to engage more with his own or outsiders' ideas to find new and vibrant sources of attention. He can then get rather caught up in his own flights of imagination rather than staying in touch with the situation.

Consequently the Absent Professor puts more energy in seeking new initiatives outside than in paying attention to possible initiatives inside. Despite that, in relations with others within the organization he continues to put forward quirky ideas whilst offering very little direction as to why or what should be done.

At his worst therefore he is experienced as holding the team or organization to ransom with his own absences and unpractical demands for creativity. When it comes to giving direction or implementation he remains unavailable, inaccessible or confusing. As if he lacks interest in or even awareness of the feelings or agendas of those around him. In addition he is often seen as being physically absent or going off on a tangent. This means that despite his authentic brilliance he is not around to engage with others in a way that can help them or himself make the potential come to fruition.

FIGURE 7.8   The bright and shadow sides of the Creative Daydreamer

Analysis

The Creative Daydreamer can be recognized as the 'schizotypal' personality adaptation (see also the *Diagnostic and Statistical Manual*, American Psychiatric Association, 2013). In terms of working style his main drivers are 'be strong' and 'try hard' (Kahler, 1975; and see Chapter 2).

Ways to support this individual are usually through his 'thinking' styles: looking at his eccentric thought processes, his creativity, his absent-mindedness, and then thinking about 'doing' something differently, such as change his contribution to innovation and leadership. He may then understand that, although his greatest passion has been innovation and creative exploits, he hasn't helped that agenda at all, perhaps even hindered it by abdicating so much responsibility.

The best approach towards the Creative Daydreamer is therefore through his 'thinking' styles, taking his creative and eccentric ideas seriously (which is his 'open door' in terms of Ware's 1986 model); from there he may be open to 'behaving' in such a way that he gains more acceptance and also takes on board others' ideas more (Ware's 'target door'). The third leadership domain, that of 'feeling', may be hardest to reach (Ware's 'trap door').

With the help of one of his greatest strengths, championing ideas or creativity, we can think about how he may be getting into trouble. His robust championing of the cause of innovation may develop into absenting himself and obscure daydreaming. Mentoring others and championing ideas may thus descend into absent folly. He gets carried away and becomes unavailable to others. At this point the strength becomes a 'pitfall' and this executive goes into overdrive.

From the pitfall it is usually relatively easy to see the challenge, as it is the natural opposite of the pitfall. In this case the challenge would be 'presence' with others and their differing ideas. Another way of finding the challenge is to ask oneself what we find most irritating in other people. In the case of the Creative Daydreamer this may be those people who are overly present, in a straightforward, ordinary, common-sense, earthy sort of way. This is the 'allergy' area of the Creative Daydreamer, the area where he easily becomes deflated, or annoyed, or frustrated (Figure 7.9, Ofman, 2002).

FIGURE 7.9   The core qualities quadrant of the Creative
Daydreamer

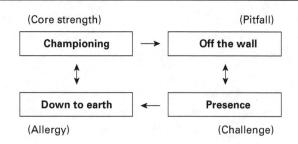

The sense one gets in the presence of this kind of leader is of imagination going overboard. We pick up distinctly odd beliefs, magical and eccentric thinking, and peculiar or over-the-top ideas, and from these a rather strong push to leave reality and its demands behind us. Playfulness and innovation seem strong interests, and seem forever unfulfilled. When the pattern is strongly developed we find it hard to understand the Creative Daydreamer and we may find him lost in self-absorption. The Creative Daydreamer is at pains to have great ideas and launch initiatives, but doesn't seem to notice that he is not taken very seriously or even ridiculed. What is projected onto us is confusion, dullness and drabness, fragmentation, and being at a loss – all sensations that are rare or even unattainable for the Creative Daydreamer himself. If the same person is placed over us and holds some power over us, we may become swamped with outlandish ideas and find ourselves the occasional target of some 'shooting from the hip'.

In working with this executive we first need to be aware of what is projected onto us and not allow ourselves to become confused and ineffective. We may then help him think about what he can learn from those that irritate him the most, and what sort of challenges he can realistically set himself. If he can balance the drive for innovation with a form of presence with others, he may avoid going into overdrive whilst continuing to draw on his core strengths. This is the case of the senior executive who finds it difficult to just 'be' with other people or do any managing-by-walking-around. Sheer presence on the shop floor, in a helpful, understanding and guiding way, can help to offset the imbalances in this personality trait. In this way his 'schyzotypal' tendencies become more balanced without there being any pressure to 'fix' them or give them up.

In practice, this can be a great sacrifice for those that have developed extreme forms of absenteeism. It can feel anxiety-provoking to be more present, it can feel like a waste of time, and it can feel like surrendering to others' demands, to their irritating demands and to their neediness.

CASE VIGNETTE 1   The Nurturing Champion

In November 2010, a few days before his 35th birthday, Elson was appointed chief of staff of an executive office of an international medical products and services operations group headquartered in Zürich, Switzerland, and active through local country affiliate offices in markets in the USA, Latin America, Europe and across Asia. In his new role Elson was charged with agreeing an international strategy that could be translated into market and business plans with associated operational budgets for each of the country-level operating entities.

Working centrally from his office in Zürich with the support of a small team of executive staff Elson was expected to:

- set overall international goals and aims for the market entities;

- agree programme- and country-specific objectives;

- set budgets and agree management performance goals and measures;

- monitor and review performance;

- address management and leadership issues affecting performance as they arise;

- report and inform the board on progress.

Although Elson was not the first chief of staff to have overall international responsibility, he was the first for whom the specific responsibilities had been so clearly articulated. Reporting to the international board, and having agreed the key requirements, Elson was then left very much on his own to work directly with each of the country-level heads. Elson was, for his part, pleased to have this freedom. He took on the role with enthusiasm and 'gusto'.

In May 2012 a new major shareholder took the controlling interest in the business and provided an injection of capital. Having joined the board, the new shareholder began to set new expectations for raising results from the international businesses – and to do so within a short timescale. Elson was consequently given direct responsibility for new market development programmes and associated product and service introductions, to be developed centrally and then transferred quickly for implementation in countries to take the businesses into new markets and to generate new income streams. By the end of the first six months much debate and design work had gone into preparing for the new programmes and products. However, it was becoming evident that the countries with the greatest opportunities also had the most difficult and cumbersome product introduction circumstances. On the whole Elson and his centrally-located team were finding that local customers were largely uneducated regarding the opportunities presented by the proposed new products. In addition, local sales and marketing organizations often had an inappropriate skills base to introduce, sell and drive the new programmes forward. So while the new shareholding provided the funding and investment opportunity for the new introductions, the reality on the ground showed that the ambitions and expectations for a fast implementation and new returns from new income streams were clearly unrealistic.

Nevertheless, Elson persisted. He visited all the countries, to talk about their longer-term strategy and to set up new local and regional roles to monitor and direct them. He expanded the central team and assigned regional monitoring responsibilities to each of them. He prioritized key areas to focus on and key markets to develop and personally took direct interest in developing a new marketing and sales strategy and in developing training courses for the sales teams to prepare themselves for their required 'new sales drive'.

By the end of 2012 it was evident that all was not going well. A number of older established products, having received less management attention, started to falter and to drop in sales and profitability. The new programmes were all struggling to get off the ground and consuming cash, with limited actual return.

Elson then embarked on a new round of assessments and changes, setting new goals, increasing controls and attempting to correct and speed up some of the programmes. He also came up with new ideas for another range of new products that he thought would be better adapted. In doing so he intervened more directly into the country-level organizations and as a result often came into conflict with some of the local senior management.

In Zürich too things began to change, without much reference to Elson. Given that Elson was rarely in Zürich, the board insisted on appointing a new Switzerland-based operations director to oversee the central board and become a new contact point for regional offices in Zürich. Whilst Elson was initially happy to have this extra resource and support, over time he gradually realized that decisions were being made directly by the board through the operations director and then also independently by the country heads. Elson felt increasingly marginalized and left out of key decisions, often finding out late through his subordinates, and after actions had been taken and his directions overruled. Eventually with more demands building up and less direct contact and influence with the board, Elson felt that his position had become untenable and unsupported. Faced with this reality and recognizing the lack of support he now had, Elson proposed to terminate his contract and leave the company.

The schizotypal personality pattern was probably already well known more than 2,600 years ago, when Aesop wrote this fable highlighting the disadvantages of being overly absorbed in idiosyncratic musings.

The astronomer

An astronomer was in the habit of going out every evening to look at the stars. Then, one night when he was in the suburbs absorbed in contemplating the sky, he accidentally fell into a well. A passer-by heard him moaning and calling out. When the man realized what had happened, he called down to him:

'Hey, you there! You are so keen to see what is up in the sky that you don't see what is down here on the ground!'

One could apply this fable to men who boast of doing wonders and who are incapable of carrying out the everyday things of life.

Aesop's Fable 65, 6th century BC

Summary: schizotypal patterns in leaders

- This schizotypal pattern of leadership will normally only come out when several factors conspire to bring it out: natural inclination, high stress levels, uncertainty and ambiguity, and a degree of over-specialization with high commitment to a particular challenge.

- Clinically, the pattern is characterized by a leader being unusually eccentric, unpractical, unpredictable or confusing. Under strain or when tested, this leader may become increasingly awkward and idiosyncratic, and may lose any real connection with the organizational context around him and his responsibilities within this context.

- Behavioural drivers that often go together with this particular pattern in leaders are tendencies to 'be strong' and 'try harder'.

- A first connection with this leader can be made through his or her thoughts, however eccentric and creative they may be. Next, it may be rewarding to enquire into the repercussions of such sublime and original leadership: lack of implementation or follow-through of ideas, lack of support and connection, possible absenteeism etc. Much harder to access is the emotional life of this leader.

The 'sensitive carers'

FIGURE 8.1   Three 'sensitive carers'

Introduction

This chapter describes three more 'overdrive' patterns in leaders, which are related to the leader's care and attention to emotion and feeling:

1 The first pattern of leadership – which we have linked to 'dependent' characteristics – feels for other people and wants to be a good team player for them.

2 The second pattern of leadership – which we have linked to 'histrionic' characteristics – overflows with feeling, particularly their own private feelings.

3 The third pattern of leadership – which we have linked to 'avoidant' characteristics – also overflows with feeling, but more in a concerned and troubled sort of way.

What these three leadership patterns have in common is that they all give primacy to 'feeling' above 'behaving' and 'thinking'; hence they can be approached and worked with most straightforwardly through empathy, understanding and personal support.

The overdrive patterns underpinning the 'sensitive carers' in this chapter are all linked to the third of these three domains or functions of the leadership process:

1 *Supporting*: facilitating or enabling the team's effectiveness, enhancing the resources and competences that are available – a making or doing function.

2 *Inspiring*: supplying the team with strategy and meaning-making – a thinking function.

3 Containing: looking after or caring for the team, nurturing and providing space for processing emotions and for understanding to emerge – a feeling function.

This containing function gives primacy to emotions and care, which you will recognize in the three leadership patterns described in this chapter.

Dependent patterns in leaders

No one is useless in this world who lightens the burdens of another.
Charles Dickens (1812–1870)

A leader with dependent patterns to the fore: The Virtuous Supporter

Like the Playful Encourager (see Chapter 6) the Virtuous Supporter is present in well-established and currently understood circumstances. Unlike the Playful Encourager, however, he provides support rather than initiative. The Virtuous Supporter has a genuine desire to be of help to others and to be a good team player. He is extremely friendly, approachable and trustworthy, and is a real ally and partner for those that he has committed to. The Virtuous Supporter prefers stable environments, where his quiet, friendly and pleasant manner is experienced as constructive. However, when faced with a new and challenging role, he works more as a facilitative peer than a confident superior.

In a new role the Virtuous Supporter focuses attention on enabling others, providing the means and resources to ensure that they excel and helping them to achieve their own goals. He will take on tasks and activities that may appear below his seniority in order to demonstrate that his attention is on being supportive of the joint achievement rather than on being concerned with his own personal success.

At his best he is experienced as being reliable, consistent, unendingly patient and quietly resourceful. He is also experienced as someone who really cares: cares for the business and cares for other people. Those that relate to him feel the space he creates for them and the encouragement he gives to them, to help them grow. He provides them with the security of knowing that he is keeping an attentive and non-repressive eye on everybody's needs and for everyone's well-being.

Virtuous Supporters may suffer from the well-known 'helper's syndrome' (eg Miller, 1979) where they deal with their own underlying and acute sense of helplessness by helping others. In this regard the support given may not be entirely altruistic and may serve another function: to keep an existential helplessness and sense of being overwhelmed at bay and to work on their helplessness in a way that makes it manageable.

Here is what happens when a leader's dependent patterns go into overdrive.

The Reluctant Rescuer

The Virtuous Supporter becomes the Reluctant Rescuer when he is overwhelmed with demands for support and feels manipulated by others who use his support to help them to avoid taking responsibility. In this circumstance he finds that he is operating more as a rescuer than a supporter, increasingly feeling the pressure to do those activities that others should be doing themselves. He may quickly become despondent and rather passive, feeling inadequate and incapable of continuing in his role. He finds it rather hard to ask for help or to stand up for others in his department.

Consequently, the Reluctant Rescuer is experienced by others as behaving in a contradictory manner. They see him as needing and desiring to help, and at the same time appearing reluctant and unwilling to actually step forward and be helpful. His difficulty in addressing negative issues, criticism or anything that may be perceived as such by others now haunts him and makes it impossible for him to step out of a vicious cycle. Colleagues will understand less and less where the Virtuous Supporter stands on issues and what his views are.

At his most challenged he becomes withdrawn and sullen or falsely optimistic and pseudo-supportive. He begins to be experienced as shallow and unwilling to provide the engagement, direction or support that others need to take on full responsibility.

FIGURE 8.2   The bright and shadow sides of the Virtuous Supporter

Analysis

The Virtuous Supporter can be recognized as the 'dependent' personality adaptation (see also the *Diagnostic and Statistical Manual*, American Psychiatric Association, 2013). In terms of working style his main driver is 'please others', often accompanied by 'be strong' (Kahler, 1975; and see Chapter 2).

Ways to support this individual are usually through his 'feeling' styles: real feeling and support is appreciated even if sometimes not explicitly. The Virtuous Supporter is a feeling person who easily gets drawn in by human warmth and other emotions. Through real feeling for himself – instead of others – he may be able to change his stance. Allowing feelings to be present within himself and processing them with time will lead to a new attitude and hence to new behaviour. Such new behaviour might be the deliberate withdrawal of some support based on the realization that some people do not need his ongoing support whilst other people really value it. Or it might be the growing ability to speak up on behalf of others or even for himself, separating the issues from the person. The success of such new behaviours may also change his thoughts and views on himself, his colleagues and his organization. At the 'thinking' level he may understand his vulnerability to the helper's syndrome, but this is by no means sufficient for a better balance.

The best approach towards the Virtuous Supporter is therefore through his 'feeling' styles, offering warmth and appreciation (which is his 'open door' in terms of Ware's 1986 model); from there he may be open to 'behaving' more assertively (Ware's 'target door'). The third leadership domain, that of 'thinking', may contribute through enhanced self-understanding (Ware's 'trap door').

With the help of one of his greatest strengths, his ability to really care for others, we can think about how he may be getting into trouble. He wants others to do well and is fully attentive to them, but he also wants them to need his help which contradicts his desire for them to do well. In a similar way he reneges on his own legitimate needs in order to be present for others, and his lack of care and attention to self contradicts his care for others. When he forgets his own needs and starts working against them, this strength descends into a self-defeating purpose. At this point the strength becomes a 'pitfall' and this executive goes into overdrive, sacrificing self to others to such an extent that their own leadership and guidance fades.

From the pitfall it is usually relatively easy to see the challenge, as it is the natural opposite of the pitfall. In this case the challenge would be to be aware of his own needs, to be compassionate for self and others, and to be assertive whilst also being caring. Another way of finding the challenge is to ask what we find most irritating in other people. In the case of the Virtuous Supporter the most annoying people may be those who cling to him and are really needy in a dependent way. Or people who are demanding of his time and support, claiming him or pushing him to do more than is reasonable. This is the 'allergy' area of the Virtuous Supporter, the area where he easily becomes deflated, or despondent, or frustrated (Figure 8.3, Ofman, 2002).

FIGURE 8.3 The core qualities quadrant of the Virtuous Supporter

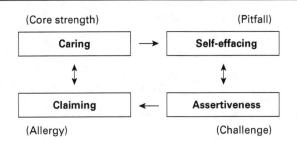

The sense we get in the presence of this kind of leader is that the Virtuous Supporter is extremely obliging and friendly towards us, and seems quite invested in making the relationship pleasant and mutually supportive. We pick up a certain element of 'needs' suppression', except for the ever unfulfilled need of caring for and looking after others. There seems to be a rather strong claim on us to reciprocate by being kind in return. Harmony and agreement seem strong areas of interest and are constantly improved upon. When the pattern is strongly developed the impression is as if the Virtuous Supporter is ready to sacrifice all his own desires and his time just to please everyone. The Virtuous Supporter is extremely alert to the needs of others. What is projected onto us is authority, egocentrism, and self-confidence – all sensations that are rare or even unattainable for the Virtuous Supporter himself. If the same person is placed over us and holds some power over us, we may suffer a lack of direction and indecisiveness, and we may experience that the generous support we are getting only goes as far as it is not controversial within the organization.

In working with this executive we first need to be aware of what is projected onto us and not allow ourselves to be seduced into being overly understanding and nice. We may then help him think about what he can learn from those that irritate him the most, and what sort of challenge he can realistically set himself. If he can balance the care for others with fearless compassion, in other words if he can be available to others without losing sight of his own needs, he may avoid going into overdrive whilst continuing to draw on his core strengths. In this way his 'dependent' tendencies become more balanced without there being any pressure to 'fix' them or give them up.

In practice, this can be a great sacrifice for those that have strayed far into supporting and helping behaviour. They will have to recognize that their helpfulness essentially derives from helplessness and does not make them a superior organizational citizen. On the contrary, their helpfulness exposes very real vulnerabilities and wounds that are very hard to heal beyond a very tender age (Miller, 1979) and that they will have to somehow live with.

CASE VIGNETTE   The Virtuous Supporter

Jim has been foreman and team leader for the health and safety team of a glass manufacturing plant in Denmark for the last two years. Before that he worked in mining firms in Australia, South Africa, Indonesia and Canada. At 40 he has already had over 20 years in the industry, having started straight from school, age 18, as a rookie trainee miner in his native Australia. He often says that he never chose his jobs but that they chose him, and he followed them wherever they took him. Over the years he learned that he is good with his hands, good with his buddies, and enjoys working hard. He also values the financial security and benefits that his work provides. He has learned that taking a tough assignment in difficult locations can bring significant rewards. In this job as well as in jobs before this one he has become well known for his practical, direct 'Aussie' demeanour, yet courteous style, with a dry sense of humour, and a willingness to investigate and address concerns on behalf of team members and colleagues. In his role as a safety team leader his job is to ensure that accidents, however small, do not happen. And indeed if they do happen that they are taken very seriously, are thoroughly investigated and follow-up decisions and changes are made.

Jim has been successful. In the last two years the number of recorded work time accidents had fallen by 20 per cent; lost time due to incidents has fallen by 10 per cent and employee confidence in the team's record for safety is rated good or excellent by over 90 per cent of the staff. The health and safety team motto is 'not on our watch' and they feel free to roam into every part of the business using this motto, using it to challenge staff and management to ever higher safety regions, assured that Jim and senior management will be supportive.

In January 2012 Jim's safety work seemed to be rapidly falling apart. The business decided to launch a new polymer-strengthened glass product, using a new polymer additive from an established and longstanding supplier. In the rush to market, the company had turned down cheaper alternative suppliers, which would have taken longer to test and certify, in preference for a well-known certified supply partner. Team members from Jim's team had grumbled about this. They sarcastically questioned why this was 'happening on their watch'. Jim had been aware of the decision and had automatically approved it but was also acutely aware of his team members' reservations. At the same time his team was expecting him to champion the cause with senior management, which he felt unable to do as he had already given his formal support. From his peers he heard about the many criticisms behind his back and had responded with a series of assessments and process reviews, as well as impromptu certification checks for longstanding suppliers. Now it was the turn of the senior team to grumble: they openly talked about 'doors being bolted after horses had fled'. This was much to Jim's annoyance and frustration. He felt they were being disloyal and became eager to allay both his own team's concerns and the doubts about the measures taken.

The knock-on effect of all the activity was that the new product roll-out was delayed and that the established supplier sued for breach-of-contract to recover development costs. In addition, safety performance in other areas began to deteriorate and confidence in the safety team and routines deteriorated. Jim's ever-increasing efforts to correct the situation consisted of more team and management meetings, safety 'get togethers' and 'action plans', but with little follow-up or actual action itself. Jim seemed unable to get the necessary commitment from colleagues to actually implement what was agreed. Eventually the director of manufacturing operations invited an external consultant in to meet with Jim and his team to help them review and prepare an action plan as well as see how they might give Jim support to rebuild team morale and commitment. Having agreed to have a team retreat, Jim found that also attending the team retreat for the first time was the manufacturing operations director himself, an occurrence that Jim objected to and raised with the consultants but somehow felt unable to raise directly with the director himself.

The gullible, naïve tendencies that inform the dependent personality pattern have always been the butt of jokes from as early as 600 BC when Aesop wrote this fable warning his readers of being overly helpful to others.

The fox and the billy-goat

A fox, having fallen into a well, was faced with the prospect of being stuck there. But then a billy-goat came along to that same well because he was thirsty and saw the fox. He asked him if the water was good.

The fox decided to put a brave face on it and gave a tremendous speech about how wonderful the water was down there, so very excellent. So the billy-goat climbed down the well, thinking only of his thirst. When he had had a good drink, he asked the fox what he thought was the best way to get back up again.

The fox said:

'Well, I have a very good way to do that. Of course, it will mean our working together. If you just push your front feet up against the wall and hold your horns up in the air as high as you can, I will climb up on to them, get out, and then I can pull you up behind me.'

The billy-goat willingly consented to this idea, and the fox briskly clambered up the legs, the shoulders, and finally the horns of his companion. He found himself at the mouth of the well, pulled himself out, and immediately scampered off. The billy-goat shouted after him, reproaching him for breaking their agreement of mutual assistance. The fox came back to the top of the well and shouted down to the billy-goat:

'Ha! If you had as many brains as you have hairs on your chin, you wouldn't have got down there in the first place without thinking of how you were going to get out again.'

It is thus that sensible men should not undertake any action without having first examined the end result.

Aesop's Fable 40, 6th century BC

Summary: dependent patterns in leaders

- This dependent pattern of leadership will normally only come out when several factors conspire to bring it out: natural inclination, high stress levels, uncertainty and ambiguity, and a degree of over-specialization with high commitment to a particular challenge.

- Clinically, the pattern is characterized by a leader being unusually keen to please, genuinely caring for others whilst also being entirely reliant on others' views and guidance. Under strain or when tested this leader may over-promise and become submissive and passive for fear of upsetting anyone by taking action.

- Behavioural drivers that often go together with this particular pattern in leaders are tendencies to 'please others', possibly accompanied by 'be strong'.

- A first connection with this leader can be made through his or her kind and open emotions, with actions including the rather dependent behaviour not coming very far behind. It is rather harder to access the more detached thinking and to engage this leader in bold reflection.

Histrionic patterns in leaders

I'm going to bed, where I may die.
Diana Wynne Jones, *Howl's Moving Castle* (2004)

A leader with histrionic patterns to the fore:
The Accomplished Thespian

The Accomplished Thespian is typically an executive who is in a role that they know well but in which they are now facing new challenges. In fact, with the Accomplished Thespian there is always this sense of a new challenge, an exciting opportunity or a grave concern, as if something unique and unheard-of, even dramatic, is about to occur.

Faced with the new challenges, his focus and resolve are channelled into what seems a highly choreographed performance. The Accomplished Thespian is focused on what is needed to achieve the desired outcome in the new circumstances. In relationships, he is attentive to what is needed to elicit the required response from those around him. But he may also over-commit and over-promise, and insist on being the centre of attention, on being seen as 'the transformational leader'.

With his experience and skill, he can easily adapt his behaviour to the requirements of others in order to get the responses that he needs. His focus is on acting the role out in the right way to get the right audience response. His accomplishment comes from paying attention to how people respond to him and from adapting his response to the demands of the situation.

At his best the Accomplished Thespian is appreciated for his ability to turn up and do what is needed. He is active and engaged, always present and reliable, and attentive to the needs of the moment. Organizations facing new challenges can rely on him performing well in front of the troops, and to be highly sociable, engaging and entertaining. He provides the interest and excitement needed for people to engage and address challenges that they are not familiar with.

Here is what happens when a leader's histrionic patterns go into overdrive.

The Performing Prima Donna

The Accomplished Thespian becomes the Performing Prima Donna when his focus is more on the performers than on the reason for the performance.

Instead of paying attention to doing what is needed, instead of listening to his counterparts, his energy goes into holding his own performance and ensuring that he is looking good in it. In that sense the performance becomes the purpose and the reward, and the wider function or organizational requirement is increasingly missed.

The Accomplished Thespian's tough resolve tips over into being unhelpful when his performances no longer elicit the longer-term outcomes and achievements that the organization seeks. Experiencing the challenge and criticism of others, he becomes less connected with their needs and becomes more concerned with showing that he is delivering or at least doing his best.

Paradoxically his attention to performance per se and ignorance of wider circumstances can create a situation where he's seen as irascible and self-absorbed. He is then experienced as being closed off to reality and not open to constructive feedback.

At his most challenged, the Performing Prima Donna is experienced as a self-obsessed and unpredictable loose cannon, a superficial talking shop, and an organizational liability. Those who work with him try to avoid his worst excesses of showing off, and to protect others from his most embarrassing outbursts.

FIGURE 8.4   The bright and shadow sides of the Accomplished Thespian

Analysis

The Accomplished Thespian can be recognized as the 'histrionic' personality adaptation and was also described by Ware (1983).[1] We have also on occasion described him as the 'enthusiastic over-reactor'. In terms of working style his main driver is 'please others', often accompanied by 'try hard' or 'hurry up' (Kahler, 1975; and see Chapter 2).

Ways to support this individual are usually through his 'feeling' styles: recognizing and validating his overflowing pathos first, validating the need to 'vent' his anxious feelings and, after exploring such feelings, which may still take place in the same slightly over-the-top, histrionic manner, moving on to 'thinking': thinking about what feelings there are and what the feelings stand for can be very helpful for the Accomplished Thespian to get things back in proportion. This may bring him back to deciding what action is needed and then accomplishing that action ('behaviour').

The best approach towards the Accomplished Thespian is therefore through his 'feeling' styles, making contact with his overflowing feeling, pathos and enthusiasm (which is his 'open door' in terms of Ware's 1986 model); from there he may be open to 'thinking' these passions into more proportion and realism (Ware's 'target door'). The third leadership domain, that of 'behaving', may be hardest to reach (Ware's 'trap door').

With the help of one of his greatest strengths, his wonderful attentiveness and reliability, we can think about how he may be getting into trouble. He attends to others and their responses, and works consistently to contribute and help at their pace. The price he pays for this ability is that he has to deny his own needs, except the need to please and to be the centre of attention. He has to go at the pace of others, and he becomes dependent on their presence and cooperation. When others threaten to turn away from him or ignore him, he redoubles his efforts and starts showing his anxiety and his dramatic feelings. At this point the strength becomes a 'pitfall' and this executive goes into overdrive, with great dramatic but little organizational purpose.

From the pitfall it is usually relatively easy to see the challenge, as it is the natural opposite of the pitfall. In this case the challenge would be to be aware of his own needs, to be modest and unassuming, to be compassionate for self and others, and to be assertive whilst also being caring. Another way of finding the challenge is to ask oneself what we find most irritating in other people. In the case of the Accomplished Thespian the most annoying people

FIGURE 8.5   The core qualities quadrant of the Accomplished Thespian

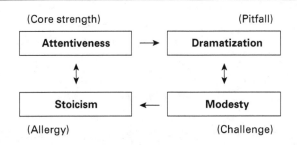

may be those who are not affected and rather stoic, not responding to his great performances and potentially even ignoring him. This is the 'allergy' area of the Accomplished Thespian, the area where he easily becomes deflated, or annoyed, or frustrated (Figure 8.5, Ofman, 2002).

The sense one gets in the presence of this kind of leader is of some superficiality and abundance, as if one needs to content oneself with the modest role of being 'in the audience'. We pick up an orientation towards immediate agreement on how attractive and entertaining they are, and a strong claim on us to indulge the showboating and flamboyant behaviour. The need to entertain and to impress seem strong themes, and seem forever unfulfilled. When the pattern is strongly developed we feel at the same time a need to be the centre of attention and to dominate any and all social proceedings. The Accomplished Thespian is extremely alert to signs of engagement in the audience. What is projected onto us is followership, pity, sensitivity and the faculty of listening well – all sensations that are rare or even unattainable for the Accomplished Thespian himself. If the same person is placed over us and holds some power over us, we may find them dominating meetings and not showing much interest in others, let alone listening well to our concerns, as if our opinions and contributions matter very little.

In working with this executive we first need to be aware of what is projected onto us and not allow ourselves to be seduced into being merely a spectator. We may then help him think about what he can learn from those that irritate him the most, and what sort of challenge he can realistically set himself. If he can balance the attentiveness to others with real modesty, in other words if he can maintain his social strengths without getting carried away, he may avoid going into overdrive whilst continuing to draw on his core strengths. In this way his 'histrionic' tendencies become more balanced without there being any pressure to 'fix' them or give them up.

In practice, this can be a great sacrifice for those that have strayed far into engaging performances and dramatization. It seems almost an impossible thing to say to a great actor that they should not get carried away. That will sound to the Thespian as if they have to kill their greatest strength, their passion, enthusiasm and responsiveness. Nevertheless, if they cannot somehow keep their cool and see their own role in proportion, they will remain very exposed to showboating, over-promising, under-delivering, and they will also eventually lose the popularity with others that they so relish.

CASE VIGNETTE   The Accomplished Thespian

The audience sat through Douglas's presentation in the auditorium of a lecture theatre at a well-known charitable foundation in London, marvelling at this young doctor's enthusiasm as he manipulated complex-sounding statistical information. In an undulating tone of voice he made his challenging comments, pausing for effect from time to time, before proceeding with an engaging smile and dramatic flourish of the hand. The occasion was an unscheduled and impromptu grant-making meeting called at the behest of the foundation chairman who had been intrigued by an application (received from Douglas) for research funding towards an HIV project in Malawi aimed at assessing the risks of HIV infection faced by midwife populations in the suburbs of Lilongwe.

John had been asked by Douglas to accompany him to this meeting when he bumped into him on the London Underground on the day of the presentation. Swept along by Douglas's enthusiasm and his own concern about the problems of HIV-AIDS in Africa, John agreed to attend. Douglas assured him that as an African he could lend credibility to the occasion. Flattered and curious John agreed and now sitting alongside Douglas as if he were a board member of the charity, he realized that flattery and mild overstatement were only two of the many ways Douglas had skilfully been gaining attention and persuading others.

On that occasion Douglas walked out of the meeting with a guaranteed seven-digit-figure's worth of support, subject to paperwork. Half the audience had appeared bedazzled and enthused by his brilliance and the other half (including John) somewhat unsure about what the funding had actually been given for.

John met Douglas again 20 years later, this time by appointment, in a restaurant in London. The two of them spent a pleasant evening catching up on what had been going on in the last 20 years. Douglas had written a number of books, started three businesses, and raised a family. His latest venture, it emerged, late in the conversation, was concerned with assembling a research team to develop a risk-assessment model for life-insurance companies. Douglas wanted to develop predictive models of malarial infection to be made available via travel-insurance websites for tourists travelling to high malarial areas, and eventually to other areas with communicable and non-communicable diseases. John was not sure he understood what Douglas was saying. So he waited for the flow of words to stem. Sensing that it was time again for his small part in keeping the dance of this conversation going, in his next bid to sound intelligent and engaged, John asked him how long he had been working on this project and what the next step would be? 'Oh I thought about it last night as I was leafing through the *New Scientist* and the *Financial Times* and I thought that it would be a great idea to develop and provide something like this. Don't you think? Would you like to join us?'

John duly made his excuses, as he needed to beat a hasty retreat if he was to catch the next train home. As he walked to the station he marvelled at the man, wondering what he would be saying next if they were to meet again in another 20 years.

Much ado about nothing, the classical pattern of histrionic presence, was already spotted and somewhat ridiculed more than 25 centuries ago in this simple fable ascribed to Aesop.

The mountains in labour

One day the countrymen noticed that the mountains were in labour: smoke came out of their summits, the earth was quaking at their feet, trees were crashing, and huge rocks were tumbling. They felt sure that something horrible was going to happen. They all gathered together in one place to see what terrible thing this could be. They waited and they waited, but nothing came. At last there was a still more violent earthquake, and a huge gap appeared in the side of the mountains. They all fell down upon their knees and waited. At last, a teeny, tiny mouse poked its little head and bristles out of the gap and came running down towards them, and ever after they used to say: 'Much outcry, little outcome.'

Apocryphal Aesop Fable, 6th century BC

Summary: histrionic patterns in leaders

- This histrionic pattern of leadership will normally only come out when several factors conspire to bring it out: natural inclination, high stress levels, uncertainty and ambiguity, and a degree of over-specialization with high commitment to a particular challenge.

- Clinically, the pattern is characterized by a leader being highly expressive and attention seeking, to the point of being dramatic and sycophantic. Under pressure or when feeling insecure this leader may become embarrassingly superficial, unpredictable, disorganized and self-obsessed.

- Behavioural drivers that often go together with this particular pattern in leaders are tendencies to 'please others' in combination with 'try harder' and 'hurry up'.

- A first connection with this leader can be made through his or her vibrant and blatant emotions. These emotions may need to take precedence as a topic of conversation, after which reflection can more easily take place. It is rather hard to challenge or discuss the behaviours and actions of this leader.

Avoidant patterns in leaders

Master, go on, and I will follow thee
To the last gasp with truth and loyalty.

William Shakespeare, *As You Like It* (1599)

A leader with avoidant patterns to the fore: The Simmering Stalwart

The Simmering Stalwart is often found in roles that already exist and in organizational situations that are familiar. He is typically a long-standing and experienced organizational stalwart. He will have observed the organization develop to its current situation and will understand well the underlying dynamics that drive its efficacy and its less effective activities. He is generally seen as somewhat introverted and endowed with deep feeling.

As a result the Simmering Stalwart is realistic, measured, well-prepared and attentive to what he thinks matters to others. He is a reliable and outstanding corporate citizen. He is also sparing in his energy and cautious about innovations that he regards inappropriate or risky. He abhors waste and quietly seeks to help the organization avoid its worst excesses. Underneath the surface the Simmering Stalwart may be more self-critical than others would imagine; more sensitive to the opinions of others than he gives out.

As the organization's trajectory is relatively stable, the Simmering Stalwart considers that much organizational activity is driven by personal needs and organizational power/political considerations rather than real underlying necessity or purpose. Consequently he will skilfully absent himself from activities where he feels that colleagues' activities are a waste of time. At the same time he will be committed and innovative within those few activities that he considers essential to the well-being of the organization.

Those who work with him will experience him as dedicated, long-suffering, reflective and committed. He will also be seen as firm and unbending in particular situations as well as highly principled, and committed to defending what is right. In matters of little significance (in his view) he will be experienced as absent and unwilling to engage but rather quietly enduring of others' foibles. One thing he abhors is being controversial in public.

Here is what happens when a leader's avoidant patterns go into overdrive.

The Suffering Misfit

The Simmering Stalwart becomes the Suffering Misfit when he is unable to engage others in those areas of concern that he believes are important. His contributions become less pertinent and his concerns are seen as irrelevant. He may also be seen as exaggerating dangers or risks. In this circumstance he becomes tortured with his inability to bring his knowledge and attention to others. His command of the wider situation is missed because of his inability to connect with the political processes that are underway in the organization. He turns within himself and spends long hours brooding about these issues.

On the outside his colleagues will notice little change in his behaviour, although he may become increasingly inappropriate in the way he raises issues. He pushes harder for attention to what he offers and what he feels is needed but receives less attention and engagement from others. He takes feedback from others very personally. Over time he becomes completely unable to bring others into a conversation with him that addresses the issues he considers important.

At his most challenged he becomes angry and suffering. He turns in on himself with self-criticism. He is unable to make this suffering available as a constructive reflection for the organization. He hates himself for missing opportunities to share his deeper feelings and thoughts constructively. He is experienced by others as unable to contribute, complaining, awkward, and inappropriate in his interventions and contributions.

FIGURE 8.6   The bright and shadow sides of the Simmering Stalwart

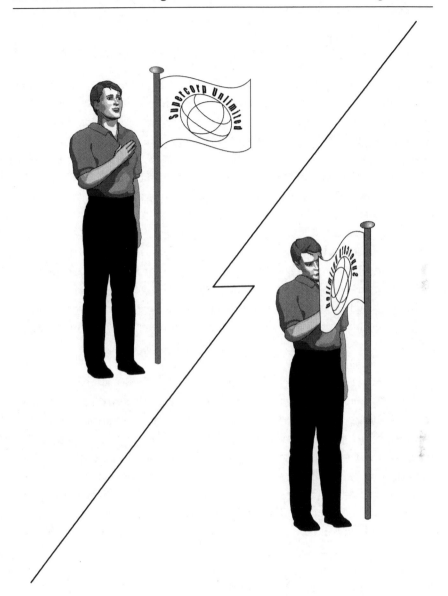

Analysis

The Simmering Stalwart can be recognized as the 'avoidant' personality adaptation (see also the *Diagnostic and Statistical Manual*, American Psychiatric Association, 2013). In terms of working style his main and overriding driver is to 'try harder' mixed with any and all of the other behavioural drivers (Kahler, 1975; and see Chapter 2).

Ways to support this individual are usually through his 'feeling' styles: recognizing and validating his overflowing feelings and helping him to verbalize those feelings in relationship, often for the first time. Changing his behaviour is difficult for the Simmering Stalwart, but not impossible once the feelings have been processed and shared. Once he recognizes his deep misgivings and the anxieties underneath, his dedication to engage with others will be rekindled. 'Thinking' is a less productive area for coaching, as he will often have spent a lot of time already ruminating about his predicament in his own splendid isolation. New thoughts will often not be sufficient to shift the existing pattern of misgivings.

The best approach towards the Simmering Stalwart is therefore through his 'feeling' styles, naming his private distress or his worries (which is his 'open door' in terms of Ware's 1986 model); from there he may be open to new 'behaving' such as reengaging with others or taking a risk (Ware's 'target door'). The third leadership domain, that of 'thinking', is less susceptible to change (Ware's 'trap door').

With the help of one of his greatest strengths, his great loyalty, we can think about how he may be getting into trouble. His loyalty is strongly wedded to the way things were done in the past and to existing relationships. In the face of change, innovation, criticism or growth, he will come across as a figure of the past with a conservative, restrained or closed outlook. When he stands up for tradition and ethics in a backward-looking way, his great loyalty descends into an obstacle for others in the organization. At this point the strength becomes a 'pitfall' and this executive goes into overdrive, an overdrive which is not visible through increased activity but rather through isolation and misgivings.

From the pitfall it is usually relatively easy to see the challenge, as it is the natural opposite of the pitfall. In this case the challenge would be a genuine interest in innovation and change, in order to create a new balance between loyalty and support. Another way of finding the challenge is to ask oneself what we find most irritating in other people. In the case of the Simmering Stalwart the most annoying things generally are whims, capriciousness and shallowness in others; in other words the unbearable lightness of being or aggressiveness of his colleagues. This is the 'allergy' area of the Simmering

FIGURE 8.7   The core qualities quadrant of the Simmering Stalwart

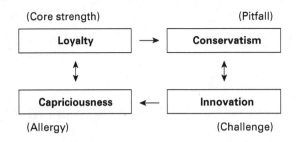

Stalwart, the area where he easily becomes deflated, or annoyed, or frustrated (Figure 8.7, Ofman, 2002).

The sense one gets in the presence of this kind of leader is of a fear of failure or criticism. We pick up an element of doubt in their own abilities, and the fear of being criticized for any potential mistakes made. This creates a kind of rigidity born of insecurity and a tendency to 'play it safe'. As a result the Simmering Stalwart may become reluctant to do anything other than what has worked in the past. Conservatism and rigour seem strong themes, and seem forever unattainable. When the pattern is strongly developed we feel at the same time a need for acceptance and an avoidance of criticism. What is projected onto us is strength, reassurance, and the power to criticize – all sensations that are rare or even unattainable for the Simmering Stalwart himself. If the same person is placed over us and holds some power over us, we may also become rather anxious that decisions are not being made and opinions are not being expressed, so that we are very much on our own, which may extend to a feeling of being 'hung out to dry', completely unprotected.

In working with this executive we first need to be aware of what is projected onto us and not allow ourselves to become directive or critical. We may then help him think about what he can learn from those that irritate him the most, and what sort of challenge he can realistically set himself. If he can balance the loyalty to the organization with a genuine interest in innovation and improvement, in other words if he can move his loyalty along with changing circumstances, he may avoid going into overdrive whilst continuing to draw on his core strengths. In this way his 'avoidant' tendencies become more balanced without there being any pressure to 'fix' them or give them up.

In practice, this can be a great sacrifice for a Simmering Stalwart who is really stuck. His conservatism stretches to a deep and philosophical outlook on life including values that are very dear to him, and it may feel to him that he is now being asked to sacrifice or abandon his core values. Moreover, his apprehension, inner tension and sense of insecurity and inferiority are not likely to change as they are so wrapped up with his personality. His continuous yearning to be accepted and hypersensitivity to what appears to be rejection or criticism is not likely to go away.

CASE VIGNETTE   The Simmering Stalwart

Joseph is external sponsorship and fundraising director for a global PR partnership. His role reporting to the senior partnership's global management committee is to persuade top global corporations to part with six-figure sums in the aid of charities and the arts. In doing so he raises millions of dollars each year and ensures that the donations are channelled through and associated with the PR partnership. The benefit to the corporations varies from country to country and is a mix of goodwill, reputational enhancement, brand image building, visible philanthropic presence and opportunities for mutual staff exchanges and internships. Joseph has a target list of companies divided into the ones that he 'has got' and the ones that he 'will get'. He also has a list of people who will help him to keep current donors engaged and/or get through to potential donors on his target list. Once he has 'got' a contact Joseph never lets go and uses every bit of organizational news, excuse for contact, argument based on their strategy, and legitimate offer available to him to keep the relationships active and the donations flowing.

In December 2010 Joseph invited himself over for a working breakfast with the director-general of an international partnership organization, as soon as he had discovered that they were engaged in a new senior management assessment centre. He had heard that the following year the make-up of the global executive committee was going to change, with a number of senior managers retiring from the committee. At breakfast he inquired if there were any meetings with new potential senior managers from India or Brazil. Joseph was concerned that if such was the case he would want to meet with them when they were at the centre to explain his own organization's work. He was concerned that if he failed to engage with the new executives early, they wouldn't understand what he did and might suggest to others to downgrade his role or decrease the donations. Up to this point he had not really spent much time proactively lobbying the previous committee members, with the exception of the few in Europe, whom he felt were able to get in touch with and influence non-European colleagues. His concern, therefore, he finally explained, was to know who the new senior managers might be and get into contact with them as soon as possible.

When his counterparts made clear that they didn't know anything and that in any case announcements would come out of the organization in due course, probably somewhat later in the year, Joseph became more assertive in his demands alternating between pleading, arguing and demanding. Gradually his counterparts spoke less and less as it transpired that each additional objection from their side only stimulated ever louder responses. With growing embarrassment and concern at the attention they were now drawing from across the breakfast room, the counterparts finally decided to keep silent and to let Joseph talk himself out. After a few minutes, they realized that even this approach was not having the desired immediate effect. Eventually without much communication between them they stood up almost in unison, saying they would remember what Joseph had said whilst reluctantly agreeing to take his card with his contact details.

How avoidant patterns curb our productivity through the workings of shame and fear has never been brought alive better than Aesop in this absurd yet true-to-life, tiny fable of two and a half millennia ago.

The fox with the cropped tail

A fox, having had his tail cut by a trap, was so ashamed that he judged his life impossible. So, resolving to urge the other foxes to shorten their tails in the same way in order that he could hide his personal infirmity in a communal mutilation, he assembled them all together. He advised them to cut their tails, saying that full tails were not only ugly but were a useless extra weight, and an obsolete appendage.

But one of the other foxes, acting as a spokesman, said:

'Hey, friend! If it wasn't in your own interest you wouldn't be giving us this advice!'

This fable concerns those who give advice not out of kindness but through self-interest.

Aesop's Fable 41, 6th century BC

Summary: avoidant patterns in leaders

- This avoidant pattern of leadership will normally only come out when several factors conspire to bring it out: natural inclination, high stress levels, uncertainty and ambiguity, and a degree of over-specialization with high commitment to a particular challenge.

- Clinically, the pattern is characterized by a leader being highly sensitive to criticism or failure, and as a consequence extremely risk-adverse and slow to make decisions. When, despite all efforts, criticism is raised or something goes wrong, these events may be seen as catastrophic and the leader becomes unable to contribute, self-defeating, weak and unassuming.

- Behavioural drivers that often go together with this particular pattern in leaders are tendencies to 'try harder'.

- A first connection with this leader can be made through his or her emotional life: from working through feelings, new behaviours and actions can become topics of conversation and eventually be undertaken. Reflection and thinking powers to evaluate and debrief may be rather harder to access.

Note

1   In fact Ware uses the term 'hysteric' but from his definition it is clear he means 'histrionic'.

Neurotic patterns in leaders

> *I told the doctor I was overtired, anxiety-ridden, compulsively active, constantly depressed, with recurring fits of paranoia. Turns out I'm normal.*
>
> **JULES FEIFFER**

N ow we have made an inventory of realistic and observable 'overdrive' patterns in individuals, we must ask ourselves the question: how do such patterns play out between executives? In our experience it is very rare to see the personality 'disorder' in extreme, textbook form and highly unusual to see one of the 'caricatures' played out in a pure sense. Rather, we regularly encounter aspects of various overdrive patterns in stressful situations or in particularly demanding careers. Also, in more senior management positions we can expect a much higher prevalence of overdrive patterns (see Kaiser, LeBreton and Hogan, 2014).

The personality patterns usually play out in a 'neurotic' way, in a way that is not completely outside socially acceptable norms and just strikes us as rather intense or unusual. Privately, during 'down time' with the family or in late solitary nights in the office, the patterns may develop distinctly beyond the socially acceptable. Similarly, in the privacy of the coaching room, where the spotlight and empathy is entirely on the executive and his or her patterns, the presentation may also be more extreme.

In this chapter we would like to present one more overview of the patterns, remind ourselves of other neurotic presentations that are not covered so much by these patterns, and then share a few early findings from research about the correlations between these particular personality styles and leadership effectiveness.

Table 9.1 presents a summary of all 11 personality patterns, making use of Ware's (1983) terminology of: 'open door' (the channel through which the

TABLE 9.1 Personality patterns

Personality pattern	Personality overdrive	Open door	Target door	Trap door	Working style and drivers*	Antidote/permission
1. The Charming Manipulator	Antisocial	Behaviour	Thinking	Feeling	You believe the rules are made to be broken Be strong + Please others	Respect others more: your rule-breaking strategy is one day going to catch up with you It's OK to be vulnerable
2. The Playful Encourager	Passive–aggressive	Behaviour	Feeling	Thinking	What you say is not what you really believe Try hard + Be strong	Just do it, or else be upfront about your resistance
3. The Glowing Gatsby	Narcissistic	Behaviour	Feeling	Thinking	You think that you're right, and everyone else is wrong Be perfect + Be strong	You look pathetic a lot of the time, being the only one not seeing that you cannot and will not be able to know or do it all Be less dependent on others' praise
4. The Detached Diplomat	Schizoid	Behaviour	Thinking	Feeling	You're disengaged and disconnected Be strong	Try to engage more with others Feelings are helpful and human
5. The Responsible Workaholic	Obsessive–compulsive	Thinking	Feeling	Behaviour	You get the little things right and the big things wrong Be perfect + Be strong + Try hard	Think big picture as well It's OK to make mistakes, and it is important for learning too

TABLE 9.1 *continued*

Personality pattern	Personality overdrive	Open door	Target door	Trap door	Working style and drivers*	Antidote/permission
6. The Impulsive Loyalist	Borderline	Thinking	Behaviour	Feeling	You're subject to mood swings Be perfect + Hurry up	Try to count to ten and relax
7. The Brilliant Sceptic	Paranoid	Thinking	Feeling	Behaviour	You focus on the negatives Be Perfect + Be Strong	Relax: there will always be a more charitable explanation
8. The Creative Daydreamer	Schizotypal	Thinking	Behaviour	Feeling	You try to be different just for the sake of it Be strong + Try hard	Try to listen and connect with other stakeholders
9. The Virtuous Supporter	Dependent	Feeling	Behaviour	Thinking	You try to win the popularity contest Please others + Be strong	Try instead to look after yourself more It's OK to want something for yourself and it is OK to disagree
10. The Accomplished Thespian	Histrionic	Feeling	Thinking	Behaviour	You need to be the centre of attention Please others	Relax about how other people see you
11. The Simmering Stalwart	Avoidant	Feeling	Behaviour	Thinking	You're afraid to make decisions Try hard	Worry less about what people will think

*NOTE: the first statements in this column have been copied from Dotlich & Cairo, 2003 particular person can be reached best); 'target door' (the channel through which the particular person can find new ways of working, insight or personal change and growth); and 'trap door' (the channel which is usually closed to the person as it is kept hidden behind the other two channels).

Neurotic responses to stress

Many of these personality patterns will emerge much more strongly under stress, duress or contretemps, which indicates that they have a neurotic base. Histrionic, passive–aggressive, schizotypal, obsessive–compulsive, paranoid and avoidant patterns can be directly traced back to stress and the phenomenon of going into overdrive. So if a stressful event presents itself, the executive is more likely to go into one of these patterns, particularly if the tendency is already there. On the other hand, narcissistic, antisocial, schizoid and borderline patterns are less visibly linked with stress. For example, when narcissistic or schizoid patterns come to the fore under stress the executive may appear relaxed or in control, even if this calm response is itself the result of an increase in the particular overdrive patterns. Ultimately, every single one of these personality overdrive patterns tends to increase in situations that are stressful or demanding.

How neurosis might surface 1: anxiety and depression

CASE ILLUSTRATION

Meet Jennifer, who always ruminates about her career. Has she made the right choices? Was it wise to leave her initial academic career behind for a consulting position in industry? Was she then right to have become a general manager? Is it not time for her to go to the next level of general management, even if that means changing company yet once more? Has her CV been weakened by all these moves between companies and even across industries? Or will this rather be seen as a strength on her CV? She often has the feeling that her job or more broadly her career is 'plateauing', ie she feels as if she masters all there is to know about her job. Also, she fears that she is doing far too humble work for the seniority level she ought to aspire to, tasks like summarizing management information or updating spreadsheets. She has a recurring dream about walking in the mountains, carrying on to the highest peak, only to find that it was a false summit, and that there is a much higher peak beyond but which is unreachable because of a ravine in between. These thoughts about not being in the right place are more stressful for her than the content of her job, and they even distract her when she is at home or on holiday. Moreover, much of her time off-work, or during the lunch hour, is taken up by 'networking' conversations about possible alternative roles, inside or outside the company, with former colleagues, head-hunters, and just anyone who seems to work in an 'interesting' organization.

Anxiety, the feeling of being unsettled, is the core of any neurosis. It can be a feeling of not being safe, of not knowing what is going on, of not being appreciated, of self-criticism, doubt, over-excitement etc. It is often accompanied by nervous behaviour such as being fidgety, pacing back and forth, somatic complaints and circular ruminations. Anxiety increases pressures on body and mind, and it can build up over time. These stress patterns only come down with appropriate levels of reassurance, success and safety. There is probably a certain level of 'eu-stress' or helpful anxiety which helps us to stay vigilant and focused, but if this level is exceeded substantially and chronically, anxiety can build up to really crippling levels. The suffering may be further exacerbated by a low mood or depressive feelings, which often accompany chronic anxiety. Where minor and manageable levels of anxiety can help us to turn our focus to the challenges of our work and other duties, high levels of anxiety will turn our attention inwards so that our focus, criticism and scrutiny turns against ourselves, which is what normally happens in depression. With prolonged exposure this may lead to loss of interest in outside events and objectives, prolonged sadness and even lethargy.

How neurosis might surface 2: mood swings

CASE ILLUSTRATION

Meet Dominic, who manages to hold down two entirely separate top careers, one as the CEO of a biotechnical corporation and the other as a professional clarinet player. Dominic can and does often talk passionately, both about the innovations in his company and his jazz music. As CEO he plays a distinguished role in selling the company through investor relations, public speaking opportunities and television interviews, where he impresses by making state-of-the-art genetics easy and exciting for wide audiences. He is also known for being the lively core of late weekend jazz concerts, after which he gets up early to do something with his children before travelling around the world for his company. He is often quoted as a truly impressive human being or as a figure larger than life.

His musician and board colleagues have also learned to live with Dominic's 'other side': once every few weeks they will find an e-mail in his inbox saying he cannot attend any further meetings until the end of the year, or urging the sale of a division 'before the beginning of next month'. These frenetic e-mails or phone calls usually announce strategies or topics that verge on the bizarre and that have not been contemplated or discussed before by Dominic or others. Colleagues have learned not to react and just to wait it out. Dominic usually takes a few days off after such e-mails and manages, with the help of his wife, to switch off from further correspondence, to recharge, and to come back fresh to the tasks of the team the very next week. The bizarre plans or over-the-top complaints seem forgotten and are best not mentioned, while Dominic is as reliable and passionate as ever.

Mood swings can be another manifestation of neurosis, where exaggerated 'highs' often full of creativity, enthusiasm, responsibility and generosity, may be followed by deep 'lows' when one gets the impression of dealing with a different person, someone who is unexpectedly despondent, angry, absent or stubborn. Just like the first manifestation above, through anxiety, such bipolar moods may become crippling and neurosis may give way to serious mental conditions such as psychosis and depression. There are many famous cases of bipolar disease where medication proves necessary, such as top executives Philip Graham (who was publisher and co-owner of the *Washington Post*) and Ted Turner (real estate magnate and founder of CNN).

Kets de Vries (2006) introduces the 'hypomanic personality' as one of the ways mood swings may play out in the workplace. People whose behaviour is hypomanic are prone to mildly manic states rather than the extreme highs and lows of full-blown manic-depressive illness (Kets de Vries, 2006). Such highs and lows can come across as somewhat similar to the borderline personality patterns that we have studied in Chapter 7.

How neurosis might surface 3: lack of confidence

CASE ILLUSTRATION

Meet Connor, who has just become VP of global marketing for an important player in scientific equipment and tools. This is his first board membership after leading the 'engine' of the company, the crucial global IT department, as he did successfully for many years. He knows he is completely daunted by this promotion, which has brought him on a par with his old nemesis Stuart, who is VP of global sales. He feels probably erroneously that Stuart, despite his ebullient and warm personality, is always looking for mistakes or faults in his, Connor's, presentations, plans or results. He regularly flushes in Stuart's presence as well as sometimes with senior clients. He just feels a cheat having made it to such a senior level. He would say he was 'only ever a software engineer' which is how he started in the company many years ago. Although he has the full trust and support of the CEO, Connor feels he needs to improve his presentation style now, particularly at trade fairs or when speaking to the 300-strong marketing and sales force. He has often left those presentations to Stuart who is very charismatic on such occasions. Nevertheless, Connor knows at some level that he has a lot more to say than Stuart and that his colleagues want to hear the full detail of market positioning and prospects for all products which can only come from him. Connor's confidence is often very low for which he compensates by spending long hours at work and reading up on the minutest detail of the many hundreds of technical products and services of his company.

Neurotic guilt is another well-known manifestation of neurosis. Individuals who suffer consistently low levels of self-esteem may dwell on and exaggerate the magnitude of past mistakes. They may retain a chronic pessimistic outlook despite evidence to the contrary and they may harbour envy of others who apparently do not suffer such misgivings. When given feedback, individuals with low self-esteem often take it negatively and personally, and can even be devastated by it (especially if they also struggle with avoidant tendencies in their personalities – see Chapter 6). This damage can be much more severe if the feedback is harsh or directly criticizes the individual's worth, moral character, achievements etc. Individuals with low self-esteem are already very self-critical and depend on the approval and praise of others for their own evaluation of self-worth. They believe that a person's approval of them is contingent on their performance and that their likeability depends on their successes.

Kets de Vries (2006) introduces the 'impostor syndrome' as one of the ways lack of confidence may play out in the workplace. Pressures to conform and achieve may become so high that we don a different persona or – conversely – do not appreciate our own success and feel fraudulent in the absence of genuine fraud (Kets de Vries, 2006). The impostor syndrome may be accompanied by an excessive will to please, in which case we will see similar behaviour as described by the dependent personality patterns that we have studied in Chapter 8.

CASE ILLUSTRATION

Jane is the senior leader of a global team within a large Australian construction company. Jane had recently been promoted for her outstanding recruitment and integration work during a period of rapid growth. However, she expressed feelings of inadequacy, something she had been prone to throughout her career but being exacerbated by her recent promotion. She felt that she had to constantly prove herself and although she knew rationally that she was good at her job (as well as in her role as a mother) she felt like an impostor leading a large team of mainly specialists. She said that she felt flat, had no energy and that she tried to combat these feelings of inertia by pushing herself even harder at work and in her private sphere. In this way she tried to pull herself out of her negative internal state. The impact was not only detrimental to herself (she seemed close to burnout) but also had seemingly alienated some of her new team members who found her restless, inaccessible and pushy. Her direct boss was now implicated and for Jane the feedback only exacerbated her low self-esteem.

How these overdrive patterns may be related to leadership outcomes

Now that we have described 11 ways of relational myopia and overdrive in the previous chapters, we are also ready to look at the first research that has

FIGURE 9.1   Self-ratings of leaders: not always the best performance
indicators

been done into the impact of these patterns on leadership effectiveness and
on the rate of leadership development.

The relationship between personality and leadership effectiveness has now
been researched for several decades. For an overview and meta-analysis of
earlier studies see Judge, Bono, Ilies and Gerhardt (2002). They show that each
of the five factors in the well-known Big-5 personality model (Goldberg, 1990)
correlates somewhat (between 0.1 and 0.3) with leadership effectiveness.

Effective leadership was correlated with low Neuroticism (–.24), high Extraversion (.31), high Conscientiousness (.28) and high Openness to Experience (.24). Interestingly, Agreeableness (.08) was not an important predictor of leadership, so the 'nice guy' was not necessarily the best leader or an effective one. Moreover, and specifically in business contexts, Conscientiousness, ie being the 'decent guy', was also unrelated to leadership outcomes.

Judge *et al* (2002) further broke down the results of leadership success studies into those examining *leader emergence*, which has to do with who becomes a leader, and those examining *leader effectiveness*, which is how people perform once they are in leadership roles. This is a similar distinction as Luthans *et al* (1988) made in their research, ie between *leadership success* and *leadership effectiveness* (see Chapter 11 for more detail). Their measures of leadership were based on others' ratings, rankings or nominations. While Extraversion was the most consistent correlate of overall leadership, it was more strongly related to leader emergence than it was to leader effectiveness. Perhaps Extraversion helps people to be noticed and to assert themselves in places where there are opportunities for taking a leadership role, whilst it is less important once you are in a leadership position.

In more recent years the first studies are beginning to appear that explore quantitative correlations between 'dark-side' personality patterns (such as the overdrive patterns in this part of the book) and leadership effectiveness, and an interesting, rather mixed picture is beginning to emerge. Moscoso and Salgado (2004), in studying 85 job applicants and correlating their self-scores on overdrive patterns with their success on the job, find a simple negative correlation between all the overdrive patterns, except the obsessive–compulsive patterns, and job performance. Khoo and Burgh (2008) explore correlations between self-reported effectiveness on a multifactor leadership questionnaire and ratings on the Hogan Development Survey (HDS; Hogan and Hogan, 1997) which covers the 11 personality overdrive patterns above, in a group of 80 New Zealand business leaders and senior managers. They find the histrionic pattern to be a *positive* predictor of self-reported leadership, whilst the avoidant and narcissistic patterns were revealed as *negative* predictors, suggesting a relationship between histrionic personality overdrive tendencies and leadership effectiveness. These findings may have more to do with the reporting of the subjects than with their actual effectiveness as leaders.

Harms *et al* (2011) have investigated the role of these personality traits as predictors of leader development over time and more rigorously, again making use of the Hogan Development Survey for reliable measurements of these 'subclinical traits'. This longitudinal study over four years with 704 cadets in the US Army showed that these subclinical traits were important moderators of the rate of leadership development. The 'rate' of leadership development was measured by yearly development reviews completed by immediate managers in the chain of command over a three-year period.

Harms *et al* (2011) found negative correlations between paranoid and schizotypal personality patterns and leadership development. Surprisingly, they also found positive correlations between some of the patterns and leadership development, namely with obsessive–compulsive, avoidant, narcissistic, histrionic and dependent personality patterns. The strongest predictors were schizotypal, which predicted 10 out of 12 review dimensions; and obsessive–compulsive and paranoid, which predicted 9 out of 12 review dimensions, in opposite directions. The other four patterns (avoidant, narcissistic, histrionic and dependent) predicted only 4 of 12 review dimensions significantly. Passive–aggressive also predicted 4 of 12 review dimensions, albeit negatively. The other three patterns of leadership showed only a mixed and weak relationship with leadership-development review dimensions, with only few significant correlations, in opposite directions.

In summary, according to this study the best predictors of leadership *effectiveness* are obsessive–compulsive leadership patterns, and the best predictors of leadership *derailment* were schizotypal and paranoid patterns of leadership. The other patterns seem to yield a mixed response which is what one would expect for all the 11 patterns, as they are patterns of 'overdrive' and should only derail a leader when they are overdeveloped and become dominant in his or her style or approach.

This is only a first large-scale study, in a very particular setting with a young age group, and with relatively junior leaders; also, the study may confuse leadership success and leadership effectiveness (see Luthans *et al*, 1988 and Chapter 11). But it is a beginning. Moreover, the study demonstrates that the amount of predictability (up to 17 per cent of the variance in the leadership-development reviews) is of the same order of magnitude as the correlations that have been found between Big-5 personality characteristics and leader effectiveness (see eg Judge *et al*, 2002). The picture is complex which means that there is more scope for interesting research. We are confident that future research will begin to unpick the healthy, driven aspects of the leadership patterns, and measure where these same healthy patterns of leadership turn into less healthy *obstacles* to leadership development or effectiveness, ie when exactly each of these leadership patterns go into 'overdrive'.

Kaiser *et al* (2014) correlate scores on the overdrive patterns (making use of the HDS; Hogan and Hogan, 1997) of 320 American and European top managers (mostly director and executive level) with their leadership performance rated by 4,906 co-workers on four leadership dimensions (forceful, enabling, strategic and operational). They showed that *both* low and high overdrive patterns can be linked to leadership excess on these four dimensions. This suggests that perhaps *both* extremes of the 11 overdrive patterns in this part of the book (antisocial, passive–aggressive, narcissistic, schizoid, obsessive–compulsive, borderline, paranoid, schizotypal, dependent, histrionic and avoidant patterns) are associated with counterproductive leadership. Not just *excessive* overdrive patterns, but also *a lack of* overdrive patterns, which would indicate that all leaders need a modicum of these patterns, and begin to develop risks in their leadership behaviour when the overdrive patterns are extremely under- or over-represented.

However, this was only demonstrated for 5 out of the 11 overdrive patterns. Here is a summary of Kaiser *et al*'s (2014) nine significant correlations that involve those five different personality patterns:

- Obsessive–compulsive overdrive patterns are significantly related to both 'too much enabling' leadership and to 'too little forceful' leadership performance.

- Borderline overdrive patterns are significantly related to both 'too much forceful' leadership and to 'too little enabling' leadership performance.

- Schizotypal overdrive patterns are significantly related to 'too much strategic' leadership performance.

- Dependent overdrive patterns are significantly related to both 'too much enabling' leadership and to 'too little forceful' leadership performance.

- Avoidant overdrive patterns are significantly related to both 'too little forceful' leadership and 'too little strategic' leadership performance.

And the most fascinating of their statistical results were, firstly, that on regression the overdrive patterns around the 50 per cent percentile (the modal scores) corresponded closely with the mid-point of the leadership performance dimensions, ie overall these dependencies are such that 'the right amount' of leadership corresponds exactly with 'the mid-point' of the overdrive patterns – and not as was perhaps expected, with the low point or absence of those overdrive patterns. Secondly, Kaiser *et al* (2014) also found that most of the found influence of overdrive patterns influences was moderated significantly by high Emotional Stability on the 5-Factor Model, to the extent that *all* the nine effects above become insignificant if the leader has high Emotional Stability.

To put this latter finding in different words: low Emotional Stability, or high Neuroticism, has now been found as an amplifier of the link between over-drive patterns and leadership importance. Kaiser *et al* (2014) have found that not just the overdrive patterns but also neurotic or emotionally unstable patterns in leaders really have an effect on leadership performance. Stable leaders are the ones that are calm, confident, and resilient; whilst unstable leaders are anxious, easily upset, negative, and moody; and that does have a significant impact on their leadership performance, at least in the eyes of their co-workers.

Although the research picture is still mixed and contains only very few studies, those investigations are already confirming that the very same over-drive or derailment patterns that can bring a leader off course and can cause serious complications, do also have something positive to offer to the leader-ship role. Harms *et al* (2011) show that five of the overdrive patterns may have a straightforward positive correlation with leadership effectiveness, which we can well understand: obsessive–compulsive patterns point to per-fectionistic hard work, avoidant patterns point to cautious double-checking, narcissistic patterns point to self-confidence and ambition, histrionic patterns point to engagement and attention-seeking behaviour, and dependent patterns point to a great willingness to help.

The research shows how important it is for a leader to bring the best out of those patterns without allowing them to go into overdrive and burn out his or her great potential and contribution as a leader. This is precisely the topic of Part Three of this book: how to make the most of your overdrive patterns whilst avoiding their worst excesses.

Here is where Aesop located the neurotic response to the stresses of business life some 2,600 years ago, as part of a character analysis that most of us in the 21st century would recognize for ourselves. For how often do we really allow ourselves to use our greatest treasures?

The man who found a golden lion

A timorous miser came across the statue of a lion made of pure gold, but did not dare to take it. He said:

'Oh dear, oh dear! I don't know what will come of this strange bit of luck! I'm absolutely terrified. I'm torn between my love of riches and my cowardly nature. For is this sheer chance? Surely some god or spirit has made this golden lion and left it here for me to find? I'm torn in two. I love the gold but fear the image of the gold. Desire says, "Take it!"... but my fearful nature says: "Hold back!" Oh, fickle Fortune! You offer yourself but at the same time do not allow yourself to be taken. Oh golden treasure which gives no pleasure! Oh favour of a god which becomes a curse! And what if I took it? How would I use it? What on Earth can I do? I know! I am going to go and fetch my servants and let them take this golden lion. I will watch from a safe distance while they do it.'

This story relates to rich men who don't dare either to touch their treasures or to put them to use.

Aesop's Fable 62, 6th century BC

Summary: neurotic patterns in leaders

- The most likely way we will see leaders derail into one of the 'overdrive' patterns discussed in previous chapters is by neurosis, meaning a type of relatively functional mental disorder involving distress but neither delusions nor hallucinations. In neurosis. behaviour is not outside or not very much outside socially acceptable norms. In fact, most psychologists would say neurosis is the norm rather than the exception.

- Neurotic patterns often involve one of the personality extremes described in Chapters 6–8, and also relatively high levels of anxiety. Other ways of detecting neurosis are through sadness, lethargy, mood swings, or loss of self-confidence. All in all we would argue that there are three key ways that neurosis may come to the fore:

  – anxiety and depression;
  – mood swings;
  – lack of confidence.

- Such neurotic patterns, as expressed through the personality overdrive patterns of the previous three chapters, spur the leader on to be even more ambitious, to remain resilient in the face of huge stress, and to gather courage in daring exploits. However, they also keep leaders off balance and hold them back from being truly high performers. Neuroses are therefore best understood and processed rather than simply raging in the leader's mind.

- Research into the various personality patterns shows that indeed there is a rich presence of mild forms of each of the patterns in the normal population. The research also shows considerable correlation between the 11 overdrive patterns and leadership effectiveness.

- At the present rather early stage of research we have a mixed picture in terms of leadership *effectiveness*: some of the patterns (such as paranoid and schizotypal overdrive patterns) truly appear to hold leaders back, whilst others (such as obsessive–compulsive, avoidant, narcissistic, histrionic and dependent overdrive patterns) instead spur the leader on to a high performance rating in the eyes of bosses and direct reports.

- The *best positive predictor* of leadership effectiveness turns out to be the obsessive–compulsive pattern, which does indicate that a leader can be very effective, being diligent, hard-working and perfectionistic.

- *Neuroticism* does seem to aggravate the negative impact of the overdrive patterns on leadership performance, whilst for five overdrive patterns (obsessive–compulsive, borderline, schizotypal, dependent and avoidant) it has been shown that *both too much and too little* of them can have an adverse relationship with leadership performance in the eyes of close co-workers.

10 | Your own leadership patterns

> *To be normal is the ideal aim of the unsuccessful.*
>
> CARL GUSTAV JUNG, *DIE PROBLEME DER MODERNEN PSYCHOTHERAPIE* (1929)

After learning about a range of leadership patterns or subclinical personality traits that we all possess to some degree, this chapter helps you to inquire into your own patterns as a leader. It is possible to self-score yourself on all 11 dimensions of the previous chapters, by taking the Hogan Personality Inventory (Hogan and Hogan, 1997, **www.hoganassessments.com**). This gives you scores for yourself on the 11 similar subclinical traits as defined by that questionnaire. If you take the questionnaire, please make sure that you talk the results through with a qualified consultant who has a Hogan Development Survey accreditation.

Here, we would like to invite you to some introspection on your own leadership patterns, by asking you a few questions about your experiences as a leader. This will give you a chance to explore your own patterns and challenges as you can identify them now.

Exploring your qualities, opportunities, threats and challenges

Start by *describing at least three unique and personal strengths that you believe you possess as a leader.* To do this, think about feedback you have received over the years, and try to use a single word, or a maximum of two words per strength. Give one example for each of them: something you handled particularly well making use of that strength.

FORM 10.1

	Name (1–2 words)	Example
Strength 1		
Strength 2		
Strength 3		

Then *describe some of the shadow sides that you realize you have as a leader*: aspects of leadership that you do not attend to, or that you struggle with, or that you struggle to find time or energy for. Think again about the feedback that you have received from others.

FORM 10.2

	Name	Example
Shadow side 1		
Shadow side 2		
Shadow side 3		

Now *choose two characters that really irritate you and get under your skin*. Choose one from public life, and one from your own organizational context, or, if you can't find one in your current organization, someone from your organizational context in the past. Ask yourself which aspect of their behaviour annoys you the most, and try to capture this particular irritation in just one or two words.

FORM 10.3

	Name	Irritation (1–2 words)
Public character		
Organizational character		

Finally, *produce three core quadrants* (Figure 10.1) with at least one based on a strength and at least one based on a real person who gets under your skin (placing a particular trait of that person which annoys you under your 'allergy').

FIGURE 10.1   Core quadrants for yourself as a leader

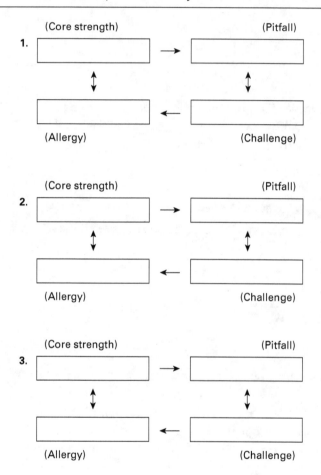

Exploring your own neurotic patterns as a leader

Now read again the summaries of Chapters 6 to 8, and in Table 10.1 give yourself points for the various patterns of leadership, from 1 ('I have no inclination whatsoever towards this pattern') to 10 ('This pattern does characterize me rather well, particularly in periods of stress and difficulties').

TABLE 10.1   Overdrive patterns in leaders

Overdrive pattern	Self-assessed rating of my tendency towards this pattern (1–10)
Chapter 6: movers and shakers	
'Antisocial' patterns: Do you find it hard to be held accountable for your actions?	
'Passive–aggressive' patterns: Do you find it hard to take responsibility for your views and actions?	
'Narcissistic' patterns: Do you as a leader often think that others are wrong and not up to their jobs?	
'Schizoid' patterns: Do you often distance yourself from the everyday running of the business?	
Chapter 7: rigorous thinkers	
'Obsessive-compulsive' patterns: Do you often fret about minutiae whilst losing focus on the big picture?	
'Borderline' patterns: Do you find it very hard to hear bad news about how the business is doing?	
'Paranoid' patterns: Do you often think that people are for or against you, and in particular against you?	
'Schizotypal' patterns: Is your picture of the future often proven wrong?	
Chapter 8: sensitive carers	
'Dependent' patterns: Are you looking after everyone and trying to make them all feel happy?	
'Histrionic' patterns: Are you obsessed with your public image?	
'Avoidant' patterns: Are you concerned or hesitant because of what other people might think or do?	

When you have done this please use the findings of the short drivers' questionnaire in Appendix A1 that you were asked to complete in Chapter 4 (or else complete it again: it only takes a few minutes). These drivers tend to propel you towards your ambitions and successes, yet they also tend to persist under stress and even go into overdrive. Bring the numbers you have found in Appendix A1 forward and into Table 10.2.

TABLE 10.2   Behavioural drivers

Behavioural drivers	My score	Cross if score is 80 or more	Cross if highest score
Be perfect			
Please others			
Hurry up			
Be strong			
Try hard			

Now check if your highest scores from both tables match, ie whether your most prevalent leadership *derailers* match your most prevalent behavioural *drivers*, with the help of Table 9.1 in Chapter 9. If there is not a good fit, take your highest behavioural driver and check (with the help of the summaries of the previous chapters) which overdrive pattern of leadership may also be strongly represented in your personal style. Consider replacing your third strongest leadership pattern with the overdrive pattern you have just found.

Exploring your own hubris

Finally, take a look into the tragic side of your own development, your own flaws and exposure to hubris, based on those core quadrants of strengths, pitfalls, allergies and challenges. Try to list a number of specific situations that are particularly stressful for you and where you go into 'overdrive'. Try to list also where you might overstretch and place unrealistic expectations on yourself and others, for example by finishing the sentences 'In my wildest dreams my career would reach the following summit: ...' or 'When they finally award me an Industry Award or Nobel Prize, this award will be for my good and irreplaceable work in the area of ...'.

After doing the various reflective exercises of this chapter you should be able to write a very personal story about your unique leadership journey, as follows:

My personal leadership journey

I am a leader with several strengths:

... which have come out in the following examples:

I know that with these strengths and with my particular personal make-up there are certain challenges that I am facing in my leadership practice. Here are a few examples of challenges with which I anticipate struggling in the longer term:

In trying to master these particular challenges I am vulnerable to certain patterns in my leadership style, in particular the following:
(*name three, based on what you have found above in terms of leadership overdrive patterns and behavioural drivers*)

... which come out mostly in the following situations:
(*name a few stressors or situations that you find difficult to handle, such as particular conversations, presentations, conflicts, relationships, work challenges, and try to describe them as specifically as possible, by giving details, names of counterparts, specific events, etc*)

If I do not master some of my challenges, then this is how I imagine my own 'downfall' or 'derailment' as a leader:
(*find words for some of your worst nightmares of what might happen to your career and your present position*)

With the self-knowledge that you have gained through this exercise, you may now be able to write a *tragedy* about yourself as a leader:

My personal leadership tragedy

Act 1: How I was raised and how my patterns were strengthened in childhood.

Act 2: How I began to achieve great personal success, eg at school, in my first employment, as an entrepreneur, in my other activities or hobbies.

Act 3: How I became a 'one-trick pony' and started to get stuck in what was initially a very successful routine.

Act 4: Where I am now, trying to learn from this personal 'stuckness' and my great vulnerabilities as a leader.

Act 5: What might happen if I am promoted a couple more times, or double my successes, and yet not learn what I have to learn regarding my challenges, given my personal patterns (*a description of my potential downfall*).

Summary: your own leadership patterns

- This chapter has helped you to explore your own patterns of overdrive as a leader.
- You were invited first to catalogue your core qualities as a leader and explore where these qualities may go into overdrive, so that a pitfall of your leadership style is encountered. Then you were invited to find your main allergies as a leader, as a way to think

about your main challenges and opportunities when operating with the particular leadership quality as described.

- Then you were invited to describe your own neurotic patterns as a leader, with reference to the 11 personality patterns that we have explored in Chapters 6–8.

- Finally, you were invited to make contact with the tragic side of your own life: your achievements, your losses, the very human limitations of your style, and the potential for derailment or downfall in your own career.

- It can be a healthy exercise to think about the unique and uniquely disturbing tragic path that we are on as a leader. We believe sincerely that if we all regularly take a long hard look at ourselves and how we are developing, alone or with an executive coach, we may actually diminish the risk of real tragedy and derailment happening in our workplaces.

PART THREE
Overcoming the excesses of leadership

Introduction: the importance of invisibility

A leader is best when people barely know he exists;
when his work is done, his aim fulfilled,
they will say: we did it ourselves.

LAO TZU, *TAO TE CHING* (CA 500 BC)

In this final part of the book we have come full circle. From the intense light of the Sun King at the start of Part One we arrive at the kind of leader who actively chooses to sit in the shade. From the absolute power and zero responsibility-cum-accountability of Louis XIV we are now glimpsing a leader who can bear full responsibility and accountability without claiming any power, ownership or merits. Lao Tzu writes in his classic text about virtue and leadership that a leader should first and foremost lead him- or herself, with humility, based on the kind of personal learning that we have tried to cover in Part Two of the book. Starting from the ability to somehow deal with incoming emotion and projection, such a leader starts to balance opposite forces and take responsibility whilst making him- or herself practically invisible.

As we have seen in Part One an organization's 'leadership function' is devoted to the effectiveness of the teams in place, so leadership is in principle selfless rather than self-aggrandizing. Some of the best leadership in any organization goes without notice, as it happens in the background, or when a leader is alone, picking up the pieces or dotting the i's.

In this final part of the book we will go through the leader's journey in much more detail, bringing in relevant research and looking from an organizational and personal perspective at maintaining effectiveness in a top leadership role.

Though there is a lot of detail in this part, we prefer to present it in Charlie Parker's words: 'Learn it all; practise, practise, practise; and then forget all that'. You cannot use much of the research in this part of the book directly but it can help you to become a better leader. As a leader you will need to work in the moment and you will need to improvise, so you may find 'bookish' knowledge of little direct practical application. On the other hand, you may ultimately be moved and inspired by the hard-won knowledge or by the trials and tribulations that other leaders went through, so in an indirect way this part of the book may have a considerable impact on your leadership style.

Over the following pages we will try to come to a deeper understanding of leadership. What are the defining characteristics of leaders? What is the single most active ingredient in effective leadership? What is the internal experience of being a leader? How do unhelpful patterns of leaders emerge, and what circumstances nurture such patterns further? How are such overdrive patterns amplified or attenuated at team and organizational level, and what can you do to face up to them and begin addressing them, whether you are the designated leader or not?

In the following chapters we want to look at maintaining balance and effectiveness in the leadership journey. The next chapter, Chapter 11, will tell the *outside story* of leadership success and failure in organizations, based on what is known generally about effectiveness and derailment. Following this, Chapter 12 looks at the *inside story* of the leadership journey: how leaders themselves experience their transitions and the difficulties of maintaining balance. Chapter 13 traces the leadership story further through wider relational dynamics, such as the dynamics of groups and teams. Finally, in Chapter 14 we offer an opportunity for reflection on your own leadership within your teams and organizations, with the help of questions that we believe are relevant for your personal journey as a leader and your own ability to handle yourself as a leader in difficult circumstances.

Coming in, staying on and going out as a leader

11

> *To my mentor Fronto I owe the realization that malice, craftiness, and duplicity are the concomitants of absolute power; and that our patrician families tend for the most part to be lacking in the feelings of ordinary humanity.*
>
> **MARCUS AURELIUS, *MEDITATIONS* (CA AD 180)**

FIGURE 11.1   Timely entries and departures

A good leader knows when to arrive on the scene and start to lead. A good leader also knows when it is time to go and how to go gracefully. Finally, a good leader is available, partly by design and partly by good fortune, at the moment when new leadership opportunities arise. Thus a key aspect of the leadership function is *timing*: when to arrive, when to act, when to take up new opportunities and when to leave them, and when to bow out in a healthy way. The Greeks had a saying: 'call no man happy until he is dead' (first found in Aeschylus' play *Agamemnon*). Similarly, we would do well to call no leader successful until he has retired. As long as a leader is still in place, there is still scope for disgraceful acts in the role, for stubbornly clinging on to a position beyond the natural expiry date, for some major conflict or for a public and humiliating derailment. In this chapter we want to look at how leaders enter new roles, how they manage their promotions and how they handle their endings. We will pay particular attention to botched endings and the derailment of leaders, building on a rich and varied research literature. We are particularly indebted to the work of Robert Hogan and to the Center for Creative Leadership (CCL) leadership derailment studies.

Leadership positions afford power in the form of the *discretion* to act one way or the other. Too much discretion or unchecked power allows our naturally selfish tendencies and behaviours to grow and lead us in the direction of abuse or leadership derailment, just like a spoiled child will throw up ever more problematic tantrums. We want to study this phenomenon in the context of what we already know about overdrive patterns of leaders (see Part Two of this book).

As we argued in the Preface to this book, before we can think about the success and derailment of a leader we first need to be clear on what leadership is. The simplest and most obvious definition is through the role of a leader: anyone so designated within the organization is by definition its leader (Rost, 1991). If you are hired as a leader and referred to as a leader, you *are* a leader. In other words, anyone on the team could in principle do the job. It is then up to the next level to nominate who fills the position. This seems rather shallow and empty as a definition. However, as we will show, it is unfortunately a definition widely and often implicitly held in organizations.

Coming in as a leader: getting into a leadership position

What makes people in organizations hire leaders or refer to their colleagues as leaders? Which criteria do they use, and which criteria are the best predictors of a leader's future success in role? As we have shown in Chapter 2, once you have a definition of leadership, then criteria for fulfilling the role follow automatically. For example, if the definition of a leader is 'whoever takes up the role of the leader', then the criterion becomes 'availability' and it becomes best to take whoever is most motivated, most willing to sacrifice and to pay, in order to fulfil the role and become a leader. Indeed, this is an important criterion at job interviews, or even at some presidential elections. However, if leadership is more than just 'being there', then it is doubtful that you will get the best person for the role if you simply take the most available, the most motivated, the most ambitious.

There are essentially two ways for leaders to get into position: through recruitment and through promotion. In both cases tangible results delivered in the past, as perhaps summarized on a CV, may count towards achieving the position. Hogan (2007) argues, however, that in both cases a more overriding influence will be wielded by the social skills of the candidate, demonstrated through the manner in which he or she comes across during the interviewing process. Obviously, many organizations try to dig a bit deeper than just interviewing a candidate. They apply objective criteria and a numerical form of scoring for shortlisting a candidate, or a psychological assessment.

Selection processes are set up in such a way that 'good qualities', 'talents', 'experiences', 'education' are sought, over and above the motivation and the presentation of the candidates. However, Hogan (2007) also notes that even the best of such procedures look for positive assets rather than excluding negatives. Serious derailment criteria such as personality disturbances are completely hidden from ordinary recruitment practice. This includes traditional assessment centres (Hogan and Hogan, 2001).

Interestingly, the best *predictor* of 'leadership success' is rarely used at the time of selection. Psychologists widely agree that the best predictor for successful, lasting leadership is *general intelligence*, often abbreviated as *g* or IQ (Hunter and Hunter, 1984; Ree and Carretta, 1998). The best single predictor of job performance – as well as training performance, job and income level, and longevity – is *general cognitive ability*, usually measured as the intelligence quotient IQ.

The idea of a single, general ability that predicts a huge variety of performance is now almost 150 years old (Sir Francis Galton, 1869), with forerunners in the imperial examinations in China dating from the 7th century AD. Ever since that first idea, a great many mental test questionnaires have been designed, which have predominantly loaded onto a single factor called general ability, *g*, with very little independent loading onto other factors such as, for example, musicality or creativity. Moreover, that single factor has been shown in countless investigations with countless subjects to correlate with human characteristics as wide apart as amount of brain myelination, brain glucose metabolism, reaction time, altruism, social skills and longevity (Ree and Carretta, 1998). Most importantly for the topic of this book, general ability *g* also correlates to a very significant extent with job performance, ranging from a correlation of around 0.4 in manual work to a correlation of 0.6 in jobs of 'high data complexity' such as leadership (see for example Hunter and Hunter, 1984). Any other specific abilities that have been proposed as alternative predictors do not add beyond about 0.02 in incremental validity to these predictions (Ree and Carretta, 1998).

However, measuring *g* as an assessment for a leadership position is very controversial as this may seem to discriminate against people with lower levels of education, people who were raised in a different country, or with different genetic origins (see Gottfredson, 2005). Quite apart from the politics of using an IQ test, it is important to know that this is the best predictor we have short of trialling the leader in the particular leadership position itself. Likewise it is important to know that even a good predictor such as this runs the risk of recruiting 'false positives' (ie selecting people that appear to but in fact do not really qualify as leaders because of interfering strong 'overdrive' patterns). Not having looked at the negative, often hidden aspects of a leader's personality may certainly cost us dearly. It is for this reason that it would be good for recruitment and assessment processes not just to look at quality and suitability of the candidate(s) but also at potential risk, such as through the overdrive patterns that we have described in Part Two of this book (Hogan, 2007).

Hogan, Hogan and Kaiser (2010) estimated the replacement costs of a single derailing board member as $0.5 million in 1988, which with inflation would be over $1 million in 2014. This is the most conservative estimate, not taking account of secondary costs such as golden handshakes and golden parachutes, lost intellectual and social capital (Adler and Kwon, 2002), disengaged employees etc. Now, clearly, the prevalence of derailment is very high, at least in the opinion of direct reports: work is experienced as stressful, the highest stress factor at work is apparently the immediate boss, and more than half of direct superiors are deemed a failure.

Here are some numbers underpinning this statement: in 1999 the influential NIOSH report found that about a third of US workers reported that their jobs are very or extremely stressful (Hogan, Hogan and Kaiser, 2010); in 2001 the UK Health and Safety Executive reported 20 per cent of workers suffered high stress levels and in 2011 stress comprised 40 per cent of work-related illnesses. Moreover, 75 per cent of working adults see the highest stress factor at work as their immediate boss (Hogan, Raskin and Fazzini, 1990). Add to this the around 50 per cent figure of management failure, as measured in many different ways (Hogan, 2007), and one can imagine huge costs, both personal and financial, to derailment overall.

In conclusion, the price our businesses and societies pay for failing leadership is enormous. Half of all leaders are already failing (see also DeVries, 1992). Moreover, there may be secondary costs related to the consequences of bad leadership over and above lost revenues, through the need to deal with symptoms such as absenteeism, turnover of staff, theft etc. Arguably even the price for non-failing leadership is very high, simply because leaders in organizations are paid extremely well. The average pay ratio between CEOs and workers has been found by some statisticians to be *ca* 350 in the USA and *ca* 100 in the rest of the western world (McGregor, 2013). At the same time there is little evidence that leaders make such a difference to their organization.

An additional problem with this kind of cost is that it is very likely to be a chronic burden, a cost that needs to be paid year-on-year until the leader's retirement, if the leadership failings are not addressed. As Freud already noted in 1914 (Freud, 1914), we are bound to keep repeating the behaviours that we cannot make sense of. We can even safely assume that such patterns may turn up in the subordinates of leaders as this is the type of leadership that they have been exposed to and take as normal. We all tend to learn leadership from those that lead us. And in abusive relationships the propensity of 'identification with the aggressor' (Anna Freud, 1936) has long been noted. Moreover, it wouldn't be surprising if some such repetition of unprocessed leadership failings stretches out across the generations, as already intuited by Freud in 1940, and by evidence found in attachment studies across the generations (see De Haan, 2012). We can safely assume that without leaders robustly and deeply looking into their own shadow sides, with a sincere and sustained intention not to suffer their worst excesses, causes of leadership derailment are likely to be self-perpetuating. After all, the kind of overdrive patterns we saw in Part Two are linked intimately with unconscious patterns and they themselves obstruct the leader's ability to learn. They have a considerable 'defensive' component which aims at coping with stressors, pressures and responsibilities.

On a personal note for the leader him- or herself and for those directly involved, this is the stuff of tragedy, or at least considerable trauma. Losing your job leads to a similar loss in well-being as a divorce, and in statistical terms appears to generate more lasting trauma even than losing a spouse (Clark and Georgellis, 2013). Moreover, what we are talking about here is not just ordinary loss of employment, but an event that can be exacerbated by being highly public and exposing. Julia Gillard, who was ousted as Australian prime minister through a Labor party leadership challenge, wrote movingly about the personal repercussions that such an experience can have:

> Losing power can bring forth a pain that hits you like a fist. Losing power is felt physically, emotionally, in waves of sensation, in moments of acute distress... You can feel you are fine but then suddenly someone's words of comfort, or finding a memento at the back of the cupboard as you pack up, or even cracking jokes about old times, can bring forth a pain that hits you like a fist, a pain so strong you feel it in your guts, your nerve endings. I know that late at night or at quiet moments in the day feelings of regret, memories that make you shine with pride, a sense of being unfulfilled can overwhelm you. Hours slip by.
>
> Julia Gillard, 2013

Staying on as a leader: lasting success in a leadership role

Before we look at how leaders can achieve lasting success in their leadership roles we have to spend a bit more time exploring some of the less wholesome practices that leaders employ to stay in their positions.

Because of the fact that for many people, both leaders and followers, the 'leader' is just the person who is there, the person who happens to officially or unofficially occupy the leadership position, we see a lot of jostling for that role and a lot of usurpation in that role. Moreover, a leadership role is usually better paid and carries more influence and power (more 'discretion' to choose your own action), so it really comes as no surprise that there is generally competition around these roles. However, when one defines leadership – even if implicitly – by 'being there' and taking up the role, this will condone abusive behaviour. In our view this implicit definition is a major factor in the disturbing statistic that so many leaders in organizations are failing in the eyes of their direct reports. Typical management behaviours associated with defining leadership as 'taking up the leadership role' are:

- *claiming the space*, eg by speaking out at meetings even when not having much to say, having views on every imaginable topic, taking up time and 'waffling' for longer than is necessary;

- *claiming the successes*, ascribing initiating or helpful contributions in a successful enterprise to oneself, and conversely blaming other people, predecessors or other parts of the business if there are failures;

- *actively building a reputation* (Petriglieri and Stein, 2012), including marketing self, brushing up positive characteristics and masking negative traits;

- *building a network of supporters and followers*, up to the point of favouritism and nepotism, in order to have some sort of a 'power base'.

Apart from these visible consequences of this particular conception of leadership, there are likely to be internal and invisible consequences as well. Firstly, the leader may begin to believe in his or her claims and successes, may begin to believe in his reputation, and thus may be primed more towards an authoritative, successful, capable self-image. Secondly, building up one's reputation often goes together with building up a matching identity internally, which sets a chain of internal mechanisms in operation that split the personality (see also Chapter 3, where we have shown that this splitting of the personality lies at the root of the leadership shadow). Within him- or herself, the leader is under pressure to bring to the foreground more 'positive', 'leaderlike' characteristics of the self and to cast aside the more 'negative', 'denigrated' or 'follower-like' characteristics of self. Petriglieri and Stein (2012) have shown how defensive mechanisms such as projection and projective identification may play an important role in building up and maintaining leaders' identities, and how as a consequence such leaders may contribute to 'ongoing conflict and a toxic culture' in organizations.

We think that these internal dynamics within leaders, which are of course a response to both the pressures on them and the leadership definitions they adopt, go a long way to explain the frequent failings of leadership and the general unpopularity of leaders with those closest to them, ie their direct reports. They go a long way towards explaining 'everyday' leadership derailment. The most unfortunate and sometimes even abusive behaviour which can be the consequence of this constant need to claim terrain, claim success, compete with peers and polish a reputation will be familiar to anyone who has spent time inside organizations. Every organizational worker or team member we speak with has at some stage been frustrated or put off by this kind of behaviour from leaders and they have felt embarrassed when noticing it within themselves. Even though all of the indicated behaviours may contribute to holding or maintaining their position, they are not generally signs of 'good' leadership, and are probably more characteristic of the opposite: 'flawed' leadership. There must be something profoundly wrong with the simple, common-sense definition of leadership as 'whoever happens to be there in the role'.

However, it is hard to go beyond the 'default' definition of the leader as being 'the person who holds that position', towards a more helpful definition from which one can deduce criteria that can in turn be used to measure leadership success of effectiveness quantitatively. Defining leadership is notoriously tricky. There is a whole literature, estimated at over 10,000 books and articles (Rost, 1991; Hogan, Curphy and Hogan, 1994) that has attempted to provide definitions. Almost every human quality, trait or skill imaginable can be and has been used to define good leadership: openness, honesty, trust, commitment, courage, persuasion, ability to transform, ability to create meaning – and there are a plethora of more situational or contingency models of leadership as well, ie models that come up with distinct qualities for different situations or with the quality of adaptation and flexibility itself as a defining leadership characteristic. However, as Plato conclusively showed nearly 2,400 years ago in his dialogue on leadership, the *Meno* (Plato, *ca* 380 BC), listing attributes of leadership excellence will never get us to a definition of what leadership excellence *is*, in essence.

Our leadership definition in Chapter 2 shows that we agree with Hogan and Hogan (2001) that a better place to start is by defining leadership as what a leader contributes to the effectiveness of a team. In fact, in an even more competitive arena than most leadership in business organizations – professional international sports – there have been more fruitful endeavours to determine the *value* of a leader. A precise figure has been put on the leadership ability of, say, a football manager, by computing how much the manager over- or under-performs by comparison to the money spent on wages for the team (Kuper and Szymanski, 2012). Kuper and Szymanski (2012) also show that there are some consistently over-performing managers, ie leaders that outperform the competition in terms of performance of their team as compared with other teams with similar levels of investment, over sustained periods of more than five years. Brian Clough and Bob Paisley were examples of such managers in the UK leagues. However, apart from those few overachievers 'the vast majority of managers appear to have almost no impact on their team's performance' (page 124), a statement backed up with hard statistics. Brown (2014) demonstrates that something similar is true in politics, ie that the person of the leader is much less influential in winning elections and in shaping policy than is often thought. It is very likely that the very same statement may also be true in business, namely that leaders and their qualities do not make much difference to the bottom line. This would be an even more serious finding in business than in sports or politics, because expenditure on business leaders, both in terms of salaries and other expenses, is proportionally much higher than in sport and politics. And even more troubling if one considers the financial and emotional costs of failing business leadership.

Similar to the sports rankings, *Forbes* has produced rankings on the 'efficiency' of US CEOs, based on very similar criteria: change in share price relative to own compensation over a six-year period (DeCarlo, 2012). After the financial crisis exposed the disadvantages of the focus on short-term shareholder benefits and bonuses, the *Harvard Business Review* has also begun publishing rankings of CEOs based on long-term increase of market capitalization of corporations (Hansen, Ibarra and Peyer, 2010 and 2013). This ranking is based on the *ca* 1,200 (2010) and 1,800 (2013) largest publicly-traded companies worldwide. They found that the best-performing CEOs during their tenure within a 12-year period were not the same as the best-paid CEOs or even the 'star' CEOs, and also that geographies and markets made little difference. Hansen *et al* (2010) conclude with the comment:

> Taking a longer perspective did bring to light a number of 'hidden gems' – quiet CEOs who delivered outstanding results year in and year out, away from the glare of the cover stories and business school case studies. Their success makes a persuasive argument for a new approach to evaluating CEOs. Only by analysing performance over their tenure and beyond can we begin to understand the nature of great leadership.
>
> Hansen *et al*, 2010

This is in line with what we are trying to argue in this chapter.

Effectiveness of leaders has also been studied in another way, namely by scrupulously measuring what they do with their time and then checking if there is any difference between how leaders with better ratings or a higher-performance organization spend their time in comparison with less effective leaders. The first to do this was Mintzberg (1973) who collected detailed data from a week's work of five CEOs. Luthans *et al* (1988) analysed detailed data from two groups of 44 and 248 'real managers' from many sectors and all levels. They found that there are substantial differences between how 'successful' and 'effective' managers spend their time.

They first identified four major clusters of activities:

- *routine communication* such as exchanging information and paperwork (29 per cent);
- *traditional management* activities such as planning and decision making (32 per cent);
- *networking* such as interacting with outsiders and socializing (19 per cent);
- and *human resources* such as staffing, developing, motivating and managing conflict (20 per cent).

'Successful' managers, defined as the leaders who are promoted quickly in their organizations, spend 70 per cent more time on networking activities and 10 per cent more on routine communication compared with less successful managers. 'Effective' managers, defined by a combination of business unit performance, subordinate satisfaction and subordinate organizational commitment, spend 50 per cent more time on routine communication and 30 per cent more time on human resource management than average managers. In short, Luthans *et al* (1988) confirm that, to be effective, leaders need to facilitate communication, inform, and be open to upwards communication (as we also suggested in Chapter 2), whilst politics, networking and traditional management activities are a lot less important.

The main findings of Luthans *et al* (1988) were confirmed in 2011 by Bandiera, Guiso, Prat and Sadun following a detailed time analysis of one week's activity of 94 CEOs from top-600 Italian firms. They write that the observed patterns are consistent with the hypothesis that networking time spent with outsiders is on average less beneficial to the firm and more beneficial to the CEO than time spent in internal routine communication (Bandiera *et al*, 2011).

Once we have a formal definition of leadership, as enhancing or maintaining the effectiveness of a team of high performers (see our definition at the start of Chapter 2), this can be operationalized, in terms of 'outperforming the competition' or 'increasing market capitalization'. Such rankings of leaders could help to provide clear and unambiguous criteria as to the performance of individual leaders, by comparing leaders with similar responsibilities in the same organization or the same industry.

Hogan and Hogan (2001) have also shown that with this definition in mind the best indicator of leadership competence, in the absence of specific and objective benchmark numbers for profitability, is made up of the leader's ratings by those high performers themselves, the subordinates of the leaders and in particular the direct reports. They argue that all the alternatives one might come up with are tainted and less useful. Self-ratings by leaders have been shown to have a much lower correlation with performance than the other two (unsurprisingly perhaps for those who are familiar with leaders who are wont to ascribe great talents, substantial change and impressive successes to their own role or contributions – see Harris and Schaubroeck, 1988, or Gentry, Hannum, Ekelund and de Jong, 2007); ratings by superiors correlate more with the technical competence of the leader and less with the leader-ship aspects of the role such as performance of the team; and peer ratings are contaminated by the organization's politics (Hogan and Hogan, 2001).

The best way therefore to define and measure ongoing leadership success appears to be to judge the achievements of a leader from the perspective of his or her team's effectiveness, as seen from objective results or from the perspective of the team members themselves (Hogan and Hogan, 2001). Leadership would be defined in similar terms as in Chapter 2, eg as 'the ability to build and maintain an effective team, one that can outperform its competition' (Hogan, Curphy and Hogan, 1994). The test of a good leader is then given by the extent to which they enable others to work collectively to address issues and achieve appropriate results today as well as anticipate and respond to new issues emerging. The 'damage' of bad leadership is inflicted at the level of group performance, and equally it is at this level where leaders can make a positive difference purely *as leaders*, as distinct from just co-workers. The people who will notice leadership success or failure most are those that are dependent on the leadership: the direct reports or team members. However, they are often unable to speak out or may run huge risks if they do so; therefore surveys should be organized with care, safe-guarding the subjects' anonymity. Also, upward feedback should be stimulated as much as possible, so leaders can receive the relevant data for monitoring and maintaining or enhancing their own performance (Milliken, Morrison and Hewlin, 2003).

Even with this definition of leadership in mind, countless managers have been distracted and do not spend enough time on enhancing the effectiveness of their team per se. For some reason or other they are catering too much to the other definition of leadership, the one about 'being in post'. Paradoxically, their intense attention to being the leader precludes them in large part from truly leading others.

What is often forgotten is that most employees can lead themselves most of the time. They do not need someone to tell them what to do. They need someone, but only occasionally, to enhance their effectiveness, in other words to guide or coach them towards a better performance.

There have not been any conclusive studies on 'leadership competence' from this perspective, yet there are several helpful field studies on the topic of 'leadership incompetence' defined in these terms (Bentz, 1985; McCall and Lombardo 1983; Van Velsor and Leslie, 1995; and see Gentry *et al*, 2007). They are usually based on psychometrics of leaders or interviews with those that stay behind about the leaders that have failed them. These studies collectively bring to the fore the following main causes for derailment of leaders:

1 breakdown in interpersonal relationships;

2 failure to meet agreed objectives and expectations;

3 inability to build a team;

4 inability to adapt to change; and

5 too narrow a functional orientation.

These aspects can all be viewed as relational and seem all underpinned by the leader's personality patterns in working with others. They do not seem to be directly reducible to focused leadership skills or behaviours. In fact, all the studies report good correlations between derailment and (perceived) strong social skills. In other words, it is probably not the quality of social interaction that precludes a leader from derailing.

Causes of leadership success and derailment are probably doubly hidden: under the surface of the leader's reputation, ie underneath the behaviour that a leader demonstrates in most meetings, and also underneath the organizational power structures. Leadership which is going awry is not easily visible and only apparent to those closest to the leader. The outward behaviour of the leader may still be very elegant, smooth, upbeat, attentive, persuasive or encouraging (or whatever trait is associated with 'good' leadership), even when in actual fact the leader is in real trouble. Failing leadership may be more visible in the privacy of a leader's home, where all the work-related stress, turmoil, despondency and grievances may come out. And it may also be more visible to the leader's direct reports, who experience the person more intimately and on a day-to-day basis, in good times and bad. However, both of these arenas are rather private or at least hidden even from employees who are only slightly removed from the leader's practice, which in many cases includes peers and bosses of the leader, so it may take a long time for failings in leadership to emerge in an organization, if ever. The 'home' views on the leader are not known in the organization, and the direct reports' views also remain hidden beneath the real risk and awkwardness of becoming a whistle-blower.

Although derailment patterns may be hard to detect for an outsider, they cannot be hidden inside the leader's team or department as they work directly on leader–report relationships. Thanks to Robert and Joyce Hogan's work it is now also possible to self-assess one's own derailment patterns with the help of a simple questionnaire, the Hogan Development Survey. This psychometric instrument was designed in such a way that derailment patterns correlate with likely views of reports and close relationships on the leader so it gives some indication of how reports will experience their leader (Hogan and Hogan, 2001).

Just to summarize briefly what we have said so far about the selection of leaders:

1 Intelligence correlates with sustainable success as a leader.

2 Social skills only correlate with success at the recruitment or promotion stage and have no clear correlation with the leader's performance.

3 Both intelligence and social skills also correlate with derailment in some studies.

4 Derailment may be best predicted with 'having the wrong stuff' (dark-side personality material) as it is entirely unrelated with 'lacking the right stuff' such as intelligence or social skills (Lombardo *et al*, 1988).

5 This means that ongoing leadership success is probably mostly a function of a balanced character together with the ability of taking in and responding to upwards feedback.

Letting go as a leader: ways and snares when going out

There are many ways to take your leave as a leader. Your time may be up in the eyes of your employers, or you might decide to jump before you are pushed. Very successful leaders can end up in the predicament of having to be chaperoned out, for the simple reason that they cling on to their roles and literally wait for someone else to tell them that it is really time to go. It is of course also possible to go well, and to go at the right time, but that it is a delicate matter even if you are in full control of your retirement.

CASE ILLUSTRATION

Philip is Global VP for sales for a manufacturing company with a billion dollars in sales this past year. The company is privately owned and sells into almost 100 countries around the world. He has a recognized presence in the industry and also holds most of the power and influence in his company. Being a privately-owned family business, a family member is the president, but is not necessarily the most influential executive. Philip has been that figure for several years, always respectful of the hierarchy but very powerful nevertheless. Philip has realized for several years that he needs to think about his transition out of the company and into retirement. He has been working with an executive coach.

He is a 'driver' and a great deal of the coaching work over the years has been around impulse, control, pace, patience, balance, communication style along with enriching his many executive and leadership skills. He has developed himself whilst carrying out his professional responsibilities to an exceptional standard.

He had planned for retirement to be activated last year. Plans were in place to turn over his position to another VP. After the announcement to both the company and the industry, he had some regrets and found it was so hard to let go, but he remained committed to the process. His future was starting to evolve and he was in the process of creating a plan to realize that future.

His move back to his home country was a move that had never been sanctioned before by the company. They requested all their VPs to be on-site, but as the president said, if anyone could carry this off, Philip could. The purpose of moving back was to be closer to family and especially to his young grandchildren. He was determined not to be the absent grandfather as he sees himself as an absent father.

A few months after moving back home the decision was made by both Philip and the president to have him stay on another year to make the transition smoother for the VP who would assume Philip's responsibilities, and also for the industry and the company as a whole.

It will soon be another year and the new beginning that Philip thought he was moving towards has been interrupted by the year's delay and may now not be feasible. He has always been good at making plans and carrying through on them. This time he thought he had planned a journey into a new professional identity after 35 years of a managerial career. It is so unusual for him for any of his plans to get stalled that he is becoming increasingly frustrated. He keeps forcing himself to develop this plan for a 'new beginning' but he is less and less clear about what that new beginning should look like.

This major transition of retirement has forced him into sombre introspection, something he does not like at all. He would prefer a quick mini-transition; he just wants to get out fast and find a different purpose. But he cannot bring himself to do it. He has also experienced some loss of power and influence as he moved back to his own country and is not a physical presence anymore at headquarters. He feels a bit on the outside looking in and fears that this will only get worse.

Let's first look more closely at the causes of derailment in leaders. The existing literature is mainly based on what those who have worked for derailed leaders have to say about them. What they have to say about them retrospectively of course, not during their tenure, because that kind of 'whistle-blowing' is very risky and as a consequence courageous and rare.

The earliest research, by Bentz (1967, 1985), done within the large workforce of the department-store chain Sears in the US, appears to confirm the *one fatal flaw* characteristic, the idea that leaders who derail have one fatal flaw such as emotional instability which brings them down. These early studies are very meticulous, but also, as they were done by one person inside the personnel department of his own organization, fairly subjective and indeed retrospective. There is a risk of subjective biases unrelated to the object of study. Bentz's earlier research (Bentz, 1967) shows that initial test-battery scores taken on hiring a manager clearly distinguish between those who are to become successful managers and those who consequently derail and leave the organization (102 'derailed' leaders versus the total sample of 2,458). The group that went on to derail later in their careers was different from the base group against many criteria, with emotional stability, social skills, leadership skills and vocational interests the largest factors, all *before* mental ability (*g*) which was also tested for.

In the empirical literature the factors of derailment seem more comprehensive and they are summarized by Hogan and Warrenfeltz (2003) into: leadership factors; business factors; interpersonal factors; and intrapersonal factors. Their conclusion seems to show that all and everything that makes up a leader can also contribute to his or her downfall. Be that as it may, Hogan, Hogan and Kaiser (2010) summarize the earlier research as:

- 'The reasons managers fail involve poor business performance, leadership, self-control, and especially relationship management' (page 559).

- 'Derailment can almost always be traced to relationship problems. When relationships are strong, people will forgive mistakes; when relationships erode, tolerance disappears and mistakes get managers fired' (page 562).

In fact, co-worker ratings of self-awareness predict risk of derailment (Gentry *et al*, 2009) and getting fired up to five years later (Gentry *et al*, 2007). Gentry *et al* (2007) also show that the 'self-awareness gap' widens for more senior leaders, due to inflated self-ratings.

There seems to be a natural process in which a new leader who has recently come into power is at his or her most vulnerable and experiences the least control or influence. Slowly, over time, through some kind of osmosis, power clings to a leader and becomes ever greater. With this accumulation of power, the leader's *discretion* to choose their behaviour or make decisions also increases. It is through discretion that leaders can begin making a difference in their organization. However, discretion is both the currency with which leaders get things done *and* the bribe that will inevitably corrupt them.

Discretion can be used for the benefit of the organization, enhancing the leader's team effectiveness – but it can also contribute to derailment, when leaders serve their own agendas or where leaders become less accountable as they increase their freedom.

With increasing discretion personality aspects will become more relevant, and may show up as 'derailers' of the discretion of a leader. This is when leaders begin to wrestle with their own shadows, with their very own personality patterns – a broad overview of which we have presented in Part Two of this book.

Kaiser and Hogan (2007) argue that discretion also increases with hierarchical level, and that there is likely to be more discretion in younger and in smaller organizations, and in those organizations with 'weaker' cultures and limited governance or control mechanisms. Hambrick and Abrahamson (1995) have done an exploration of the amount of discretion per industry that shows:

- Academic experts and security analysts agree with each other and across groups that there are significant differences of discretion between industries.

- These same experts agree on which industries have top leaders with more discretion: the software, engineering, pharma and entertainment industries.

- There are four factors in those industries that predict 49 per cent of the variance in the panellists' rankings: R&D intensity, advertising intensity, market growth and (inversely) capital intensity.

Thinking about leadership, power, influence and corruptibility has not just appeared on the scene with the advent of large corporate organizations. It has been of all ages. Leadership has been studied as relevant to society since the creation of the polis, ie probably at least since the beginning of the Bronze Age, when humans started to settle in larger groups. Famous older sources that are even today frequently drawn upon include:

- Sun Tzu's *The Art of War* which is probably more than two thousand years old and advises leaders about how to win the ruthless competition with other leaders and lead teams in direct competition.

- Machiavelli's *The Prince* (1514) is a guide for the fledgling leader with precious little discretion, advising on how to survive in the role throughout the first few dangerous months and years.

From ancient times much drama production has also been devoted to leadership, and to the derailment of leaders. The art of tragedy is the dramatization of leadership derailment, from the earliest days in ancient Athens. It is worthwhile contrasting Greek tragedy (accumulation of hubris in families, and the need to purge these waves of hubris and guilt) with Roman tragedy (the emergence of personal responsibility and degeneration when responsibility is not taken), and those two with Shakespearean or more widely Elizabethan tragedy (the emergence of the 'one fatal flaw' hypothesis for leadership derailment).

In fact, the earliest study of McCall and Lombardo (1983) can be summarized as proposing three core dynamics of derailment similar to the ones in the tragedies:

1 An early strength becomes a weakness (eg technical prowess becomes less important as one advances) – which matches the 'one fatal flaw' hypothesis in Bentz (1967) and Shakespeare.

2 A deficiency such as an inability to work with peers eventually matters – which matches the hypothesis in Roman tragedy (Seneca).

3 Bad luck, such as being caught up in a business downturn or tainted unfairly by circumstances – matching the broad background of the Greek tragedies, as it is mainly the hubris of ancestors that damages the protagonists of those plays.

Just to summarize briefly what we have said so far about the derailment of leaders:

- Derailment seems to be a clear function of leadership *discretion* (which would be confirmation that power does indeed corrupt and absolute power corrupts absolutely, as Lord Acton said), which again increases with seniority in rank, younger organizations, looser control, R&D and advertising intensity and market growth and inverse capital intensity.

- Derailment can be predicted from lack of self-awareness (which in leaders usually means inflated self-ratings, something that also increases with seniority in rank).

- From retrospective research we know that derailment can almost always be traced to self-awareness and relationship issues (Hogan, Hogan and Kaiser, 2010). The combination of lack of self-awareness, relationship issues and unbridled discretion brings us back to the personality patterns of Part Two of this book and to the concept of hubris, which we will return to in the next chapter.

As our society reveres leaders and leadership so much, one wonders where this is leaving our leaders morally, and how it is affecting them that they get such disproportionate reward and recognition for their good work? In ancient Greece Aesop approached leaders with biting satire.

The mice and the house ferrets

The mice and the house ferrets were at war. Now the mice, always seeing themselves beaten, convened a committee, because they imagined that it must be the lack of a leader which caused their setbacks. They elected some generals by raising their hands. Now, the new generals wanted to be distinguished from the ordinary soldiers, so they fashioned some horns and fastened them to their heads. The battle got under way and it happened that the army of the mice was defeated by the house ferrets. The soldiers fled towards their holes, into which they escaped easily. But the generals, not being able to enter because of their horns getting stuck, were caught and devoured.

Thus, vainglory is often a cause of misfortune.

Aesop's Fable 237, 6th century BC

Summary: coming in, staying on and going out as a leader

Leadership has been notoriously difficult to define, and yet the definition one uses, implicitly or explicitly, influences how one leads or interacts with leaders.

Most people in organizations operate on the assumption that 'the leader is the one who is in charge'. This implicitly defines leadership as having or claiming the leadership role, with disastrous consequences in terms of bad leadership and unhealthy leader–follower relationships.

A better definition is 'the leader is charged with building the overall effectiveness of the team'. From this perspective useful criteria for measuring quality of leadership are:

- objective results of the team compared with other teams (outperforming the competition);
- assessment of leadership by the leader's direct reports (subjective but relevant views on performance).

In terms of success in the leadership role as defined in this way, indications are that intelligence correlates best with success whilst social skills only correlate with success at the recruitment stage. The strongest predictors of derailment are the kind of 'overdrive patterns' we have described in Part Two, so derailment is probably more to do with 'having the wrong stuff' (ie, dark-side personality patterns) and less with 'lacking the right stuff'.

Derailment patterns are a complex function of personality and context, leaders' and followers' characteristics. One important ingredient is probably leadership *discretion*, the freedom to make or influence decisions. Power corrupts and power with discretion corrupts incrementally, to paraphrase Lord Acton's famous saying.

To sum up:

- there are demonstrable and significant differences between *successful* leadership (ie promotions, ratings from superiors) and *effective* leadership (ie organization performance, team ratings);
- the best predictor of 'successful' leadership that we have is intelligence;
- the best predictor for effective ('good') leadership that we have is attention to routine communication and human resources;
- the best predictor of 'bad' leadership (derailment) that we have is a cross between personality patterns and discretion;
- the ability to receive upward feedback can be useful for leaders to determine their true impact in relation to those they lead and in determining when to leave.

Balancing your patterns as a leader

12

The enemy is within the gates, it is with our own luxury, our own madness, our own wickedness, that we have to contend.

MARCUS TULLIUS CICERO,
***THE SECOND ORATION AGAINST CATALINE* (63 BC)**

In the previous chapter we have largely explored the leader's fortunes *from the outside*, by defining leadership and success and effectiveness as a leader, and by looking into the successes, contributions and failures of executives largely from an organizational perspective and from what can be learned from the research literature. In this chapter we want to relate the *inside* story: how does it feel to be a leader and what might a leader do to minimize the risks of derailment?

The experience of complexity

If you don't stumble and fall at the first post, by spending all your time and credibility as a leader claiming or defending your leadership position rather than truly leading (see Chapter 11), then the leadership landscape is still remarkably challenging. We have already outlined some of the changes in our society and business world, which contribute to making it ever more complex (see Part One of this book). We must not underestimate how subtle the contribution of a leader is, even when disregarding the pace of change and the increasing connectivity and speed in our societies. A leader has to work with the most complex structure known, our central nervous system (CNS), and particularly with interactions between several or many of those systems. It is incredibly hard even to begin to think about how humans might work together, how they might become more effective at what they do, and how to influence them at achieving that.

Executives are constantly battling with questions such as:

- How do I make sense of the effectiveness of my team as it is?
- How can I support us as a team to become more effective?
- How do I help to meet the multiple needs that I and team members have, and balance this process with meeting the needs that other stakeholders have of our team?
- How can I help implement the kind of change that I believe we need to see?

The three domains or functions of leadership which we distinguish as underpinning the three groups of overdrive patterns in Part Two are:

1 *Supporting*: facilitating or enabling the team's effectiveness, enhancing the resources and competences that are available – a making or doing function.
2 *Inspiring*: supplying the team with strategy and meaning-making – a thinking function.
3 *Containing*: looking after or caring for the team, nurturing and providing space and boundaries for processing emotions and for understanding to emerge – a feeling function.

Together these three functions of a leader very much describe the role broadly taken up by parents or carers for children. We have seen in Part Two how these leadership functions may go into overdrive (Dotlich and Cairo, 2003). Here is that summary from Chapter 5 again.

Overdrives of the supporting (doing) function

- Antisocial patterns: you believe the rules are made to be broken. Do you find it hard to be held accountable for your actions?
- Passive–aggressive patterns: what you say is not what you really believe. Do you find it hard to take responsibility for your views and actions?
- Narcissistic patterns: you think that you're right, and everyone else is wrong. Do you as a leader often think that others are wrong and not up to their jobs?
- Schizoid patterns: you're disengaged and disconnected. Do you often distance yourself from the everyday running of the business?

Overdrives of the inspiring (thinking) function

- Obsessive–compulsive patterns: you get the little things right and the big things wrong. Do you often fret about minutiae whilst losing focus on the big picture?

- Borderline patterns: you're subject to mood swings. Do you find it very hard to hear bad news about how the business is going?

- Paranoid patterns: you focus on the negatives. Do you often think that people are for or against you, and in particular against you?

- Schizotypal patterns: you try to be different just for the sake of it. Is your picture of the future often proven wrong?

Overdrives of the containing (feeling) function

- Dependent patterns: you try to win the popularity contest. Are you looking after everyone and trying to make them all feel happy?

- Histrionic patterns: you need to be the centre of attention. Are you obsessed with your public image?

- Avoidant patterns: you're afraid to make decisions. Are you concerned or hesitant because of what other people might think or do?

As we have seen in the previous chapter, when you get more settled in your leadership role, you will sense that your control and your authority gradually grows. You will feel that your discretion to take decisions for the team grows alongside your growing strengths in the role, and you may begin to reach out to more challenging aspirations. You may also find that the way of relating towards you changes, sometimes pushing you towards aspects of your own behaviour that you'd rather not emphasize. You may feel a lot of freedom to do the role, or you may feel that you are butting up against powerful forces in the organization. In both cases the risk of 'hubris' looms large, which is why we want to spend some time on that ancient concept.

The risks of hubris

As leaders get more immersed in their roles their own influence tends to grow, along with (both countervailing and supporting) organizational forces and expectations. This means that with growing discretion there is more and more risk that leaders will live out their overdrive patterns at work. Emotionally, they will make their organizational contexts similar to their homes, and they may increasingly recognize aspects of their own nuclear families (both past and present) in their closest networks in the company. At the same time, unavoidably, because of habituation, they will let their guard down more and more. Gradually they will both become more impactful and more at risk of living out their overdrive patterns, patterns such as the ones we have seen in Part Two. At that moment they will increasingly come under the spell of hubris, ie under the spell of pride and presumption.

CASE STUDY A case of hubris or of appropriate executive discretion?

Sidney is a 38-year-old MBA recently appointed to lead the administrative core of an international family foundation that is just about to celebrate its 150th anniversary.

There is much excitement because the celebration of this anniversary comes after a period the chairman of the foundation referred to as being 'the most difficult and destructive time in the foundation's history'. The clear expectation is that with all the work that Sidney has done to revive the fortunes of the foundation, it is now time to go public and to show that the foundation will be able to survive and flourish for another 150 years.

Sidney was recruited after an extensive search that involved some of Europe's top head-hunters. The foundation was keen to bring in new thinking and new blood, and in particular, to put behind it the previous 'failures' in recruitment: the last two CEOs had lasted less than three months which had resulted in board acrimony, staff demotivation and loss of discretionary funding from family members (the foundation relied on members of the family making regular annual contributions to the administrative core funding).

Sidney has therefore joined with much at stake and with much promise. He was seen as a fresh pair of hands, not connected to any of the family, or the other non-family factions that had sought to control the foundation. He also joined as an experienced, independent and highly-skilled executive, with a practical vision and international perspective that the board felt was really needed to take the foundation into a new direction.

But even as preparations were being finalized for the tremendous 150-year celebration, there were signs of rumblings amongst the staff that Sidney was possibly overreaching himself and making decisions without 'consulting' anyone. Anonymous letters had been written to the board treasurer complaining that Sidney had disbursed funds for approved projects without getting signatures required from other board members (a requirement given the scale of funds being disbursed).

When confronted, gently, in a board meeting, Sidney pointed out that given the board members' locations around the world it was not possible to get all signatures before timely disbursements could be made. He noted that he had raised this with the board and that his actions were merely fulfilling the board's wish to expedite payments and to ensure that the bureaucratic aspects of board procedures did not get in the way of the foundation's day-to-day duties.

Sidney was somewhat irritated that despite his hard work and the effort and attention he was already putting in and successes he had achieved already, the board appeared to be focusing on this minor infringement. He felt he was essentially being unfairly and naïvely 'carpeted' for something that he was doing for the good of the organization.

That would have been where the matter might have rested, had the treasurer (who also acted as ombudsman) not suggested that a conversation about ethics and boundaries for the board and the executive should be held at the next board meeting and at the next joint executive board retreat. He added that it was essential that this very capable CEO should not be in a position where he is accused of overreaching himself and overstretching his authority when dealing with policy and procedure in routine matters such as this. The treasurer stated that he felt this was necessary for the CEO's own protection as well as the protection of staff, the board and the organization as a whole.

Sidney disagreed, stating that he felt that his authority and executive independence were being challenged inappropriately and that he had no choice but to tender his resignation, and in so doing became the third CEO to resign from the foundation within less than 18 months.

Hubris literally means 'outrage' or 'overstepping the mark'. In ancient Greece this meant mostly overstepping the mark towards the gods (or if you wish, the unassailable forces of nature) but also towards fellow mortals, by abusing them or shaming them and thus challenging society's norms. Hubris is not just the same as over-confidence, as some authors seem to imply (see eg Hayward, 2007); hubris also contains an element of transgression, of going beyond a natural boundary or imposed structure. In our view hubris may even be accompanied by a *lack* of confidence, such as in the avoidant overdrive pattern (see Chapter 8).

Here is an example, one of the many we could take from Greek mythology, one that is relevant for this book as it is the founding myth of narcissism. Narcissus was a very beautiful and arrogant hunter from the ancient city of Thespiae, who disdained the ones who loved him. His excessive arrogance brought him down eventually. Nemesis (divine retribution) lured him to a pool where he saw his own reflection in the water and fell in love with it, not realizing it was only an image. He was unable to leave the beauty of his reflection and he eventually perished.

We would argue that a leader can overstep the mark in several directions. Upwards, towards higher authority, but also downwards by imposing decisions which only limit the team's effectiveness or the individual team members' contributions. Moreover, the leader can overstep the mark towards peers and wider society, by violating ethical boundaries, and leaders can overstep the mark towards 'self', by forcing themselves to do things they are not capable of or that cannot be sustained physically or otherwise.

Here is an overview based on these four ways of overstepping the mark, with examples:

1 *Presumption towards authority or the larger organization.* Here the leader oversteps the mark with regard to the hierarchy or the institutional order. If done against oppression, such as we have described with Michael Woodford at Olympus in Chapter 5 or such as whistle-blowers do in a variety of contexts, then this kind of hubris could be very positive and in fact, heroic.

2 *Presumption towards designated role and own team.* This is when a leader suppresses the creativity or contributions from his or her team, using discretion to limit rather than enhance the team's effectiveness. Or conversely, when a leader caters to demands of key members of

the team that go beyond the reasonable expectations laid down by the role, including ethical considerations. A good example is the case of Lance Armstrong and his behaviour towards his team members and the cycling fraternity.

3 *Presumption towards own context.* This is when a leader oversteps the mark towards society as a whole, by engaging in non-ethical leadership practices such as abuse of office or fraud. A classic example is the case of Enron, where future CEO Jeffrey Skilling developed a staff of executives who, by making use of accounting loopholes, special purpose entities, and restricted financial reporting, were able to hide billions of dollars in debt from failed deals and projects.

4 *Presumption towards the self.* Here a leader exhausts his- or herself so that he or she isn't able to function or cope. There have been some high-profile cases in recent years, such as CEOs António Horta Osório at Lloyds TSB and Ton Büchner at Akzo Nobel, who both were off from work with 'fatigue' for a couple of months, and Sir Hector Sants at Barclays Bank who took leave related to exhaustion and stress and then resigned from the bank on 13 November 2013.

These four types of hubris have been brought together in Figure 12.1, where the space opened up by managerial discretion is represented by a rectangle. However, if a leader truly uses up all the space that he has in terms of managerial discretion, and allows his or her decisions to stretch all the way to the edge of that field, then very real occasions of hubris with serious consequences are to be expected. A wise leader therefore stays well within the bounds of his or her discretion, within a self-imposed new rectangle as drawn below, as the 'impact zone' (Figure 12.2). As Potter Stewart at the US Supreme Court famously said, 'Ethics is knowing the difference between what you have a right to do and what is right to do'. In our view the same is true for leadership.

This makes leadership into an art – the art of staying inside the box voluntarily, restraining oneself whilst using one's managerial discretion to help the team become more effective. This sounds straightforward but in our view is really something that has to be earned. There are just too many forces that pull the leader into the 'hubris zone' and make it so much easier to overstep the mark. Just as a breach of ethics may be tempting because of its rewards, in the same way lashing out at or competing with subordinates may be ever so alluring. And in similar ways, relational overdrive patterns that hark back

FIGURE 12.1 Managerial discretion: four areas where a leader could transgress but needs to hold back

FIGURE 12.2 Managerial discretion in a rectangle with different 'zones' of action

FIGURE 12.3   The unbearable lightness of getting the right balance

all the way to early childhood and characterize the private person may play up in a leader who is under pressure.

In our experience of working with leaders, particularly those in entre-preneurial fast-changing environments the ability to challenge themselves and subordinates to 'work at the edge' and to stretch and change existing norms can be remarkably effective at creating new opportunities or turning around fossilized, tired and failing organizations. Yet we also find that 'overstepping' the mark and going too far is a real risk. Many succumb and fail, some recover and 'learn' from experience(s) in order to have another go. Indeed many successful entrepreneurs and leaders point to earlier failures as being significant in enabling their future successes. Some however may never learn and appear fated to repeat and to pay (and make others pay as well) for their repeated errors.

In the Greek myths a divine spirit of retribution, personified by the three Fates or by Nemesis, follows on hubris. This haunting spirit metes out a divine punishment for the pride and presumption of the ordinary mortal. In our modern business world, this natural drive for balance or cleansing after hubris is often represented by some form of derailment, which can take the form of a very public 'outing' as well as ousting. In modern times it is as important as ever to restrain hubris and to bring back balance to the business of leadership. In the final section of this chapter we want to look at different ways this balance may be achieved.

The need for balance

General management is an exhausting function, where it becomes tempting to overstep the mark and use the limits of discretion to get results. The limits of discretion open up the risk of hubris which can bring even the best and brightest executives down. It is very hard to know from the inside what degree of risk we are taking, yet retrospectively hubris – exaggerated pride or overdrive patterns – are often found at the heart of derailment. In this section we want to offer four ways of recognizing the degree of risk and thus balance hubristic patterns with counter-measures.

The ancient Greeks called the antidote to hubris *sophrosyne*, which literally means healthy-mindedness. *Sophrosyne* also stands for humility, restraint, self-control and temperance, in short, anything that brings us back from the abyss of hubris and that placates the nemesis of retribution, so that we remain capable of offering the very best of our leadership.

In our view there are essentially four starting points for *sophrosyne*, as follows:

1 *Owning*, realizing and reflecting on our weaknesses or vulnerabilities.
2 *Building up* our strengths and resilience.
3 *Balancing* our strengths with our weaknesses by finding the strengths or challenges in our weaknesses.

4 Truly *focusing on our team and other stakeholders*, in a generous and even self-effacing way.

These four are all complementary and can therefore be practised in a coherent, mindful way, all at the same time. We will say more about each of them using the models that we have ourselves found useful.

Know thyself: own your vulnerabilities

'Know thyself' is an ancient motto in the temples of Luxor and Delphi, and seems to have had a connotation of knowing your boundaries, ie knowing where you might overstep the mark and invoke the wrath of the gods. Knowing yourself is a balancing act: by understanding your vulnerabilities you can acknowledge and own them, and in true *sophrosyne* sense, begin to apply moderation and restraint, cultivating ego strength. You actively try to stay away from acting out your vulnerabilities, by not giving in to temptation and by restraining your managerial discretion.

In reading this book you are increasing your knowledge of leadership effectiveness, derailment and psychology, so in a way you are gathering more understanding of your limitations, and perhaps also, by doing some of the exercises in the book, of your vulnerabilities. A more effective and in-depth way of doing this is with the help of a more personalized programme, using psychometrics, feedback instruments, executive coaching and other forms of leadership development.

Part of knowing yourself honestly is taking on board your real and true resistance to doing something about your limitations. Schein (1993) says that for any learning to happen we have to find a balance between two countervailing anxieties:

1 One can be called the 'fear of learning' which testifies to the acute pain and frustration in learning, where you know what you need to give up and change but do not know what you will get in its place. As a result of this fear, most of us will try to suppress any information and avoid any action that confronts us with the fact that we have not yet learned something.

2 The other can be called the 'fear for survival' or the fear of *not* learning, and is often associated with feelings of despondency and powerlessness. If this fear gets the upper hand, we will be forced to make an effort to learn.

This reminds us of the significant internal defences that we need to overcome in the practice of knowing ourselves better, defences that protect and often mask our vulnerabilities, shame and frailties. To balance those defences it is very helpful to cultivate an ongoing interest in learning about yourself and others. This means being open to new experiences and views, in particular upwards feedback in terms of your performance as a leader. And it means taking every opportunity you can to expand your repertoire of understanding and insight as well as action. Leaders who are good at learning relate positively to the possibility of finding out something new that helps them to engage better with their reality and with their team. They learn from immediate experience and are also able to take a step back and reflect on wider experience that might inform and change their assumptions and frames of reference.

Work on your resilience: build up your strengths

Resilience is a topic that is receiving a great deal of interest amongst those responsible for performance and well-being in organizations, as work environments become increasingly challenging and uncertain. In the main, however, resilience-focused selection and development interventions are still quite limited, and there is probably more that the scientific study of resilience, well-being and performance has to offer the organizational practitioner (Flint-Taylor and Robertson, 2013).

Resilience has been defined by psychologists in a variety of ways across a number of settings, including 'the ability to bounce back or recover from stress, to adapt to stressful circumstances, to not become ill despite significant adversity and to function above the norm in spite of stress or adversity' (Carver, 1998; Tusaie and Dyer, 2004). By adopting this view, those working in or with organizations that have been experiencing high levels of pressure should acknowledge that resilience involves three pillars: an internal, an external and an 'in-between' or relational pillar:

1 A number of key individual characteristics or 'internal pillars' such as ability, personality, attitude, mood.

2 The experience of pressured situations or challenges, or the 'external pillars' that underlie the experience of resilience.

3 The productive coping that occurs as a result of these experiences, all the responses that happen at the boundary between internal stamina and outside pressure, in other words the 'relational pillars' such as bouncing back, keeping going, learning, driving forward.

It is important when helping leaders develop resilience that attention is paid to individual factors, but it is equally important to understand how these individual factors interact with the situations they are encountering and finally how we can capture the outcome at an individual, team and organizational level. Our colleague Alex Davda has identified six key areas of resilience, which he describes as 'resilient attitudes' which have been shown to affect how an individual thinks about, feels about and then responds to pressured or stressful situations (Davda, 2011). These six attitudes are:

1 *Emotional control*: controlling emotions and taking personal responsibility for thoughts, feelings and behaviours.

2 *Self-belief*: belief and confidence in the self and personal capabilities.

3 *Purpose*: setting and organizing goals and identifying a broader meaning from these.

4 *Adaptability/adapting to change*: adapting readily to change and responding to uncertainty in a positive and developmental manner.

5 *Awareness of others*: demonstrating self-awareness and an understanding of other people's situations and perspectives.

6 *Balancing alternatives*: generating and managing alternative options, opinions and choices.

Davda has developed a resilience questionnaire based on these six attitudes, a shorter version of which can be found in Appendix B. These resilient attitudes are generally found to be helpful for individuals when under pressure as they help them manage particular stressors in a more proactive, adaptive and positive way. However, each of these helpful attitudes can become counterproductive if it is 'over-used' (used inappropriately for the particular situation).

A good example is 'confidence' or what we describe in the resilience framework as 'self-belief'. In a lot of potentially pressured situations, having a strong belief in yourself as a leader has been shown to be important.[1] For example, if you need to have a difficult performance conversation, lead a new team, manage a high-profile project or take people through a significant change. This is because it is your own confidence that helps motivate you and others to draw on capabilities and experience and to keep going. This confidence can also help you believe that any tough choices you make as a leader are the right things to do.

However, if you are an extremely confident leader, dealing with a team who are anxious, apprehensive and even fearful of the impact of change on them, your own confidence may in fact impact negatively on the team and make you appear as 'arrogant', 'cocky', 'uncaring' and even naïve. You may also acquire the characteristics of narcissistic leaders that we have described in Chapter 6. Team members may then think to themselves and ask each other questions such as: 'Why is he or she so confident when we are all so nervous because we do not know what this new change will bring?'

They will then start questioning whether you really understand, care or are able to empathize with them. This could put additional stress and pressure on you, as you are not getting the reactions or results you feel you should from your team.

Therefore, it is important for you as a leader to develop your attitude towards pressure, taking into account the types of situations you typically experience both at work and at home. However, you also need to be aware that behaving in a particular way may help you maintain your own resilience (being confident), yet at the same time may have a detrimental impact on the resilience of those around you (raising the anxiety levels in your team).

Developing resilience takes work and time, but there is now growing evidence of how resilience training can boost individual and organizational success (Proudfoot *et al*, 2009). The work of the Comprehensive Soldier Fitness Programme (Seligman and Fowler, 2011) also gives a clear example of a large-scale resilience-development intervention that is beginning to show benefits for individuals and a whole organization.

From our point of view, developing resilience involves:

- An awareness of the characteristics you already possess and whether they help or hinder you under pressure. (For example, are you extremely planned and organized and find adapting to uncertainty and ambiguity difficult, as may be the case for an obsessive–compulsive pattern? – see Chapter 7). The questionnaire in Appendix B can help with understanding your coping characteristics.

- An intention or motivation to develop a resilient attitude towards pressure that can either help you overcome certain individual predispositions or build on your strengths. (For example, as a naturally pessimistic person can you develop a more optimistic approach by focusing on what you can learn from situations when you are reflecting on them?)

- An understanding of what is difficult about certain situations and what resources you feel you need to manage them.

- An ability to consider a number of outcomes that you may experience as a result of certain situations.

Find value in your own 'dark side': balance strengths and weaknesses

Self-knowledge and understanding of your vulnerabilities is one thing. Strengthening your resilience is quite another. It is very clear that both together do not alone make a 'character', a well-balanced, mature and mindful leader. Well-developed toughness and resilience can make for a great champion, and profound self-knowledge can make for an eminent sage. However, if the two are not balanced then the champion will suffer from dark areas that are out of consciousness or out of grasp, such as momentary pride, arrogance, addictions or weakness. Or conversely, the sage will recoil into introspection, experiencing moments of not being able to face the world or act in the market-place. What makes for a truly mature leader is a certain balance in strengths and weaknesses, a sense that the greatest strengths are allowed to look silly and weak, and the greatest weaknesses bear some hidden treasure.

The core competences model (Ofman, 2002 and Chapter 3) is based upon exactly this principle that great characters are built on the transformation of polarities, where they manage to allow their greatest strength to become their most acute pitfall, and their greatest weakness to become their most treasured challenge.

Essentially, what the core competence model does is identify for every espoused strength a corresponding overdrive. The espoused strengths are self-reported, so the view that this quality is indeed developed above average will be subjective. From this, a challenge will be identified: a quality that is not readily accessible (ie a weakness) or does not carry conviction (ie a blind spot), and that is worth aspiring to. By taking on the particular challenge the leader commits to strive for a form of balance to his or her own (perceived) strength. The leader therefore chooses to balance out strengths and weaknesses.

One aspect of balancing strengths and weaknesses is the process of *taking back projections* to counteract a process that happens very frequently under stress, and in particular also for leaders. It is the process of splitting strengths and weaknesses, and, in order to build up a positive identity (Petriglieri and

Stein, 2012) or to feel safer and less anxious, attributing strengths to oneself and weaknesses to others. When leaders set themselves the challenge of befriending their own allergies and vulnerabilities, draw inspiration and challenge from their strengths going into overdrive in order to develop their own (perceived) weaker sides in such a way that they balance their strengths, we can say that on a less conscious level they are working against the ubiquitous pattern of splitting and projecting in response to pressure.

As a result of this process strengths become more marked and humbled by substantial challenges, so that hubris or excessive pride are much less likely.

The process is very simple and will again be facilitated in the final – practice – chapter of Part Three of the book: ask yourself what you can learn from those that annoy you the most. Spend slightly more time than you would ordinarily on those people that you do not rate and to whom you wouldn't want to give a second's notice. Promote precisely those people to the main object of study for your 'further education in leadership'. Learn something important about yourself precisely from what irritates you the most in others. Make more use of the conflict, irritation, and frustration in your leadership role, just as you would of 'the dung on your fields which will make new shoots grow' (Dutch proverb).

Lead without the self: truly focus on your team

As we have been focusing on the leader and what the leader can do to face up to hubris, derailment and overdrive, we have forgotten slightly what the task and definition of leaders is. Was it not something about growing the effectiveness of the team for which one holds responsibility? This core task of leaders also offers important clues on how to manage the excessive pressures of top leadership positions or in challenging transitions. A humble, selfless leader who focuses on the very ordinary aspects of his or her team (Binney, Wilke and Williams, 2004), the everyday challenges of strategy formation, operations and people, a leader who is perhaps less self-conscious and less central to his or her own leadership, will run a smaller risk of overdrive and hubris. The busy bee has less time for mis-steps than the queen bee.

We believe it is possible to grow your compassion in equal amounts to your energy, drive, focus and toughness. For many executives, however, this is almost like a Copernican revolution, in which they move away from placing themselves and their ambitions at the centre of the universe, and start paying full attention to others' ambitions and growth. It is the further development of our capacity to *listen*, where we try, even if only for limited periods, to allow not our own thoughts and challenges to be central to our minds, but those of others. We open up our minds to the interests and drives of other people, and discover that our world does not actually revolve around us but really revolves around other people and their interests and needs. A leader's task is fundamentally altruistic and selfless, just like the task of an executive coach: to intervene so that others can perform.

Regaining balance: you do not have to do it alone

The one thing that all leaders in overdrive seem to struggle with is a certain lack of *compassion*, sometimes a lack of compassion for themselves and perhaps more often a lack of compassion for others. The four ways of balancing that we have introduced here all endeavour to grow compassion and acceptance, for oneself, for others, and for the consequences of difficulties, disappointments and loss.

The best place for a leader to grow compassion and to address the excesses of hubris and relational overdrive is in a tailor-made, confidential and personal relationship, such as can be established in the privacy of *executive coaching*. By working in such a personal one-to-one helping relationship other relationships can be brought under scrutiny, and overdrive and derailment patterns can be observed and explored in depth. The coaching relationship can be used as a preventive intervention but also as a remedial intervention, provided the executive can feel safe enough to talk freely about very sensitive areas, which are possibly burdened by shame or frustration.

As we saw in the previous chapter, the research literature, which is primarily based on statements from colleagues in the same organization, can be summarized by concluding that the derailment of senior executives can mostly be attributed to shortcomings in self-awareness and interpersonal expression (Hogan, Hogan and Kaiser, 2010). Both of these can be addressed well in a coaching relationship. Self-awareness can be enhanced by feedback and the production of new insight, in terms of potentially self-defeating mechanisms like the overdrive patterns we have explored in Part Two of this book, and in terms of defences and what underpins them, as well as resistances against change. Interpersonal expression can be enhanced by experiencing oneself in a relationship that explores relational phenomena explicitly. Leadership development programmes may also be useful, although we agree with Hogan, Hogan and Kaiser (2010) that simple leadership 'training' is probably too basic and general to make a difference regarding the derailment patterns. So, we conclude with these authors that 'personalized coaching is probably more effective for preventing derailment than leadership development programmes because such programmes focus on the leadership and business skills rather than on the interpersonal and intrapersonal deficits at the root of derailment' (Hogan, Hogan and Kaiser, 2010, page 569).

Kaiser and Kaplan (2006) and Nelson and Hogan (2009) go on to suggest that effective coaches must be prepared to confront the subtle fears of failure, inadequacy and rejection that can cloud the executive's judgement and impair interactions with subordinates and peers. In our experience a rigorous process of contracting for safety and confidentiality is needed before overdrive patterns can be addressed directly. It is important that the leader can freely associate to his or her pressures and concerns, and can gradually learn that doing so in a safe coaching relationship can actually provide new ideas, help and insight. Once this has been done a coach can be bolder in addressing the overdrive patterns that are at play.

Summary: balancing your patterns as a leader

The inside story of becoming a leader is a gradual experience of stepping into role, finding one's feet and growing one's understanding and authority. With this growing external influence come growing internal pressures, as well as a growing similarity of the leader's responses to those learned in one's 'home turf': the core nuclear families that shape all of us and the core features and patterns of one's character. This is where overdrive and derailment patterns come into play, and the leader comes under pressure to find a way to balance those patterns out with resourcefulness.

We listed three core functions of leadership:

1 *Supporting*: facilitating or enabling the team's effectiveness, enhancing the resources and competences that are available.
2 *Inspiring*: supplying the team with a vision, strategy and meaning-making.
3 *Containing*: looking after or caring for the team, nurturing and providing space for processing emotions and for understanding to emerge.

We have used the ancient concept of hubris or presumption to illustrate how the growing management discretion of a leader may go overboard if left unchecked.

Within the management discretion of a leader in authority, so within the possible behaviours and decisions of a leader, we can identify four hubristic routines, four ways of overstepping the mark:

1 overstepping the mark towards authority;
2 overstepping the mark towards your own team;
3 overstepping the mark towards the team's environment and wider context;
4 overstepping the mark towards the self.

These can lead to proper derailment and serious repercussions, even if there may not be any immediate short-term consequences, because of the fact that they are all well within the discretion of the leader.

In order to make sure that being driven does not turn into hubris or any of the overdrive patterns that we have studied, it is important to find a form of balance. In this chapter we have described four ways of balancing out excessive overdrive:

1 owning and exploring weaknesses and vulnerabilities;
2 building up strengths and resilience;
3 balancing strengths with weaknesses by finding the challenges in weaknesses;
4 truly focusing on the team in a generous and self-effacing way.

Each of these practices helps to grow compassion and acceptance, both for one's own frailties and disappointments, and for those of others. Natural and honest compassion is probably the best antidote to hubris, short of derailment and humiliation which tend to be the ultimate consequences of hubris.

Leaders do not have to go through such painful balancing processes in isolation. Conversations with an executive coach who has psychological knowledge and can help generate self-awareness, insight and acceptance can be extremely useful in overcoming hubris and derailment.

Note

1 There is not much empirical evidence to show that self-esteem leads to better performance, with the notable exception that high self-esteem facilitates persistence after failure (see eg Baumeister, Campbell, Krueger and Vohs, 2003).

13

Balancing relational patterns in organizations

> *The temptation to tell a chief in a great position the things he most likes to hear is one of the commonest explanations of mistaken policy. Thus the outlook of the leader on whose decision fateful events depend is usually far more sanguine than the brutal facts admit.*
>
> **SIR WINSTON CHURCHILL,** *THE WORLD CRISIS 1916–1918* **(1931)**

For simplicity's sake, we have rather ignored our *interpersonal* or *relational* theory of leadership in the previous two chapters. It is now time to remind ourselves that if leaders succeed or fail in their role, they always succeed or fail for *someone*. Leaders always achieve and thrive in their dealings with others as looked upon with their own eyes and those of their counterparts. Success and failure in leadership are therefore always relational. By definition, leaders work for their team, for their colleagues, for their organization. Failing in isolation does not exist. As a matter of fact, a fair amount of failing leaders would not know that they are failing. You wouldn't be able to tell either, when you meet them and talk with them by themselves. You would only notice when you pull their relationships into view.

In other words, derailment, or leadership failure, is a relational, interpersonal phenomenon. Just like leadership performance and success. It is also a continuous, gradual phenomenon: we all fail only to some extent whilst we are successful to some extent as well. This makes all the broad strokes about leadership from the previous chapters a lot more complex in reality. Similarly, if you had asked someone else about the leaders in the examples of this book, you might have got an entirely different account.

We speak about *relational* leadership because leadership does not just take place in constant interaction and conversation (of all kinds, including e-mail and other written communication) with others, but is also a constant meta-reflection on those very relationships as it seeks to optimize relationships so as to foster a higher team performance. As we emphasized before in Part One, relational leadership means working relationally at two levels: fostering strong and dependable relationships and inquiring into these relationships as they evolve in this very moment.

Traditionally, since the 'launch' of transformational leadership in 1978 (Burns, 1978) there has been a furious debate regarding the question of whether leadership is *transactional* (ongoing meaning-making, collaboration and negotiation within relationships which are in principle equal as they are between adult professionals in different roles) or *transformational* (largely top-down, inspired by a charismatic, visionary, 'excellent' and change-driven individual or group of individuals). Partly because of the great appeal of terms such as 'excellence', 'visionary' and 'transformational' the latter model of leadership has mostly had the upper hand in the leadership literature over the past 35 years. Increasingly, however, transformational leadership has been exposed as not very different from the leadership that one finds in cults, sects and totalitarian regimes, so the model is in a lot more difficulty now (see Tourish, 2013, for a highly critical and well-informed review of transformational leadership). Rather than transformational leadership being seen as helpful, there is increasing evidence that highly charismatic and visionary, 'transformational', leaders may have a very stifling effect on their followers' creativity, initiative and well-being in large corporate organizations.

We want unequivocally to come out on the 'transactional' side in this long debate, because we firmly believe leaders and followers are equals who are constantly (re-)contracting and negotiating from different roles. We do however prefer the term 'relational' to 'transactional' because it comments more on the essence of leadership as working within a relationship with a difference of roles, and also because it avoids the negative connotations of a 'transactional' relationship based only on self-interest. Moreover, relational leadership affords more room in our view for compassion, altruism and generosity which are important characteristics (or painful absences) of any leadership bond. We acknowledge that relational encompasses the 'good and effective' as well as the 'challenging, difficult and the problematic'. Last but not least, we believe leadership is relational in the true sense of the term, being not just about optimizing but also about (self-)reflecting relationships (see Chapter 2).

This is why the 'patterns' approach that we introduced in Part Two can be so helpful: we all recognize *each* of the overdrive patterns for ourselves and for everyone that we work with, *to some extent*. Things only become

FIGURE 13.1   Teamwork: an odd passing game and more complex than is assumed

a problem and only for some leaders for some of the time, when we see these patterns moving towards their more extreme expressions. This chapter rehabilitates the team or organization perspective on leadership, and looks more into group, inter-group and organizational phenomena.

Teamwork is a 'passing' game

One of us (Erik), growing up in Rotterdam, got early exposure to the game of football. He remembers a moment from one of his first football training sessions as part of his physical education. He received a big compliment from the teacher, who said something like, 'I want you all to learn from how Erik is playing'. To which he added, 'Erik is one of the worst players on the field. But unlike most of you he seems to know about his shortcomings and therefore tries to get rid of the ball as soon as he receives it. He tries to play off to a teammate as quickly as he can. And that is the right thing to do in football. You have to learn to give the ball away.'

This PE teacher seems to have been on to something: Kuper and Szymanski (2012) note that ever since the time of Johan Cruyff, ie since the early seventies, the football teams that have consistently come out on top play a quick passing game focusing on possession, ie on keeping the ball in the team shared by different players.

We believe that the same is true for most teamwork in organizations as well. Team or departmental work is essentially a passing game. It is crucial in particular for leaders, but for the other 'field' players as well, to be able and content to pass on the initiative and allow others to score.

What is passed around exactly? Not just jobs, tasks, pieces of work... more importantly for the topic of leadership is the fact that mental 'energy' is passed around as well: praise, blame, frustration, enthusiasm, loyalty, projections, rumours etc.

It is really hard to get a handle on the complexity of a team or organization, precisely because so many things are passed around between its members at any given time. All conversations in organizations are essentially passing around opinions and views about the work and the workers, and as such they help passing around not just basic information, not just more elaborate information such as strategy, opinions and decisions, but also, and in particular, psychological 'information', packed up in reputations, impressions of styles and leadership, praise, blame, expectations, psychological contracts, idealization, shaming etc.

In order to keep reflecting on a team *as a team* with all its richness of demands, obligations, tasks and goals, we need to take on board those manifold subtle and psychological passes and exchanges as well. These exchanges can be thoroughly enriching, such as when actionable feedback is passed on at the right time, or when motivation is boosted by relevant and specific praise. The exchanges can however also be stifling to team members and to a team's production, such as when conflicting signals are passed on, or when unhelpful, exaggerated criticism is communicated or half communicated, or even worse, is communicated without offering help with improvement, or at a time when it cannot realistically lead to improvement, or with a content that is so saturated with projections that there is only a 'grain' of truth for the other person.

It is well known that a dominant style of the 'passing game' in organizations can invite more 'passes' of the same style. There are many strengthening 'feedback loops' in organizations that can amplify messages and projections, such that they emerge as an organizational theme. Leadership patterns, such as the ones in Part Two of this book, can easily be strengthened by these mechanisms, such that larger parts of an organization are affected by them than just those that the leader meets and works with in person. Such strengthening of existing patterns can be very helpful, such as when 'team spirit' or 'company pride' is propagated and amplified. And it can happen in rather more devious ways, such as when blame games are passed on in endless cycles.

An example of the passing game

A very large accountancy organization is struggling with the fact that the best accountants leave well before they achieve partner level, so that partners have to be recruited from the outside and larger numbers of graduates have to be trained up than would normally be necessary. An anonymous opinion poll is conducted in the organization, where the style of leadership is severely criticized: partners and senior managers are not seen as conducive to development, they don't seem to be able to listen and younger staff find it hard to guess what the partners' views are.

A consultancy is hired to help all the partners of this organization to improve their development of younger staff. The coaches from the consultancy get their instructions at head office and go out to work with small groups of partners and later senior directors, to improve their capacity to develop younger staff.

What the consultants only very gradually find out is that this is an organization where indirect feedback is the order of the day. Practically all the messages about performance are relayed to a third party, with an expectation on the third party to pass on the messages to the leader. It turns out to be very significant that the partners receive their feedback on their leadership style through an (indirect!) opinion poll, managed by HR. Hence they receive most of its messages from paperwork produced by HR, or from their bosses, including the managing partner. The team of consultants also receive their messages about what to do with the partners indirectly, namely from other consultants and occasional phone calls with HR – not from the partners or the performers directly. After a programme of group coaching for partners has been running for some time, indirect criticism starts to emerge: some partners are not attending, others speak with HR about the limited value of these activities, and many speak amongst each other about the money and time spent on this leadership improvement programme, and how little return they are seeing.

Very slowly this situation starts to escalate: individual consultants are being scapegoated for not being worth their reputation: they are told not by their clients but by HR and by the consultancy company directors that they should change their coaching style and some are even advised to step down from the programme, to be replaced by other consultants. Similarly, when the groups with senior directors start to form, they offer profound and biting criticism of the earlier partner groups, underlining how little those partners have learned thus far, in their eyes. This is a message those directors share with each other and with the facilitating consultants, but have not mentioned to any of the partners. As a result of the low 'yield' of earlier programmes, the directors find it very difficult to engage themselves, despite the fact that large numbers are saying they agree with the original feedback from within the organization. Many even add that they themselves are great champions of leadership coaching and are in favour of a different, more engaging style of development of younger staff.

It isn't long before those difficulties of engagement within the senior directors' groups also start to escalate, whereupon the remaining consultants are advised by HR – not by the participants in the groups themselves – to improve their coaching and to offer more usable and practical tools and tricks. By the end of the programme both clients and senior external consultants are feeling rather depleted and exhausted although they find it difficult to understand why they are feeling so tired.

Here is an example of an organization where there is a lot of passing on of rumour and gossip, or indirect feedback, and very little passing on of usable information, or actionable direct feedback. This leads to increased levels of suspicion, frustration, and ultimately, disengagement. Without any particular individual leadership pattern being to blame, the organization has begun to derail as a whole, as less and less direct feedback leads to further attrition of the most talented staff. An opinion poll taken two years after the previous one shows even greater levels of criticism regarding the way partners and senior managers develop accountants and advisors in the firm.

Vicious cycles in organizations

We can safely assume that the literature about leadership derailment provides inspiration for team and organizational derailment as well, simply because one leads to the other. In most of Shakespeare's tragedies we can observe how the crisis around a leader can spread into strife, civil war and the downfall of a nation.

We expect similar patterns in teams as we identified in Chapter 11 (see eg Van Velsor and Leslie, 1995) for individual leaders:

- unhelpful team dynamics leading to breakdowns or ruptures in interpersonal relationships;
- lack of a sense of urgency and a shared vision and perspective – leading to failure to agree and subsequently to meet objectives and expectations;

- inability to go beyond competing and establishing the altruism that is needed for real collaboration;
- inability to learn, innovate and adapt to change.

Sydney Finkelstein has reported in *Why smart executives fail* (2003) how he and his team have studied unhelpful patterns in 51 disastrous and very public company failures, such as Enron and Motorola, by studying public records and interviewing many of the executives involved. The book exonerates many a CEO as the findings moved away from the 'single person culpable' and also from the 'single fatal flaw' theory of derailment.

First, the book argues that some seven common-sense ideas about the causes of failure are either wrong or have very limited explanatory value. They are (Finkelstein, 2003):

1 top executives were stupid;
2 executives could not have known what was coming;
3 there was a failure to execute;
4 executives weren't trying hard enough;
5 executives lacked leadership ability;
6 executives lacked the necessary resources; and
7 executives were simply a bunch of crooks.

Later, when he comes to what his research did find and what he thinks explains the 51 disastrous corporate failures, he lists the following (Finkelstein, 2003):

1 Brilliantly fulfilling the wrong vision or in other ways being deluded, ie cognitive dissonance often compounded by group cohesion dynamics. So in most cases clear patterns of overconfidence compounded by conformity, in the form of a surplus of 'team spirit' or 'group think' (see also Asch 1951). Overconfidence compounded by conformity.

2 Lack of open debate in executive boards, usually because of conflict avoidance or disruptive, unhealthy dynamics based on either a surplus of raw, unprocessed conflict or the opposite, conflict avoidance.

3 Excessive or insufficient oversight, ie too high or too low levels of managerial discretion. Insufficient oversight mainly of those executives with 'exceptional personalities' who have delivered spectacular results in the past.

4 Personality characteristics ('spectacularly unsuccessful people'), often found in conjunction with truly admirable qualities. These are the disturbing sides of driven, successful leaders, the kinds of things we talked about in Chapter 11 and in Part Two of this book. The specific aspects Finkelstein points to, the *seven habits of spectacularly unsuccessful people*, include: omnipotence; absence of boundaries between themselves and their organizations; 'infallibility' (thinking they have all the answers); ruthlessness; being obsessed with their company's image; underestimation of obstacles; and stubborn reliance on what worked in the past.

Inspired by Finkelstein's book and many other cases that we have seen, we would like to attempt to create a short-list of unhelpful dynamics in teams, a list of core 'vicious' patterns that we can encounter in many large organizations. They are all linked, either directly or indirectly, to the way multiple agendas and talents are handled in an organization. Essentially, for us, there are only three types of vicious circles in organizations: those informed by *(in-)fighting* – or a bellicose spirit; those informed by *fear* – or a propensity to be shamed; and those informed by *fatigue* – or an active turning away from the agendas that matter.

In our own search for 'spectacularly unsuccessful relationships' we can see these three patterns recurring again and again. Relationships can become antagonistic, unsafe or unfocused and confused, through the emergence of (in-)fighting, fear or fatigue, respectively. Let's look at these vicious relational patterns in a bit more detail.

Fighting: being wrapped up in conflict and competition

All collaboration is negotiated in a field between mutual support and mutually exclusive competition. Conflicting ideas about what to do abound, as well as competing demands from the outside world and contrasting talents in the membership of a team. These are sources of conflict that need to be constantly managed. They are never totally absent or suppressed, nor will they be the only dominant force lest they burn up the organization and allow its members to be sacrificed to competing ambitions. In any organization at any time some compromise solution is always being found. Either individual team members eat up some of the conflict by suppressing their own ambition and ideas, or a strict hierarchy channels the conflicting desires and powers in the team with the help of prohibitions and regulations, which leads to a similar pruning of ambitions and ideas. In organizations both of these processes work together to manage conflict, and the price they pay is a serious curbing of ideas and drive.

Both processes are examples of defence mechanisms (Freud, 1894): one individual (suppressing one's own ambition or creative energy, putting a stop to one's own desires to dominate, to shine and to lead), another organizational (suppressing disagreement and informal action, sticking to formal hierarchical positions, contracts and rules). Defence mechanisms help to channel raw energy and allow team members to collaborate and to accept their places in a team and an organization. Such mechanisms do come at a price though: individual talents may not be expressed, energy and motivation of individuals may be held back, and healthy development and growth, both for individuals and teams, may be blocked by this need to channel, suppress and regulate energies.

Some of the common patterns we have seen around conflicts are:

- Raw competition and debate, where aggressive energies are let loose. Team members spend huge amounts of time and even more energy competing for attention and defending or attacking ideas and arguments.

- Passive aggression as a response to the suppression of creative energies: team members do not turn up nor do they give of their best when they are there, and individuals devote more energy to their own future career or outside-work activities than they devote to the team and its challenges.

- Scapegoating and bullying, which are much more frequent phenomena in organizations than is usually assumed. A simple e-mail from a team leader shooting down one of their team member's ideas in public can already be a strong indication of a bullying mentality in the team. When power goes unchecked and unchallenged by team members, bullying and scapegoating by senior members of the team become almost unavoidable in most organizations.

As consultants to organizations where fighting is the norm we have often been surprised at how much the consulting role lends itself to scapegoating. Differences between us and the dominant culture, differences of accent, clothing, heritage, are quickly pointed out to us in such cultures, in a way that implies inferiority and disapproval of the way we are.

CASE ILLUSTRATION   The Fight Cycle – Disney and the 2003
boardroom battles

In 1984 Michael Eisner was brought into the Disney company by Roy Disney, major shareholder and board member and nephew of founder Walt. Through the 1980s and 90s Michael Eisner transformed the business, fighting off takeovers, and diversifying and expanding the corporation.

By the time he departed in 2005, the corporation's revenue had grown from US $1.5 billion in 1984 to US $30.75+ billion in 2004. The share price had grown by 1,646 per cent and the number of theme parks from 3 to 11.

Despite this remarkable success the corporation was to face a number of internecine infighting incidents and boardroom battles. During the Eisner period, a number of key executives were to be involved in well publicized internal feuds and disagreements. In a high-profile departure Jeffrey Katzenberg left to join Steven Spielberg to create DreamWorks SKG. In a later disagreement in 1996, Michael Ovitz, who had himself been brought in by Eisner, left after 14 months. In 2003 Roy Disney and Stanley Gold, two major shareholders who had previously been supportive of Eisner, were to be involved in an intense internal battle with him. The battle led to the attempted ousting of Eisner from the top of the Disney Corporation. The attempt failed – leading to the resignation of both Disney and Gold from the Disney board. In 2005, finally and quietly, Eisner himself retired from the Disney organization.

Fear: internalizing conflict and competition

Separate from the workings of aggression, but not entirely disconnected, are the workings of *shame* in any organization. Shame appears when the aggressive bully becomes internalized and unconscious. Many organizational cultures have prohibitions against speaking out, not so much because of the 'objective' risks in a competitive environment, but more because of internal inhibitions that are nurtured by team members.

Some of the common patterns we have seen around shame are:

- Avoidance and indirectness, such as in the accountancy example above. There can be such a premium placed on being polite and diplomatic, and not causing trouble of any kind, that an indirect culture emerges, more aptly named a 'gossiping' culture.

- Fear of getting close to colleagues, fear of surveillance, even a fear of touching and being touched, ie fear to give a compliment or show vulnerability.

- A depressed feeling of impotence and dependence, as if the team member and even the leader is still a child that has to know his or her place, seen but not heard.

As consultants to organizations where fear is the norm we have often been surprised at how quickly we ourselves picked up similar feelings of being inadequate, small or rude and abrasive. Even as a relatively 'untouchable' outsider we have learned to live with fear and shame relating to our interventions, in such organizations.

CASE ILLUSTRATION   The Fear Cycle – the UK National Health Service and Berwick safety report

---

In 2013, following a number of safety scandals and crises in the NHS, a renowned international expert was asked to carry out an independent study of patient safety in the UK National Health Service. The findings, widely published and commented on in the media, indicated how vicious cycles of 'fear' have created subcultures of secrecy that have prohibited staff and leaders at all levels from speaking out or addressing real issues or problems facing the organization. The report concluded that the challenges that the NHS faced in relation to patient safety were created by the systemic effect of a cultural fear, a lack of clear responsibility, the undermining of staff effort, commitment and goodwill, and application of rules and regulations without associated learning support to address and improve the situation in the organization.

Amongst other recommendations the report concluded that in particular it is necessary to develop a culture of learning that could only come from outlining key messages to start with incentives that delivered the right outcomes in patients' best interests. In addition, more attention is needed to be given to improving and acting on complaints as well as putting in place clear responsibilities for safety.

Alongside the possibility of introducing criminal offences associated with neglect or mistreatment of patients the report recommended more attention to development and training in ways that could support staff to work more effectively to create 'no harm' environments for patients.

Fatigue: turning away from conflict and competition

At this level many team members pretend that conflict and competition are absent, or that they have somehow miraculously been overcome, or were never very important in the first place. Organizational leaders and membership develop exaggerated views of what the organization and its leadership can do, and of the sublime future that is held in store for this organization, almost as a rightful, pre-eminent place in the organizational pantheon or marketplace.

Some of the common patterns we have seen around fatigue are:

- Blind belief and idealization of the status quo, as gleaned from marketing materials and press releases, self-gratifying statements from senior management, or 'good news stories' in the wider press.

- Delusional ideas about how new products or services are going to save and transform the organization, such as going into a new continent or creating a miraculous new application that everybody in the whole world will want to buy.

- Hedonism and a feeling of 'we have worked hard enough now, let the next generation take over'; sometimes in blissful innocence, at other times more like calculated laziness.

CASE ILLUSTRATION　　The Fatigue Cycle – BP and the Deepwater Horizon oil spill

In April 2010 the worst oil spill in US history occurred. The spill was a result of an explosion that killed 11 workers and resulted in 4 million barrels of oil being spilt into the Gulf of Mexico. The oil leak was to take months to plug, and resulted in widespread ecological as well as social, economic and political fallout.

The report published by the US oil spill commission found that, whilst BP had overall responsibility for the scale of the disaster, there were a number of multiple causes and parties involved. In particular, it was noted that, despite being aware of the challenges and hazards of exploring for deepwater oil in harsh environments, BP had pushed ahead with exploration and drilling without paying adequate attention to the risks and communication with the key parties they were responsible for overseeing. Amongst the issues identified as contributing to the vicious cycle and events that led to the accident were issues such as: poor risk management, frequent and late changes in plans, and inadequate attention to critical indicators within a very hazardous and changing environment.

Bion (1961) summed up these and similar vicious patterns rather nicely by talking about groups where the 'passing game' had lost contact with the primary task of the team and had become only a pretence of maintaining a shared task and goal. He called these groups 'as if' groups because they were operating as if they were creating something together, whilst in reality they were not. He distinguished three different 'as if' or 'basic assumption' groups: *fight–flight* groups which are similar to our 'fighting organizations'; *dependency* groups which are similar to our 'fear organizations'; and *pairing* groups which are similar to our 'fatigue organizations'.

When you work with an organization you can often quickly pick up whether the dominant energy, the dominant 'passing game', is one of fighting, fear or fatigue. In the first, 'fighting', culture there is frantic movement, palpable conflict and debates galore. In the second, 'fear', culture there is unimaginable shame, risk-averse caution and a distinct politeness. In the third, 'fatigue', culture there can be quite considerable denial of reality, idealization and inertia.

Each of these dominant cultures may be traced to a dominant leader. A leader's serious derailment patterns as summed up in Part Two of this book are wont to amplify unhelpful dynamics in the teams that he or she leads. The impact of a single 'derailed' leader cannot be offset easily by others who lead in a more balanced or compassionate way. It is a useful rule of thumb to assume that one single powerful person can hold the team and the organization back, whilst one single person cannot easily get it moving again. To change a 'vicious' cycle in an organization, many 'virtuous' patterns are often needed, in which many balanced and helpful leaders play a role over a sustained time period.

Virtuous cycles in organizations

Just as we all have some understanding and experience with 'vicious' organizational patterns, so we can also recognize relatively straightforward 'virtuous' cycles in company cultures. Usually a well-oiled, effective, focused or 'virtuous' organization is characterized by a sense of clarity of task and purpose, a shared idea (or strategy, vision) of what is important, good enough internal relationships, and sufficient resources for investment (a healthy bottom line is also part of a healthy culture…). One could say the organization has something extra, some energy, health, openness at its disposal, in order to keep focusing on the task even at difficult moments or in adversity. Conversely, the organization does not have to constantly pay attention to a frightened, vulnerable or needy unconscious which may express itself through fighting, fear or fatigue. The organization can afford itself to be on-task because it does not have to constantly look after itself and its own unsettled nature.

Very capable leadership expresses itself by being able to help a struggling organization, which is at the mercy of derailment patterns or vicious organizational dynamics, to become more 'virtuous' and better functioning. This links in with our definition of leadership in Chapters 2 and 11: 'making a team or organization more effective at achieving results'. Leaders – and also team members – who know how to contribute to this kind of movement, really prove their mettle as leaders. In our experience, virtuous cycles that provide an antidote to the three 'F's' above of fighting, fear and fatigue, are almost always born out of a fourth 'F' – *frustration* – provided frustration can be approached with openness and a certain tolerance.

Frustration is the salt of life. No matter how wealthy or successful you are, you will not be able to avoid profound frustration. You can pretend you are 'not bothered', turn away from the experience of being frustrated, but you cannot avoid entirely this state or this feeling within you. If you are open to the presence of frustration you will notice that you will return to it again, and again, and again, many times even on a single day. It is the basic cycle of living, which the vicious cycles above are trying to avoid and which a virtuous leader manages to tap into. Buddhism is founded on the centrality of frustration (or 'suffering') in our lives. The Buddha is not the only one who noticed though. Interesting in this regard is the book *Auch Einer* by Vischer (1879). This novel is all about the little irritations in your body and daily life, such as the recurring experience of the common cold. In the book Vischer developed the concept of the 'spite' of objects, a comical theory according to which seemingly inanimate objects conspire against humans to give them endless irritation and frustration. We would maintain that, however ironic this book appears, it is actually about the essence of life, inside and outside of organizations: little irritations and frustrations that frequently take us entirely off track but may also indicate to us a new way to go.

Here is a short overview of how we can tap into and lead from this common experience of 'frustration'.

Sit with frustration, or just stay with the passing game

Sitting with frustration means you are open to what is happening around you at the present time. You defer your judgement on what is going on, and you allow the issues that emerge to touch you. You feel the difficulties and absorb the vicious cycles, attacks, perceived attacks, shame, desire or fatigue, without passing judgement. On a meta-level this means you halt 'automatic' responses which would only amplify the existing dynamics. You sustain the dynamics without playing into them.

In sporting terms this means that you don't give off the obvious frustrated response, but that you hold your response and manage to endure it or somehow observe it. You don't play fouls, neither do you just respond with the obvious passes which the game is imposing on you. At least your head stays out of these vicious and automatic routines.

Reflect on frustration, or read the passing game

Personal reflection and inquiry *in situ* helps you to attenuate dynamics and open them up for processing. It is difficult to reflect on what we are doing whilst we are doing it. Yet precisely that brings a high reward, namely: enough detachment for choice. With a modicum of reflection we give ourselves the opportunity of choosing how and when to respond. Personal reflection includes thorough reflection on the relationships we are engaged in. In attachment theory this type of reflection is called *reflective-self function*, the ability to read one's own and other minds (De Haan, 2012). It is based on the Buddhist idea of mindfulness (De Haan, 2012), and is related to thinking in action (Schön, 1983): you become a professional who can lead or work whilst at the same time reflecting on leading or working.

In sporting terms this means that you can reflect whilst you play, imagine yourself in other people's shoes whilst you receive and pass. Reading the game means anticipating movements, positioning yourself on the field, and observing other players' movements even whilst joining in and playing.

Name and deal with issues as they emerge, or make a 'meta-pass'

The best way to stop dynamics that are problematic is just to name them. However, because problematic dynamics are precisely the ones that are going on under the surface and mostly out of awareness, finding the right 'name' is hard. Moreover, naming them is bound to be novel and may therefore entail a certain amount of risk.

It is frequently observed in the work of coaching that simple 'naming' or the attainment of a new realization can be a critical and life-changing experience (De Haan, Bertie, Day and Sills, 2010). The same is true in organizations: after the spotting of a pattern and naming it, it becomes entirely impossible to proceed in the same way. There are still several responses possible, essentially one defensive – defending the status quo – and one more virtuous – taking the message on board. The essential step though is in the naming of the vicious patterns, revealing them for all to see.[1] This is why whistle-blowing is such an important organizational asset even if rarely rewarded. There is always a degree of courage needed to name and deal directly with issues as they emerge. As we have seen in Chapter 5 and the Olympus scandal, sometimes there is an incredible amount of courage needed to be a whistle-blower, even if you are yourself the CEO.

In sporting terms this means that you can speak up about the course of play and point out an issue that others are not yet aware of. It may be an issue that you yourself are experiencing, but equally well it may be a vulnerability, short-sightedness or obstacle elsewhere.

Being able to rebalance oneself in the midst of play

See Chapter 12 for what we mean by rebalancing: owning and exploring weaknesses and vulnerabilities; building up strengths and resilience; balancing strengths with weaknesses by finding the challenges in weaknesses; and truly focusing on the team, in a generous and self-effacing way. This is a closing of the loop, preparing ourselves for new frustration, attaining that little 'extra' we need to again sit with frustration, until the next meeting arrives or when the phone rings another time.

In sporting terms of course this has to do with general fitness, being prepared and rested ahead of the game.

These are very ordinary and not very heroic attributes of leadership and in that we very much agree with Binney, Wilke and Williams (2004) who show that such humane and ordinary actions really make a difference. There is something very humanly and humbly heroic in this capacity to sit with frustration and speak one's own truth without fear. We believe that these 'virtuous' actions can be taken by leaders but just as well by followers. In fact, one needs both leaders and followers to engage in such 'virtuous passing games' of organizing for this to work. We know from many examples that although a single derailed leader can destroy an organization, you need many more leaders as well as followers to turn back the tide of toxic team dynamics. Having said this, leaders will have more influence on the dynamics, in either direction, than anyone else in their organization.

CASE ILLUSTRATION   Virtuous Cycles (frustration) – the Virgin Atlantic experience

In June 1984 Richard Branson reached a deal with Robert Fields which created Virgin Atlantic out of the trail-blazing entrepreneurial Laker Airways. Following that, the growth of Virgin Atlantic to become one of the world's best-known airlines is a litany of mini-cycles of frustration creating responsive leadership and innovation. In 1993 following the changes in the London air traffic distribution rules that allowed newcomers to fly from Heathrow, Richard Branson, faced with the frustration of needing to raise money to take advantage of the opportunity, was forced to sell the jewel in the crown of the Virgin empire (Virgin Records) to EMI to fund the airline.

Subsequently, the frustrations of competing with the mammoth British Airways, and the threat of the British Airways/American Airlines' merger, forced the organization to create distinctive products and offerings that could generate revenue as well as customer loyalty and 'fun'. The Virgin experience started to illustrate that whilst leaders in organizations may not be able to change their environment and the rules of the game it is possible to influence the outcome and ultimately to contribute to reshaping the industry by living with and through the 'underdog' frustrations and seeking creative and innovative ways to play the game.

A caveat is in place though at this point. It is always so much easier to notice toxic dynamics of *others* rather than ourselves, and to assign to ourselves mentally the role of observer regarding dynamics or of consultant to the team, rather than the role of protagonist in the team. We have too often encountered leaders who are very clever at pointing out games and dynamics of others in their team and can express themselves articulately on other teams in their organization, whilst failing to muster the courage and clarity it takes to register and name their own disturbing dynamics. For a leader to be truly courageous it is crucial to look frankly at their own contribution as well and to name those dynamics that they themselves are a main protagonist in. In fact, the most courageous pattern to name and to inquire into publicly is one that you are yourself involved in and have an active part in.

We cannot overstate the importance of executives themselves receiving frank, challenging and direct feedback regarding their own leadership practice, including style, ideas and attitudes. In this regard, Tourish (2013,) relates a very common experience of consultants working with leaders:

> ... in the course of conducting assessments of communication practices and climate in numerous companies with a number of colleagues ... we were invariably struck by the following pattern. The leaders of the organizations concerned generally accepted positive findings uncritically. Indeed, they often claimed that they knew them already. However, they were frequently shocked by negative information. It appeared that the surveys we conducted were often their first opportunity to find out what their people really thought about such issues as the priorities of its senior leaders and their style of communication. Evidently, formal communication channels tend to filter out crucial bits of information, leaving those at the top more out of the loop than they realized.
>
> Some leaders took data indicating problems as an alarm call and immediately went to work on action plans designed to remedy them. But many bitterly contested the findings. They argued that no one had ever brought such issues to their attention before and that the data were therefore flawed. Paradoxically, we rarely found that problems of morale or communication were any surprise to those further down the organizational hierarchy.
>
> Tourish (2013, page 78)

Other authors also recognize the important and pervasive issue of *employee silence* (see eg Milliken *et al*, 2003, and Tangirala and Ramanujam, 2008). In the first of these studies 85 per cent employees in the sample said they had been in situations where they were concerned about raising an issue with a superior. From their data Milliken *et al* (2003) infer that 'employees are very concerned about the complex *relational* implications of speaking up about problems and concerns' (our italics).

As there are so many obstacles to open and fluid communication, ranging from fear of repercussions, problems of ingratiation, common etiquette, power differentials and groupthink, to narcissism and cultural pressures (Tourish, 2013), external consultants or new leadership remain in many cases the only way of breaking the employee silence. Consultants can make use of interview data or 360-degree feedback instruments. Also, external executive coaching can make a real difference. The leader's false attributions, lazy reflections and defensive observations can be exposed by an independent coach, and a mirror can be held up to the grandiosity of the leader who conveniently believes, sometimes even against considerable evidence, that he or she is taking a healthy, constructive stance inviting sound dynamics from the team.

To summarize, here are four contributions that leaders themselves can make specifically and personally to work towards more 'virtuous' dynamics in their teams. To develop each of these well can be a lifelong job in our view:

1 Listen carefully and with empathy, trying to understand how you and your actions are viewed. Remember that nobody can ever become truly excellent at listening as there is always more to learn and to discover from the colleagues you work with.

2 Practise fairness and avoid bullying, favouritism, and all other inequalities. This includes the inequality between yourself and 'your' people. Remember you get paid a whole lot more than the others, possibly because they are 'in your care'.

3 Facilitate the business of upwards communication including reflection on patterns within your organization, by setting up quality assurance, feedback and protective systems for your staff. Good models for such systems are based on supervision (De Haan, 2011), as we can see in the helping and medical professions that have a longer tradition of looking after people 'in their care'.

4 Try to gain the best possible understanding of your own overdrive patterns, derailment tendencies, and hubris.

Summary: balancing relational patterns in organizations

Team relationships in organizations can be characterized by a 'passing game':

- Members and departments pass on tangibles such as information, knowledge, resources and products.

- They also pass on information on this process itself, in the form of views, perspectives and feedback. In other words they 'meta-reflect' on how the passing game is going.

- Finally they pass intangibles, often without realizing what exactly it is they are conveying: gossip, rumour, projections and introjections, which forge links between unconscious patterns within teams and their members.

A healthy passing game is where knowledge, meta-reflections and projections are passed in such a way that other team members are generously allowed to play with the right information at the right time, with support and helpful feedback, and with trust in their abilities and in their leaders and colleagues.

An unhealthy passing game is characterized by *vicious cycles* of energy being passed around and amplified to the point of becoming a counterforce to good teamwork. The most common of these vicious cycles are characterized by three F's:

1 *Fighting or infighting*: passing around aggressive energy in such a way that it moves against colleagues' best actions and intentions.

2 *Fear*: passing around shame that inhibits the development of spontaneity, liveliness and the refuelling of aggression and creativity.

3 *Fatigue*: passing around idealizations and delusions that take away from the reality now, towards the possibilities and resolutions in some unknown future.

Vicious cycles can be heavily influenced by leaders who are suffering over-drive or derailment patterns. Such leaders may be powerful sources of infighting, shame, surveillance, and hubristic delusions.

Virtuous cycles are often much slower to take hold and need a modicum of collaboration and support from a variety of team members. They need to be maintained to remain fresh, and they are usually characterized by a single F:

4 *Frustration*: the ability to sit with experience, reflect on it, name it and work with and through it, without arguing with it, inhibiting it or expecting to magically transform reality.

The vicious cycles in this chapter demonstrate the pervasiveness of *bullying*, *favouritism* and *scapegoating*, and the virtuous cycles demonstrate the need for more courageous *upwards feedback* and *whistle-blowing* in organizations and also for the protection of whistle-blowers.

Note

1 Although contributing to virtuous cycles in organizations generally does not require any specialist knowledge, experience or expertise, in our view this particular aspect of 'naming' can be greatly helped by psychological training and insight. We welcome the fact that leaders in the 21st century are increasingly interested in psychology and are increasingly seeking therapy or coaching for themselves and sophisticated training in coaching skills and expertise.

14 Balancing your own organizational patterns: do-it-yourself

Reviewing your strengths and overdrive patterns as a leader

Identify your strengths

Based on your earlier work in this book, and your answers in Chapter 10, we invite you to summarize what you see as your greatest strengths in improving the performance of your team.

List three qualities that you have that make the team achieve better results than (you think) they would do without those qualities. Give one specific example of when you used those talents, from the last few weeks:

FORM 14.1

Strength No 1
Recent specific example of using Strength No 1:

FORM 14.1 *continued*

Strength No 2
Recent specific example of using Strength No 2
Strength No 3
Recent specific example of using Strength No 3

Assess your leadership functions

In order to find some more of your core strengths, now *go back to the three leadership functions of Chapter 11 and assess how you are doing with regard to each of these:*

FORM 14.2

1. *Supporting* – facilitating or enabling the team's effectiveness, enhancing the resources and competences that are available	
Give yourself a mark out of 10 for this function	
Give an example of where you supported or facilitated well (eg where you chaired a meeting in a way that brought out more of the team's capacity, ideas, strengths etc):	
2. *Inspiring* – supplying the team with a vision, strategy and meaning making	
Give yourself a mark out of 10 for this function	
Give an example of where you contributed or inspired well, such as where you gave of your own ideas, expertise and vision:	

FORM 14.2   *continued*

3. *Containing* – looking after or caring for the team, nurturing and providing space for processing emotions and for understanding to emerge	
Give yourself a mark out of 10 for this function	
Give an example of where you handled emotions particularly well and nurtured the team or one or more of its members in a distinctly helpful way:	

Estimate overdrive potential

Now, on the basis of the last exercise, where you placed yourself on the map of these three leadership functions, *estimate in which function you are most likely to go into overdrive.* You can think about:

1 The leadership function that gives you most worries, doubts or anxiety; or the leadership function that you are most reluctant to take on.

2 The leadership function where you feel the most emotional, irritated or frustrated with other people. So, do you feel most frustrated when you facilitate your team ('bring them together'), inspire your team ('teach them'), or when you contain them ('coach them')? When do you feel the most nervous?

FORM 14.3

Write this single most anxiety-provoking leadership function down for yourself (A):

Identify leadership derailment patterns

Now, go back either to your answers in Chapter 10 or to your scores on the Hogan Development Survey instrument of 'derailment patterns' in leaders which we recommended to you if you wanted to find out about your derailers in more detail. *See which one of these patterns is troubling you most at the moment.* You can think about:

1 The pattern of 'overshooting' that seems to be most familiar to you at the time, or even during your whole career as a leader.

2 The interactions where you felt most emotional, irritated or frustrated with your team members or at home, thinking about your work.

Helpful tips

Remember the 11 derailers are (Dotlich and Cairo, 2003):

Overdrives of the *supporting* function:

● antisocial patterns: you believe the rules are made to be broken;

● passive–aggressive patterns: what you say is not what you really believe;

● narcissistic patterns: you think that you're right, and everyone else is wrong;

● schizoid patterns: you're disengaged and disconnected.

Overdrives of the *inspiring* function:

● obsessive–compulsive patterns: you get the little things right and the big things wrong;

● borderline patterns: you're subject to mood swings;

● paranoid patterns: you focus on the negatives;

● schizotypal patterns: you try to be different just for the sake of it.

Overdrives of the *containing* function:

● dependent patterns: you try to win the popularity contest;

● histrionic patterns: you need to be the centre of attention;

● avoidant patterns: you're afraid to make decisions.

FORM 14.4

> Write this single most pertinent leadership derailer down for yourself (B):

Identify functional groups

You can check whether your most anxiety-provoking *leadership function* (A) and your number-one self-reported *leadership derailer* (B) above belong to the same basic group of leadership functions through the links: inspiring – thinking, supporting – doing, containing – feeling.

This need not be the case. If they are from different groups, we invite you to look at which aspect of that leadership function it is that you are struggling with, as follows:

FORM 14.5

> 1. Find one of the three or four leadership derailment patterns above within the group characterized by your most anxiety-provoking leadership function that conform to your answer above at (A). Make sure you choose one that you have to admit is a possible derailing pattern for you:
>
> 2. Find an example of the particular leadership function which corresponds with your chosen single most pertinent leadership derailer above at (B). Make sure you give an example of being challenged in that particular function:

Results

Now you have reflected on your most prominent strengths and your most conspicuous derailer at the moment, answer two final questions:

1 Is there a relationship between one of the *strengths* that you have noted above and one of the *derailers*, in such a way that they hang together in a core quadrant (see Chapter 3)? If this is the case, the *pitfall* should come out as an exaggeration of the *core strength*.

If you have found a link between one of your greatest strengths and one of your main derailers, please complete the core quadrant in Figure 14.1, adding the corresponding *allergy* and *challenge* for yourself:

FIGURE 14.1 Core quadrant

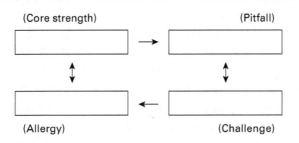

2 What are you going to do about your most significant *derailers*? How are you are going to make sure other people do not suffer, and that your leadership performance is not brought down by them?

FORM 14.6

Write down only what you think will realistically help with that derailer and also something that you can realistically do:

Now make a note in your diary in a few weeks' time to review your progress in handling your derailer. If you find making progress difficult, please talk it through with your executive coach or mentor, if you have one: confidentially involving a trusted person in these efforts can significantly enhance your leadership practice.

Reviewing your capacity to 'balance' as a leader

Complete the resilience questionnaire in Appendix B of this book.

Now look at where you are most at risk of 'overstepping the mark' and growing out of kilter, or in other words where you are most at risk of developing hubris.

Look at the four areas of hubris and ask yourself a few questions about each of them:

FORM 14.7

1. Overstepping the mark towards authority	Do we as a team often take decisions on our own that should be checked with our leaders and/or stakeholders? Do you often think it is better to proceed and then to be corrected afterwards?	
	How do I rate my boss and the higher authorities that I am accountable to?	
	On a scale of 1 to 10, how would you rate your own 'overstepping the mark' towards the people that lead you or to whom you are accountable?	
2. Overstepping the mark towards your own team	If I am completely honest with myself, could I be accused of bullying or at least hampering creativity and self-expression within my team?	

FORM 14.7 *continued*

	Do I give any particular favours to any particular people in my team? Do I have soft spots for some team members? Am I claiming to be 'helping them in their development' but really just treating them better than others?
	On a scale of 1 to 10, how would you rate your own 'overstepping the mark' towards the people that you lead and who are accountable to you?
3. Overstepping the mark towards the team's environment and wider context	Answer perfectly honestly and seriously the following question: what is the most unethical practice I am engaged in at the moment? What is the most unethical practice I am engaged in at work?
	Again, use some deep introspection to answer: what is the most unethical action I have undertaken in the last five years? What led me to do such a thing?
	On a scale of 1 to 10, how would you rate your own 'overstepping the mark' towards wider society and simple common-sense ethical behaviour:
4. Overstepping the mark towards the self	Review patiently, scrupulously and conscientiously the last few weeks of your life: when did I just go too far, lived unhealthily, usurped my own energy and health – and why did I do that?

FORM 14.7 *continued*

	Am I sacrificing myself for work? And if I am, why is that: for my family, for a vision, for power, wealth or fame, for my pension or self-expression – why?!
	On a scale of 1 to 10, how would you rate your own 'overstepping the mark' towards your own resources, resourcefulness and resilience?

You have now mapped your own 'hubris', or the temptation you experience to stretch your management discretion to areas of risk.

Look again at your four scores and ask yourself which medicine (or '*sophrosune*') you would recommend to yourself, to reduce this risk. Think about the four starting points for *sophrosyne* that we recommended in the previous chapter: owning your vulnerabilities, building up resilience, rebalancing your strengths, and focusing generously on your team.

Then reflect on how you can stay resourceful and use your management discretion to implement the challenge or challenges you found at the end of Figure 14.1:

Improving the dynamics in your own team

FORM 14.8

1. Make an exploration of at least two virtuous and two vicious cycles in your own core team and another pair of these cycles in your wider organization, as you experience them. Make sure that you describe your own contribution to these cycles:

FORM 14.8 *continued*

Virtuous
Virtuous
Vicious
Vicious

2. Over the next few weeks, take a courageous stance to challenge one of those 'vicious' dynamics in your own team. Prepare the intervention where you make sure you also name your own contribution to those dynamics:

Afterwards write down what you have learned from this experience and how you might improve 'naming' patterns in teams next time:

What more is needed to really change that dynamic and to make that change sustainable?

Think about other opportunities to name the dynamic or remind others of its continuing presence in the team:

Summary: balancing your own relational patterns

This chapter has helped you to explore your own *potential for balancing* as a leader. It is a bad sign if you haven't completed the chapter with great care and attention: unfortunately many derailed leaders do not engage in the processes that would really help them to turn back from the abyss until they are forced to, which is usually at far too late a stage.

You have been invited to:

- review your core strengths as a leader;
- compare those strengths to your particular performance on the three leadership functions of supporting, inspiring and containing;
- re-examine your core neurotic and derailment patterns as a leader;
- bring strengths and derailers together in a mini development programme for yourself as a leader, in which you engage yourself in an exercise to address the worst excesses of your main derailer.

Then you were invited to explore your own resilience and find ways to rebalance your overdrives.

Finally, you were invited to make a difference in the teams that you lead. With the help of a few open questions you explored the core dynamics of those teams and you were invited to name those core dynamics to your team members, so as to enhance the reflection in your team.

Just as in Chapter 10 regarding your own personality, you will find that taking a long hard look at your team and organization, and how you and your team are developing and mutually influencing each other, may actually diminish the risk of overdrive, personal tragedy and derailment.

Note

1 The Hogan Development Survey can be obtained through the following website **www.hoganassessments.com/content/hogan-personality-inventory-hpi**. We recommend that you contact a properly trained consultant to talk through your personal scores from this questionnaire.

Epilogue: historical models of leadership

> *Therefore the sage says:*
> *I take no action and people are reformed.*
> *I enjoy peace and people become honest.*
> *I do nothing and people become rich.*
> *I have no desires and people return to the good and*
> *simple life.*
>
> LAO TZU, *TAO TE CHING* (CA 500 BC)

Rost (1991) demonstrated in his critical analysis of 20th-century theories of leadership that a lot more work will have to be done to understand what leadership is, what it is for and how it is implemented well. He also showed that leadership thinking in the industrial age has been extremely biased towards modernist, positivist and rationalist approaches. Rost (1991) stated that *all* the 221 definitions in his meticulous overview of leadership books and articles to date were technocratic, male-dominated, linear, biased towards quantitative as opposed to qualitative appreciation of leadership, and towards content as opposed to a process concept of leadership. Together with others such as Drucker (1993) he showed that in the emerging post-industrialist knowledge society, we are in need of a new more relational and process-oriented definition of what leadership is all about. This book has endeavoured to answer Rost's call and to go back to a clear process-oriented definition of what leadership is and is for, so that criteria for effective leadership could be developed.

As part of the research for this book we have delved into some non-Western models and traditions of leadership in order to find alternative definitions and emphases. In this Epilogue we would like to present three models with a large following that have been studied extensively by historians, and yet have been virtually ignored by the mainstream 'industrialist' leadership literature. All three models have been born out of trials and tribulations, out of the self-assertion of a small state, a suppressed majority, or a counter-ideology. All three leadership models can thus be associated with the emancipation of an oppressed people or group that through sheer originality and high-quality reflection has found lasting answers to questions of leadership, power and oppression.

The first model comes out of the 'warring states' period in China where some craftsmen and spiritual teachers in smaller independent states were able to formulate a critique on the much more dominant, bureaucratic and rule-based Confucianism. This theory that later acquired the name 'Taoism' can be seen as a paradoxical or anti-leadership approach to effective leadership.

The second model comes out of the 'warring states' period in Greece where Athens and Sparta rivalled for domination and schooled their men in opposed models of military strategy and leadership. Sparta's famous leadership model was based on drilling, from an early age, just like that of the Persians: total control and unremitting focus. Athen's model, which we will describe below, was instead based on fragility and freedom.

The third model comes out of the Bantu communities of central and southern Africa, gaining prominence through the reassertion of African dignity, associated with the struggle for freedom in Zimbabwe and South Africa. This theory that embraces sociability and humanity through the concept of 'Ubuntu' is based on an *enabling* conception of leadership, a model of leadership that is entirely based in the community.

1 The shadow king: a Chinese model of leadership

Chuang Tzu was a lacquerer–philosopher who according to Chinese early historians lived in the town of Meng in the state of Song, one of the smaller so-called 'warring states', in the 4th century BC. These were the fermenting times of Taoism and Chuang Tzu was clearly inspired by the great *Tao Te Ching* book on virtue and leadership.

We have already referred to the *Tao Te Ching* at the start of Part Three of this book. Here is a short summary of Chapters 57–75 of the *Tao Te Ching* which are most directly about leadership:

- Lead by being straightforward, fight by being crafty, but win the world by doing nothing. The more rules, the poorer people will become. I take no action and the people are of themselves transformed. I enjoy peace and people become more honest. I have no desires and people return to the pure and simple life.

- When leadership is muddled, people are happy. When leadership is alert, people are cunning. The sage is sharp but not piercing, straightforward but not unrestrained, brilliant but not blinding.

- In governing others there is nothing like using restraint. Restraint begins with giving up one's own ideas. If a man knows no limits he is unfit to be a ruler.

- Ruling a big kingdom is like cooking a small fish. When done in the right way, evil tendencies lose their power and the virtue in leader and followers combine.

- A large kingdom is like the low ground – all streams flow in and it is a meeting ground for smaller states. Those who would conquer must yield and a big country should place itself low. Why is the sea king of a hundred streams? Because it lies below them. If the sage would guide the people he must serve with humility. If he would lead them he must follow behind. The whole world will support him and will not tire of him. And because he does not compete he does not meet competition.

- Achieve greatness in little things. The sage does not attempt to do anything very big and in this achieves greatness. Because the sage always confronts difficulties he never experiences them.

- Why is it so hard to rule? Because people are so clever. Rulers who try to use cleverness cheat the country. Those who rule without cleverness are a blessing to the land.

- I have three treasures which I hold and keep. The first is mercy, the second economy, and the third is daring not to be ahead of others. This is known as the ability to deal with people.

- Why are the people rebellious? Because the leaders interfere too much. Why do the people think so little of death? Because the leaders demand so much of life.

Leadership in this tradition means refraining from action, initiative or active sense-making, and instead adapting to circumstances, living with paradox and striving for balance. The following passage is from Chapter 2 of Chuang Tzu's book:

> A Penumbra asks a Shadow, 'Formerly you were walking on, and now you have stopped; formerly you were sitting, and now you have risen up. How is it that you are so without stability?'
>
> The Shadow replied, 'I wait for the movements of something else to do what I do, and that something else on which I wait waits further on another to do as it does. My waiting, is it for the scales of a snake, or the wings of a cicada? How should I know why I do one thing, or not do another?'

Chuang Tzu follows the *Tao Te Ching's* advice to rulers to shun fame and glory yet take full responsibility. A real leader's authority and wisdom reaches all, he says, yet no one relies upon him and his name need not be mentioned.

The essence of leadership in Taoism is giving up control and actively doing nothing in order that others can lead themselves. This means moving out of the way, such that the team can get on with their work. And it means the lifting of restrictions and prohibitions. The more a leader tells others what they cannot do the more they will do what the organization does not need.

Taoist leadership seems much more nurturing and welcoming than prominent Western forms of leadership, and more aimed at stimulating connection and upwards feedback, something that we concluded in Chapter 2 is probably the most reliable criterion of effective leadership. It appears more as a 'feminine' model of leadership, or perhaps more correctly a model that rigorously and fluidly balances female and male principles, as in the famous Taoist yin-yang concept.

2 Democracy: an Athenian model of leadership

In the ancient Greek world one of the greatest models of leadership was personified by Pericles, who was the defining leader of the golden age of Athenian civilization in the 4th century BC.

Pericles was the champion of a radical democratic experiment that had started in his city a little over a century earlier. In the period roughly between 460 and 430 BC Pericles was the undisputed leader in Athens, even though he took no titles other than that of (elected) general and (elected) spokesperson of his democratic party. Athens was at its strongest and produced exceptional results in almost every craft and art, a period of unsurpassed cultural ascendancy. Power and leadership were in the hands of the male Athenian citizens, who elected all officials based on merit. 'No one', says Pericles in his famous funeral speech, 'is kept in political obscurity because of poverty. Everyone has a fair chance to contribute. And we extend this freedom and tolerance even to our citizens' private lives.'

Pericles spoke in this oration in defence of a leadership model that was based entirely on democratic choice, merit and fragility. Right at the beginning of the speech he underlines the difficulty of keeping balance when many of the listeners or followers find it difficult to be convinced. 'It is my duty to do my best to meet the wishes and the expectations of every one of you.' Pericles' own position was rarely secure and yet he managed to offer leadership and initiate and supervise the great works on the Parthenon. He could only undertake such works and the leadership in several great wars, with Sparta and others, by convincing his fellow citizens and carrying their vote again and again.

3 Ubuntu: an African model of leadership

Since the late 19th century, and most recently in the 21st century in the case of South Africa, African leadership has been characterized by a conception of liberation from the colonial and post-colonial oppressor. African leadership theory has been a narrative of liberation from the post-colonial oppressor. In some of the literature that emerged after apartheid we see a leadership definition that is different from the industrialist Western picture. Leadership is defined as interventions devoted to fostering collaboration, a spirit of community and deeper intimate relationships (Mbigi and Maree, 1995). The leadership model is based on Ubuntu, a principle that signifies that 'man can only be a man through others'. Ubuntu sees the organization as more than a mere economic unit: a thriving, enterprising community of people who need each other to survive.

Interestingly enough this view also embraces its own shadow side, in this case the shadow side of the solidarity principle. Mbigi and Maree (1995) suggest that the shadow side of Ubuntu is exemplified by the fact that failure to support the community will meet harsh punitive measures from the community (page 58). The book continues, 'Unless there is a burning platform to address these shadows, it is difficult for change interventions ... to be effective and sustainable.'

This leadership model of Ubuntu asserts that we are part of each other and that we are who we are only through what we are together. It suggests that leadership is not embedded in any one person solely as an individual. Leadership is a quality we in a community own together and owe to each other. 'We create each other and need to sustain this otherness. And if we belong to each other, we participate in our creations: we are because you are, and since you are, definitely I am' (Eze, 2010).

Conclusion

These three radically different and ancient leadership models have one thing in common, namely that they each recognize the importance of our leadership 'shadow' and the essential need to deal with one's own highly personal leadership shadows, if one is to lead effectively and healthily. Moreover, they approach the leadership shadow positively, as something creative that can inform us and help to balance excesses, very similar to the way we have approached the leadership shadow earlier in this book. Here is what each of the 'schools' makes of the leadership shadow:

1 Taoism entirely embraces the shadow of leadership: the idea of in-action, non-assertion and not-leading. Taoism puts the highest value on precisely these attributes, *in particular* for leaders, and in this way encourages leaders to lead from the shadow rather than lead from the front.

2 Pericles emphasizes at every turn of his famous speech the shadow sides of his democratic model, such as paralysis through debate, the fragility of leaders (many Athenian top leaders were ostracized at some stage of their career, ie expelled from Athens for 10 years), and the vulnerability of an open society where rich citizens are at liberty not to fight to defend the society. Pericles recognizes these shadow sides but goes on to explain how Athenian awareness of these shadows helps to discipline his great city and civilization.

3 Ubuntu, as applied to leadership by southern African authors such as Mbigi and Maree (1995), recognizes its shadow side that is inevitably associated with tensions around elevating individual excellence and contribution above the needs of the community. Ubuntu leadership tries to use community leadership ('burning platforms') precisely to integrate the shadow within Ubuntu leadership practice.

The three models also present clear criteria for measuring the success of a leader:

1 Taoism: to be a sage who is psychologically mature, balanced, non-interfering, non-demanding, non-assertive.

2 Democratic Athens: to be a good soldier yourself, to be convincing and charismatic, and to be able to face disappointment.

3 Ubuntu: to be loyal and generous, to give generously and selflessly without needing a prompt.

As a final exercise in this book, please try to compare these criteria with your own priorities in your leadership role and then with those criteria for effective leadership we have suggested in Chapter 2.

These leadership models highlight that leadership is about outcomes for others. It is about what we together are able to achieve. Indeed one could say that leadership at its most effective is not about the leader. It is about others. It is about what they are able to achieve and create as a result of being in relationships with, committed to and focused on the well-being and sustenance of others. A good and effective leader is always described in terms of what they have enabled. Leadership is seen through experiences of the many who benefit from being connected, finding 'wholesome' solutions to problems and being part of integrating and resolving outcomes during episodes of distress.

Paradoxically this means that for leaders to lead, the focus cannot be merely on them: it has to be on others. At the same time, for leaders to be able to focus on others they have to be aware of and be focused on themselves. This paradox mirrors very much the way leaders are judged. We judge leaders by their results (the benefits that they 'bring to us') and the effect and impact they have on helping us in society resolve difficult issues. We critically appraise leaders' contributions to our desired futures. We do not always recognize, however, that leaders' contributions depend on their ability to understand for themselves, that at a very deep and personal level, their contribution depends on how well they examine (and if necessary) confront their own shadow sides. Leadership is about them as they are, not simply about them and what they are.

Hence in this book we have focused on a leader as she is, not simply because her self-awareness matters to her, but particularly because her self-awareness matters to others. Put more succinctly: leadership is both entirely about her as a person and not at all about her as a person.

Drivers' questionnaire

We do not know the origin of this questionnaire. It is based upon behavioural drivers that were first proposed by Taibi Kahler (Kahler, 1975).

Drivers are:

- unconscious internal pressure that makes us do things certain ways, eg with speed, perfection, little emotion etc;
- often (although not always) inappropriate or unhelpful in obtaining results. They tend to satisfy inner needs rather than actual events;
- a warning sign that strong internal processes may be at play.

Completing the questionnaire

Study every section listed in Table A.1 carefully, reading through the five statements listed. From these five statements pick out the one which is the *most true* for you and give it a high mark (between 7 and 10) in the right-hand column. Then find the statement that is *least true* for you and give it a low mark (between 0 and 3). Then arrange the other three statements in between, giving each a mark which ranks them between your lowest and highest. **Please ensure that one statement is given a mark of 5.**

Scoring the first section may take a little while. Once you get going the others will not take as long. The whole questionnaire should take between 20 and 30 minutes to complete.

Scoring

TABLE A1 Drivers' questionnaire

Section		Statement		Score (0–10)
1	a	Endurance is a valuable asset.	a	
	b	I like to see people doing their best to get things right.	b	
	c	Considering all the effort I put into things I should get more done.	c	
	d	I find myself doing too many things at the last minute.	d	
	e	On balance I adapt more to other people's wishes than they do to mine.	e	
2	a	Casualness and carelessness bother me.	a	
	b	It's keeping on doing things that interest me more than finishing with them.	b	
	c	When people are slow about saying something I want to interrupt or finish the sentence.	c	
	d	I have a fair amount of imagination when it comes to guessing what people need.	d	
	e	When someone gets emotional my reaction is often to make a joke of it or else be critical.	e	
3	a	I don't mind things being hard. I can always find the energy.	a	
	b	I prefer to use just the minimum necessary time to get to a place.	b	
	c	If someone doesn't like me I either try hard to get them to like me or I walk away.	c	
	d	It is rare for me to feel hurt.	d	
	e	If it's a question of doing something properly I'd rather do it myself.	e	

TABLE A1 *continued*

Section		Statement		Score (0–10)
4	a	I get impatient with slow people.	a	
	b	Normally I prefer to take people's wishes into account before deciding something.	b	
	c	I show a calm face even when my feelings are running high.	c	
	d	I don't make excuses for poor work.	d	
	e	There's something about coming to the end of a job I don't like.	e	
5	a	I put a lot of effort into things.	a	
	b	Sometimes it is better to just do something and leave the discussion until later.	b	
	c	I'm cautious about asking favours.	c	
	d	I don't let people look after me much.	d	
	e	I sometimes find it hard to stop myself correcting people.	e	
6	a	Sometimes I talk too quickly.	a	
	b	I'm uncomfortable when people are upset or displeased with me.	b	
	c	I dislike people making a fuss about things.	c	
	d	Things can always be improved on.	d	
	e	I don't believe in the 'easy' way.	e	
7	a	I think I do a lot to be considerate towards others.	a	
	b	I usually manage to cope even when I feel I've had more than enough.	b	
	c	I prefer doing things really well even if it takes longer.	c	
	d	I tend to start things and then gradually lose energy or interest.	d	
	e	I want to get a whole lot of things finished, then I run out of time.	e	

TABLE A1   *continued*

Section		Statement		Score (0–10)
8	a	I'm not what you would call soft.	a	
	b	I prefer to do things right first time, then have to re-do them.	b	
	c	I sometimes repeat myself because I'm not sure I've been understood.	c	
	d	My energy is often at its highest when I have a lot of things to do.	d	
	e	It's quite hard to say no when someone really wants something.	e	
9	a	I like to use words correctly.	a	
	b	I like exploring a variety of alternatives before getting started.	b	
	c	It's quite like me to be already thinking of the next thing before I have finished the first.	c	
	d	When I'm sure someone likes me I am more at ease.	d	
	e	I can put up with a great deal without anyone realising it.	e	
10	a	People who just want to finish something tend to irritate me.	a	
	b	I prefer to just plunge into something rather than have to plan.	b	
	c	If a person doesn't' know what I want I'd rather not have to ask directly.	c	
	d	Other people start whining and complaining before I do.	d	
	e	I prefer to correct myself rather than have other people correct me.	e	

TABLE A1   *continued*

Section		Statement		Score (0–10)
11	a	If I had 20% more time I could relax more.	a	
	b	I often smile and nod when people talk to me.	b	
	c	When people get excited I can stay very cool and rational.	c	
	d	I can do something well and still be critical of myself.	d	
	e	There are so many things to take into account it can be hard to get to the end of something.	e	
12	a	I have a good intuitive sense if someone likes me or not.	a	
	b	I think duty and reason pay off better than emotion in the long run.	b	
	c	I tend to see quickly how something could be improved on.	c	
	d	Some people have a habit of over simplifying things.	d	
	e	Sometimes the more there is to do, the more I get done.	e	

When you have finished scoring all the sections, transfer the marks onto the scoring sheet (Table A.2), listing each mark you have given it against the appropriate letter (a, b etc) and add them up to give you a total for each of the five drivers.

TABLE A.2 Drivers' questionnaire: Scoring chart

Question No	Item number	Your score	Item number	Your score	Item number	Your score	Item number	Your score	Item number	Your score
1	a		b		c		d		e	
2	e		a		b		c		d	
3	d		e		a		b		c	
4	c		d		e		a		b	
5	d		e		a		b		c	
6	c		d		e		a		b	
7	b		c		d		e		a	
8	a		b		c		d		e	
9	e		a		b		c		d	
10	d		e		a		b		c	
11	c		d		e		a		b	
12	b		c		d		e		a	
Totals	Be strong		Be perfect		Try hard		Hurry up		Please people	

The five drivers

Be perfect
Hurry up
Please people
Be strong
Try hard

Example: Imagine you have a set of children's building blocks and plan to make a column

Be perfect: 'I'll have to square up the blocks exactly' (as if perfect accuracy was important)

Hurry up: 'I'll have to see how fast I can build the column' (as if speed was important)

Please people: 'I'll look around to see who is watching me' (as if their approval is important)

Be strong: 'I'll sit on the floor rather than sit at a table' (as if the discomfort gives it added merit)

Try hard: 'I'll try it out horizontally first' (as if the extra effort was worthwhile).

Analysis

The most common patterns are:

a for two rather than one driver to show up strongly. This seems to fit with experience, which is that people favour a combination of drivers rather than a single one; and

b one of the drivers is particularly low, which is also useful feedback.

Scores usually range between 40 and 80. Anything over 80 is high. Only 2 per cent have scores of over 100 or under 30.

Any combination of drivers appears possible. Although it would seem difficult to combine **Hurry up** with **Be perfect** (one intent on detail, the other on speed) it does happen. **Be perfect** with **Please people** would seem especially vulnerable, particularly if combined with a low score for **Be strong**. But they do exist. People evolve clever combinations that enable them to capitalize on the strong points and minimize their losses.

Drivers give us an insight into people's behaviour and help us to build relationships more effectively. Table A.3 lists some of the main insights to be drawn.

TABLE A.3 Insights gleaned from the drivers' questionnaire

	Be perfect	Hurry up	Please people	Be strong	Try hard
Strengths	Attention to detail Accuracy Getting it right Never good enough	Project start up Meet deadlines Energetic Enthusiastic	Good team worker Gets on well with others Good communicator Innovator not inventor	Strong in crisis Not obviously panicked	Well motivated 100% effort Look for alternatives Self-motivated
Weaknesses	Slow Pedantic Never finished Irritating Miss deadlines Effective but not efficient	Arriving on time / finishing Miss essential detail Do not work well with Be Perfects	Reluctant decision maker Too busy considering others Not inventors Too sympathetic	Bottle things up Snap in private Can't solve problems (bottle up)	Misdirection? Expensive Effort for sake of it De-motivate Make complicated
When are they effective	Contracts Legal documents Patents Proofing Inspection Research	Getting things going Action more important than accuracy	Teams Arbitrator Training Building good relationships	Cornerstone in a crisis Good negotiator	Design stage Alone Clear criteria

TABLE A.3 *continued*

	Be perfect	Hurry up	Please people	Be strong	Try hard
When are they destructive	Tight time scales Finishing projects High-level plans, strategy	Detail required Rule breaking Legal/contracts	Self-assertion Can't deliver criticism	People issues	Expensive Uncomfortable with short time scales Difficulty when many options available Unwilling to get help
Key learning/change points	Willing to give in at 95% Deliver on time, regardless of detail	Being early is not a crime	Just get on with it	Allow yourself emotions OK to admit weakness	Initial effort, then see if you can offer more Be sure to take appropriate rests and holidays
How to handle these people	Agree rules Stress time over accuracy Check progress	Encourage them to be on time	Encourage Support	Trust Confidence	Set clear requirements Monitor progress Make a contract

APPENDIX B
Resilience questionnaire

This questionnaire was designed by Alex Davda at Ashridge Business School and we are grateful for his help in including this questionnaire in this book.

1 Before completing the questionnaire please think about how you are currently coping with pressure today:

Today....
1 = I feel stressed
2
3
4 = I feel neutral
5
6
7 = I feel resilient

2 Please now think of one or two situations in which you felt under pressure (the more recent the better). You may wish now to record some notes about these situations.

Note: You can provide as much information (a full detailed description) or as little information as you like (just a few key words or phrases). The words, phrases or sentences you may decide to record should help you reflect on how you would respond to these pressured situations.

....
....
....
....
....
....
....
....
....

3 Now answer the questions in the following table:

TABLE B.1   Ashridge Resilience Questionnaire

Please use the rating scale provided to answer the following questions based on the extent you would respond in that particular way to the situation(s) you have identified. **In responding to these pressured situations I would:**	1 = Strongly disagree 2 = Disagree 3 = Somewhat agree 4 = Neither agree nor disagree 5 = Somewhat agree 6 = Agree 7 = Strongly agree	
1. Take responsibility for my emotional reactions		
2. Have influence over my feelings		
3. Be able to control my mood		
4. Manage my emotional triggers		
5. Experience very few emotional lows		
Total 'emotional control' =		/35
1. Be sure of myself		
2. Know my own strengths		
3. Rely on my own resources		
4. Know that I will succeed		
5. Believe in my own viewpoint		
Total 'self-belief' =		/35
1. Find it easy to set aims and objectives		
2. Know what my long term purpose is		
3. Be clear on what I need to achieve		
4. Identify what I really care about		
5. Identify my goals		
Total 'purpose' =		/35

TABLE B.1 *continued*

1. Be attentive to the needs of others		
2. Relate to others by identifying with their point of view		
3. Empathise with others		
4. Know how I should interact with others		
5. Be aware of how others interact with me		
Total 'awareness of others' =		/35
1. Be comfortable with the unknown		
2. Adapt my behaviour to the challenges I face		
3. Look for learning opportunities		
4. React quickly to the unexpected		
5. Find it easy to adapt to changes		
Total 'adaptability' =		/35
1. Do something that makes me happy		
2. Identify something to do that lifts my spirits		
3. Make the choice to do something that I will enjoy		
4. Find something to do that I find amusing		
5. Give my attention to different parts of my life		
Total 'balancing alternatives' =		/35

4 Now reflect on your scores for each attitude and also consider how you felt at the beginning about how you are coping with pressure today.

Note

The Ashridge Resilience Questionnaire is a measure of personal resilience that was developed by Alex Davda at Ashridge Business School in 2011. The six resilient attitudes measured in the questionnaire are based on Ashridge research, which explored the effectiveness of different ways of thinking, feeling and behaving in stressful situations. The questionnaire you have completed is a shorter version of the most recent questionnaire. Each item in the questionnaire has been assessed for its relevance by a panel of six resilience experts. The six scales of the questionnaire have also been found to have acceptable levels of internal consistency (.73–.88). Internal consistency relates to the correlations between the items within a scale and the extent these items are seen to measure the same variable. Research is now being undertaken to determine the construct, concurrent and predictive validity of the Ashridge Resilience Questionnaire.

GLOSSARY

Attachment

Attachment is conceptualized as a core, biologically-based instinct which informs behavioural and motivational drives. John Bowlby introduced the concept in a series of papers starting in 1958 with *The nature of the child's tie to his mother*. Bowlby also hypothesized that individual differences in the functioning of this 'attachment system' are linked to individual working models of self and others. Infants become attached to adults who are sensitive and responsive to them in social interactions, and who remain as consistent care-givers during the period from about six months to two years of age. When infants start to crawl and walk, they begin to use these attachment figures as a secure base to explore from and to return. Responses from care-givers (usually parents) lead to the development of patterns of attachment. These, in turn, form internal working models which will guide the individual's perceptions, emotions, thoughts and expectations in later relationships. Behaviour associated with attachment is primarily the seeking of proximity to an attachment figure.

Boundary/Relational boundary

Boundaries are the places where team members 'touch' each other, where our gestures are perceived and our words begin to be heard. A boundary is not a concrete object or space, but you can be sure boundaries exist, as you will notice them when you cross them. Boundaries are the interfaces between leaders and/or team members, they are the in-between spaces in relationships, not owned by any of the team members, so they are the 'neutral zone' where parties meet and the place they co-own and co-create.

Individuation

In Jungian psychology individuation is 'a process by which a person be-comes a psychological "individual", that is, a separate, in-divisible unity or "whole"' (Jung, 1934). Individuation is a developmental process that takes place later in life, if at all, during which innate elements of personality, the components of the immature psyche, and one's life experiences become integrated over time into a well-functioning whole. Other ways of expressing this process are 'self-realization' or 'maturation'. In terms of the arguments of this book, with individuation one is finally able to integrate leadership shadow aspects and overdrive patterns (see Part Two of this book) into one's personality and leadership style. So individuation equates to the point where one stops being unaware or ashamed of these hidden traits and drivers.

Parallel process

Parallel process is a name for the phenomenon that whenever people are coming together for (say) a meeting or conversation, they will in their emotions and actions carry over interactions from other places. For this reason any meeting can be seen as partly a 'parallel version' or 'parallel process' echoing the process in another relevant meeting. The topic and occasion of the meeting and the people that are there will often influence which aspects are carried over into such a parallel process. This phenomenon is informed by transference, the overall term for carrying over emotional experience. The first reference to parallel process was made by Harold Searles in 1955, who labelled it a reflection process. Searles writes about the supervisor's experience of the parallel process. What he writes is relevant to leaders as well, namely that leaders can intuit the nature of relationships in other places from the relationship they are experiencing here and now. Searles suggested that processes at work currently in the relationship between a leader and colleague are often reflected in the relationship between that colleague and their direct reports.

Reflective-self function

Reflective-self function or mentalization was introduced by Peter Fonagy and others in 1991 and can be described as an awareness of what is going on in the minds of self and others, in the present moment. Reflective-self function can be understood as a form of mindfulness, and has been shown to be correlated with secure attachment (see De Haan, 2012).

Role/Organizational role

Roles are the spaces that are delineated by boundaries. They define the potential space that a person senses within an organization, in other words they are the sum total of their boundaries for them. Mintzberg (1973) defined a 'role' as an organized set of behaviours belonging to an identifiable office or position. Individual personality may affect how a role is performed, but not that it is performed (Mintzberg, 1973). A role is therefore more than the name, function description and list of responsibilities – a role signifies the moulding of all of that into everyday organizational experience.

Shadow

In Jungian psychology the shadow is an inferior part of the personality, the sum of all personal and collective psychic elements which, because of their incompatibility with the chosen conscious attitude, are denied expression in life and therefore coalesce into a relatively autonomous 'splinter personality' with contrary tendencies in the unconscious. The shadow behaves as compensatory to consciousness; hence its effects can be positive as well as negative. In *The Archetypes and the Collective Unconscious* (1934) Jung says, 'The shadow personifies everything that the subject refuses to acknowledge about himself and yet is always thrusting itself upon him directly or indirectly – for instance, inferior traits of character and other incompatible tendencies.'

Transference/Transferential

Transference was coined by Freud in 1905 and defined in *Zur Dynamik der Übertragung* (1912) as that part or those parts of the person's highly individual, highly personal and largely unconscious loving impulses which is not being satisfied in her relationships. Freud suggests that everyone will repeat one or several of such 'clichés' regularly in the course of a lifetime. Transference is a phenomenon characterized by unconscious redirection of feelings from one person to another, or the redirection of feelings and desires to a new person, and especially of feelings and desires unconsciously retained from childhood. The idea of transference is clearly a precursor to the idea of attachment as transference also conceptualizes earlier relationships to become working models of later relationships. Countertransference is the same phenomenon of emotional entanglement as experienced by a leader, consultant, coach or therapist in working with a client in a helping relationship.

Valency

A valency is a natural preparedness or susceptibility of an individual to enter into a special relationship with the rest of a group, team or organization (Bion, 1961). In other words, this term indicates that one individual because of his or her highly personal history has the capacity to 'pick up' and often express an emotion before everybody else does. As an example, just after a successful stock market flotation there may be 'triumphalism' or 'euphoria' around but nobody is expressing this because most of the organization is still busy working away and presenting a serious, 'professional' front to the outside world. The first leader who goes 'yippie!' can be seen to have a valency for triumphalism.

REFERENCES

Adler, P S and Kwon, S (2002) Social capital: prospects for a new concept, *Academy of Management Review*, 27, pp 17–40

Allen, J A R (2011) Relational practice and interventions: neuroscience underpinnings, in *Relational Transactional Analysis: Principles in practice*, eds H Fowlie and C Sills (pp 221–32), Karnac, London

Appelbaum, S A (1973) Psychological-mindedness: Word, concept and essence, *The International Journal of Psychoanalysis*, 54 (1), pp 35–46

Asch, S E (1951) Effects of group pressure upon the modification and distortion of judgments, in *Groups, Leadership and Men*, (ed H Guetzkow) Carnegie Press, Pittsburgh, PA

Bandiera, O, Guiso, L, Prat, A and Sadun, R (2011) *What Do CEOs Do?* Harvard Business School Working Paper

Baumeister, R F, Campbell, J D, Krueger, J I and Vohs, K D (2003) Does self-esteem cause better performance, interpersonal success, happiness, or healthier lifestyle?, *Psychological Science in the Public Interest*, 4, p 1

Bentz, V J (1967) The Sears experience in the investigation, description, and prediction of executive behaviour, in *Measuring Executive Effectiveness* (eds F R Wickert and D E McFarland) (pp 147–206), Appleton-Century-Crofts, New York

Bentz, V J (1985) *A view from the top: a thirty year perspective of research devoted to the discovery, description and prediction of executive behaviour*, paper presented at the 93rd Annual Convention of the American Psychological Association, Los Angeles, August

Binney, G, Wilke, G and Williams, C (2004) *Living Leadership: A practical guide for ordinary heroes*, FT Prentice Hall, Harlow

Bion, W R (1961) *Experiences in Groups*, Tavistock Publications Ltd, London

Bion, W R (1963) *Elements of Psychoanalysis*, William Heinemann, London

Bird, A and McEwan, M (2011) *The Growth Drivers*, Wiley, Chichester

Brown, A (2014) *The Myth of the Strong Leader: Political leadership in the modern age*, Bodley Head, London

Brown, D G (1977) Drowsiness in the countertransference, *International Review of Psychoanalysis*, 4, pp 481–92

Burns, J (1978) *Leadership*, Harper and Row, New York

Campbell, D T (1956) *Leadership and its Effects Upon the Group*, Ohio State University, Columbus

Carver, C S (1998) Resilience and thriving: Issues, models and linkages, *Journal of Social Issues*, **54** (2), pp 245–66

Clark, A E and Georgellis, Y (2013) Back to baseline in Britain: Adaptation in the British Household Panel Survey, *Economica*, **80**, pp 496–512

Collins, J (2001) Level 5 leadership: The triumph of humility and fierce resolve, *Harvard Business Review*, **79** (1), pp 66–76

Davda, A (2011) Measuring resilience: A pilot study, *Assessment and Development Matters*, Autumn, pp 11–14

DeCarlo, S (2012) America's best and worst CEOs, *Forbes*, 04 April 2012: http://www forbes com/sites/scottdecarlo/2012/04/04/americas-best-ceos/

De Haan, E (2008) *Relational Coaching: Journeys towards mastering one-to-one learning*, Wiley, Chichester

De Haan, E (2011) *Supervision in Action: A relational approach to coaching and organisation supervision*, Columbus: McGraw-Hill/Open University Press

De Haan, E (2012) Back to basics II: how the research on attachment and reflective-self function is relevant for coaches and consultants today, *International Coaching Psychology Review*, **7** (2), pp 194–209

De Haan, E, Bertie, C, Day, A and Sills, C (2010) Critical moments of clients of coaching: towards a 'client model' of executive coaching, *Academy of Management Learning and Education*, **5** (2), pp 109–28

DeVries, D L (1992) Executive selection: advances but no progress, *Issues and Observations*, **12**, pp 1–5

Diagnostic and Statistical Manual of Mental Disorders (7th ed, 2013), American Psychiatric Association, Arlington, VA, pp 646–49

Dotlich, D L and Cairo, P C (2003) *Why CEOs Fail: The 11 behaviors that can derail your climb to the top – and how to manage them*, Jossey-Bass, San Francisco, CA

Drucker, P F (1993) *Post-capitalist Society*, Harper Collins Publishers, New York

Eze, M O (2010) *Intellectual History in Contemporary South Africa*, Palgrave Macmillan, New York

Finkelstein, S M (2003) *Why Smart Executives Fail: And what you can learn from their mistakes*, Portfolio, New York

Flint-Taylor, J and Robertson, I T (2013) Enhancing well-being in organisations through selection and development, in *The Fulfilling Workplace*, eds R J Burke and C L Cooper (pp 165–86), Gower, Farnham

Fonagy, P, Steele, M, Steele, H, Moran, G S and Higgitt, A C (1991) The capacity for understanding mental states: The reflective-self in parent and child and its significance for security of attachment, *Infant Mental Health Journal*, **12** (3), pp 201–18

Fourier, J B (1822) *Théorie analytique de la chaleur*, Didot, Paris

Freud, A (1936) *Das Ich und die Abwehrmechanismen*, Internationaler Psychoanalytischer Verlag, Wenen

Freud, S (1894) Die Abwehr-Neuropsychosen, *Neurologisches Zentralblatt*, 13, pp 362–64, 402–09, translated as *The Neuro-Psychoses of Defence* by James Strachey in collaboration with Anna Freud in *The Standard Edition of the Complete Psychological Works of Sigmund Freud*, Volume III, pp 45–61

Freud, S (1900) *Die Traumdeutung*, Verlag Franz Deuticke, Vienna, translated as *The Interpretation of Dreams* by James Strachey in collaboration with Anna Freud in *The Standard Edition of the Complete Psychological Works of Sigmund Freud*, Volumes IV and V

Freud, S (1905) Bruchstück einer Hysterie-Analyse, *Monatsschrift für Psychiatrie und Neurologie* Band XXVIII, Heft 4, translated as *Fragment of an Analysis of a Case of Hysteria* by James Strachey in collaboration with Anna Freud in *The Standard Edition of the Complete Psychological Works of Sigmund Freud*, Volume VII, pp 3–125, Hogarth, London

Freud, S (1914) Erinnern, Wiederholen und Durcharbeiten, *Zeitschrift für Psychoanalyse*, Vol II, translated as Remembering, Repeating and Working Through by James Strachey in collaboration with Anna Freud in *The Standard Edition of the Complete Psychological Works of Sigmund Freud*, Vol XII, pp 145–56, Hogarth, London

Furnham, A (2010) *The Elephant in the Boardroom: The causes of leadership derailment*, Palgrave Macmillan, Basingstoke

Gentry, W A, Hannum, K M, Ekelund, B Z and de Jong, A (2007) A study of the discrepancy between self- and observer-ratings on managerial derailment characteristics of European managers, *European Journal of Work and Organizational Psychology*, 16, pp 295–325

Gentry, W A, Katz, R B and McFeeters, B (2009) The continual need for improvement to avoid derailment: A study of college and university administrators, *Higher Education Research and Development*, 28, pp 335–48

Gergen, K J (2009) *Relational Being*, Oxford University Press, New York

Gillard, J (2013) Julia Gillard writes on power, purpose and Labour's future, *The Guardian*, 14 September 2013

Gilligan, C (1982) *In a Different Voice: Psychological theory and women's development*, Harvard University Press, Cambridge, MA

Goldberg, L R (1990) An alternative 'description of personality': the Big-Five factor structure, *Journal of Personality and Social Psychology*, 59, pp 1216–29

Goleman, D (1996) *Emotional Intelligence: Why it can matter more than IQ*, Bloomsbury, London

Gottfredson, L S (2005) What if the hereditarian hypothesis is true? *Psychology, Public Policy and Law*, 11 (2), pp 311–19

Grant, A M (2001) Rethinking psychological mindedness: Metacognition, self-reflection, and insight, *Behaviour Change*, 18 (1), pp 8–17

Greenleaf, R K (1970) *The Servant as Leader*, Greenleaf Center for Servant Leadership, Indianapolis (reprint 1991)

Hambrick, D C and Abrahamson, E (1995) Assessing managerial discretion across industries: a multi-method approach, *Academy of Management Journal*, 38, pp 1427–41

Hansen, M, Ibarra, H and Peyer, U (2010) The best-performing CEOs in the world, *Harvard Business Review*, January–February, pp 104–13

Hansen, M, Ibarra, H and Peyer, U (2013) The best-performing CEOs in the world, *Harvard Business Review*, January–February, pp 81–95

Harms, P D, Spain, S M and Hannah, S T (2011) Leader development and the dark side of personality, *The Leadership Quarterly*, 22, 495–509

Harris, M M and Schaubroeck, J (1988) A meta-analysis of self-supervisor, self-peer and peer-supervisor ratings, *Personnel Psychology*, 41, pp 43–63

Hayward, M (2007) *Ego Check: Why executive hubris is wrecking companies and careers and how to avoid the trap*, Kaplan, Chicago, IL

Hermans, H J M and Kempen, H J G (1993) *The Dialogical Self: Meaning as movement*, Academic Press, San Diego, CA

Hersey, P and Blanchard, K H (1969) *Management of Organizational Behavior: Utilizing human resources*, Prentice Hall, Englewood Cliffs, NJ

Hogan, J, Hogan, R and Kaiser, R B (2010) Management derailment: Personality assessment and mitigation, in *American Psychological Association Handbook of Industrial and Organizational Psychology*, ed S Zedeck, American Psychological Association, Washington, DC

Hogan, R (2007) *Personality and the Fate of Organizations*, Lawrence Erlbaum, New York

Hogan, R, Curphy, G J and Hogan, J (1994) What we know about leadership: effectiveness and personality, *American Psychologist*, 49 (6), pp 493–504

Hogan, R, Raskin, R and Fazzini, D (1990) The dark side of charisma, in *Measures of Leadership*, eds K E Clark and M B Clark, (pp 343–54), Leadership Library of America, West Orange, NJ

Judge, T A, Bono, J E, Ilies, R and Gerhardt, M W (2002) Personality and leadership: A qualitative and quantitative review, *Journal of Applied Psychology*, 87, pp 765–80

Jung, C G (1912) *Symbole der Wandlung: Analyse des Vorspiels zu einer Schizophrenie*, Zürich: Rascher, translated as *Symbols of Transformation: An analysis of the prelude to a case of schizophrenia*, Harper, New York (1962)

Jung, C G (1934) *Die Archetypen des kollektiven Unbewußten*, Rhein-Verlag (Eranos-Jahrbuch), Zürich, translated as *The Archetypes and the Collective Unconscious* (1969), Princeton University Press, Princeton, NJ

Kahler, T (1975) Drivers: The key to the process scripts, *Transactional Analysis Journal*, 5 (3), pp 280–84

Kaiser, R B and Hogan, R (2007) The dark side of discretion: Leader personality and organisational decline, in *Being There Even When You Are Not: Leading through strategy, systems and structures (Monographs in leadership and management)*, eds R Hooijberg, J Hunt, J Antonakis and K Boal, (Vol 4, pp 177–97), Elsevier Science, London

Kaiser, R B and Kaplan, R E (2006) The deeper work of executive development, *Academy of Management Learning and Education*, **5**, pp 463–83

Kaiser, R B, LeBreton, J M and Hogan, J (2014, In Press) The dark side of personality and extreme leader behaviour, *Applied Psychology: an international review*

Kets de Vries, M F R (2006) *The Leader on the Couch: A clinical approach to changing people and organizations*, Jossey-Bass, San Francisco, CA

Kets de Vries, M F R (2008) *Reflections on Character and Leadership*, Jossey-Bass, San Francisco, CA

Khoo, H S and Burch, G St J (2008) The 'dark side' of leadership personality and transformational leadership: An exploratory study, *Personality and Individual Differences*, **44**, pp 86–97

Kuper, S and Szymanski, S (2012) *Soccernomics: Why transfers fail, why Spain rule the world and other curious football phenomena explained*, HarperSport, London

LeDoux, J (1996) *The Emotional Brain*, Simon and Schuster, New York

Lombardo, M M, Ruderman, M N and McCauley, C D (1988) Explanations of success and derailment in upper-level management positions, *Journal of Business and Psychology*, **2**, pp 199–216

Luthans, F, Hodgetts, R M and Rosenkrantz, S A (1988) *Real Managers*, Ballinger, Cambridge, MA

Main, M and Goldwyn, R (1990) Adult attachment rating and classification systems, in *A Typology of Human Attachment Organisation Assessed in Discourse, Drawings and Interviews*, ed M Main, Cambridge University Press, New York

March, J G and Simon, H (1958) *Organizations*, Wiley, New York

Mbigi, L and Maree, J (1995) *Ubuntu: The spirit of African transformation management*, Knowledge Resources, Randburg (SA)

McCall, M W Jr and Lombardo, M M (1983) *Off the Track: Why and how successful executives get derailed*, Technical Report No 21, Center for Creative Leadership, Greensboro, NC

McDougal, J (1978) *Plea For a Measure of Abnormality*, International Universities Press, New York

McGregor, J (2013) What if we knew how much CEOs made vs their workers? *Washington Post*, 22 August 2013

Miller, A (1979) *Das Drama des begabten Kindes und die Suche nach dem wahren Selbst*, Suhrkamp, Frankfurt am Main, translated by Ruth Ward as *The Drama of the Gifted Child: The search for the true self*, Basic Books, New York

Miller, J B (1976) *Toward a New Psychology of Women*, Beacon Press, Boston, MA

Milliken, F, Morrison, E and Hewlin, P (2003) An exploratory study of employee silence: issues that employees don't communicate upward and why, *Journal of Management Studies*, **40**, pp 1453–76

Mills, J (2005) A critique of relational psychoanalysis, *Psychoanalytic Psychology*, **22** (2), pp 155–88

Mintzberg, H (1973) *The Nature of Managerial Work*, Harper & Row, New York

Mitchell, S A (2000) *Relationality: From attachment to intersubjectivity*, The Analytic Press, Hillsdale, NJ

Morris, J A, Brotheridge, C M and Urbanski, J C (2005) Bringing Humility to Leadership: Antecedents and consequences of leader humility, *Human Relations*, **58**, pp 1323–50

Moscoso, S and Salgado, J F (2004) 'Dark side' personality styles as predictors of task, contextual, and job performance, *International Journal of Selection and Assessment*, **12**, 356–62

Mumby, D K (2001) Power and politics, in *The New Handbook of Organizational Communication: Advances in theory, research, and methods*, eds F M Jablin and L L Putnam, pp 585–623

Nelson, E and Hogan, R (2009) Coaching on the dark side, *International Coaching Psychology Review*, **4** (1), pp 7–19

Ofman, D (2002) *Core Qualities: A gateway to human resources*, Scriptum, Schiedam, Netherlands

Panksepp, J (1998) *Affective Neuroscience: The foundations of human and animal emotions*, Oxford University Press, Oxford

Petriglieri, G and Stein, M (2012) The unwanted self: projective identification in leaders' identity work, *Organization Studies*, **33** (9), pp 1217–35

Plato (around 380 BC) *Protagoras and Meno*, translated with an introduction by Lesley Brown, London: Penguin Group

Proudfoot, J G, Corr, P J, Guest, D E and Dunn, G (2009) Cognitive-behavioural training to change attributional style improves employee well-being, job satisfaction, productivity, and turnover, *Personality and Individual Differences*, **46**, pp 147–53

Rizzolatti, G and Craighero, L (2004) The mirror-neuron system, *Annual Review of Neuroscience*, **27**, pp 169–92

Rosenfeld, H (1964) On the psychopathology of narcissism: a clinical approach, *International Journal of Psychoanalysis*, **45**, pp 332–37

Rost, J C (1991) *Leadership For the Twenty-first Century*, Praeger, Westport, CT

Schein, E (1993) How can organizations learn faster? The challenge of entering the green room, *Sloan Management Review*, Winter 1993, pp 85–92

Schön, D (1983) *The Reflective Practitioner: How professionals think in action*, Basic Books, New York

Schore, A N (2003) *Affect Regulation and the Repair of the Self*, Norton, New York

Seligman, M and Fowler, R D (2011) Comprehensive soldier fitness and the future of psychology, *American Psychologist*, **66**, pp 82–86

Sifneos, P E (1973) The prevalence of 'alexithymic' characteristics in psychosomatic patients, *Psychotherapy and Psychosomatics*, **22** (2), pp 255–62

Stacey, R (2012) *The Tools and Techniques of Leadership and Management: Meeting the challenge of complexity*, Routledge, London

Surowiecki, J (2005) *The Wisdom of Crowds*, Anchor, New York

Tangirala, S and Ramanujam, R (2008) Employee silence on critical work issues: the cross level effects of procedural justice climate, *Personnel Psychology*, **61** (1), pp 37–68

Tourish, D (2013) *The Dark Side of Transformational Leadership: A critical perspective*, Routledge, London

Tusaie, K and Dyer, J (2004) Resilience: A historical review of the construct, *Holistic Nursing Practice*, **18** (1), pp 3–8

Van IJzendoorn, M H, Juffer, F and Duyvesteyn, M G C (1995) Breaking the intergenerational cycle of insecure attachment: A review of the effects of attachment-based interventions on maternal sensitivity and infant security, *Journal of Child Psychology and Psychiatry*, **36**, pp 225–48

Van Velsor, E and Leslie, J B (1995) Why executives derail: Perspectives across time and cultures, *Academy of Management Executive*, **9**, pp 62–72

Von Vischer, F T (1879) *Auch Einer, Eine Reisebekanntschaft*, Hallberger, Stuttgart and Leipzig

Wampold, B E (2001) *The Great Psychotherapy Debate: Models, methods and findings*, Lawrence Erlbaum, Mahwah, NJ

Ware, P (1983) Personality Adaptations, *Transactional Analysis Journal*, **13**, pp 11–19

INDEX

NB page numbers in *italics* indicate material within a table or figure